Windows for the Crown Prince

WINDOWS

for the

CROWN PRINCE

By Elizabeth Gray Vining

*"We want you to open windows
on to a wider world for our Crown
Prince."*
—Viscount Matsudaira

J. B. LIPPINCOTT COMPANY
PHILADELPHIA AND NEW YORK

To
HIS IMPERIAL HIGHNESS
CROWN PRINCE AKIHITO

LIST OF ILLUSTRATIONS

Windows for the Crown Prince

CHAPTER ONE

On October 1, 1946, I set sail for Japan, to tutor the Crown Prince.

The ship was the *Marine Falcon*, a former troopship of World War II. It carried about three hundred army "dependents," who were some of the first women and children to join the men waiting for them in Japan; about sixty missionaries, returning to the fields from which they had been driven by the war; some twelve hundred Japanese repatriates from Canada; and perhaps a dozen stray people, including myself, who did not fit into any of these categories.

I was assigned to a small cabin on A deck, along with five other women, two children, a large crib, a baby's "toidy chair" containing five bottles of champagne, and suitcases piled to the ceiling. Two days later one of my cabinmates and I discovered on C deck, where the missionaries were, a dormitory for twenty-four which was occupied by only three, and forthwith we moved down. We adopted neighboring upper berths, spread out our "bits and pieces" on the empty beds about us, and entered upon a friendship that was to be one of the joys of my life in Japan.

Mrs. John Kenderdine was the wife of the Canadian economic adviser to General MacArthur. She had lived all of her married life, up to the war, in Japan, where her husband had been president of a business firm. Now she was going home. In the afternoons when we took naps or at night before we went to sleep, she would tell me about Japan. A keen observer, with a gift for vivid and witty expression and a poetic love of beauty, she painted for me day after day a picture of Japan as seen by one who had lived in it and loved it. The festivals, the tiny candle-lighted boats slipping down the rivers with the souls of the dead after their annual visit to the land of the living, the fishermen on the piny shores, the vender of wind-bells, the old amah with her house wisdom, the little shops where your kimono was dyed to your own design, the salty taste of crisp *o senbei* (rice cakes): all these she made me know with her own delight as no book about Japan has ever made me feel them.

As the little ship wallowed and plunged across the rolling gray wastes of the Pacific, life settled into a sort of pattern—although things did happen that would not fit into any pattern I had ever known, such as meeting an elderly missionary emerging from a shower bath with a plate of pink ice-cream in her hands.

The Army dependents, who ranged from two generals' wives to a good-hearted Irish wife of a sergeant, had most of them not seen their husbands in several years, and many of the small children who followed at their mothers' heels like fawns after does had never known their fathers. One felt the tensions, the hopes, the unacknowledged fears that assailed them as they struggled in crowded quarters to keep the children clean and well and reasonably quiet, and prepared for the unknown future. Many a wife "found a stranger" when she met her husband again after the separation due to war and occupation. The one small lounge, jammed with card tables, was the headquarters of the women and babies, while the active children swarmed over the various flights of iron steps and the boat deck.

The missionaries walked the narrow promenade deck or congregated in the central space outside their dormitories. Half of them were Catholic, half Protestant; all had been in Japan before the war and were eager to get back. The Protestants carried their Bibles and their Japanese grammars about with them and held endless discussions and conferences among themselves. The nuns coagulated into their own groups and lived their separate lives among us, their draperies flowing out into the narrow passageways, touching us with their mystery. I was especially interested in the cloistered nuns who were returning to Hokkaido. They wore glorious white serge robes with scarlet panels down the front, and at intervals during the day they gathered together in a circle on deck and sang the Office of the Church very softly.

The Japanese were a small part of that great tide of repatriates picked up from their homes in America, Korea, China, Manchuria, Formosa, and the South Sea Islands, and washed back upon the shores of the homeland that many of them had never seen, to begin a new life without assets and without hope. Most of them stayed in their dormitories in the hold, though the children came up to play on deck and to buy Coca-Cola and chocolate and blue plastic combs in the little shop.

I spent most of my days on deck, wrapped in Army blankets which soon grew frosted with the spray. I did not read, I thought. I had a good deal to think about.

Chiefly I thought about the Crown Prince and wondered what kind of child he was. He was twelve, I knew, nearing thirteen. I had seen newspaper photographs of a chubby little boy with a direct, intelligent gaze, and I found these photographs, blurred as they were, appealing. He seemed to be so thoroughly, solidly, himself.

It was impossible to make any definite plans, for I knew too little. I did not know, for instance, how much English the Crown Prince already knew, or what other subjects he studied. I knew that I was to teach him one hour a week, that I was to "lecture" at the Peers' School, and that the Crown Prince's sisters would come to my house from time to time. When I first heard about it I thought one hour a week very little, but I hoped that if all went well the time might be extended. What was the age of the boys to whom I was to lecture, I did not know, nor on what subject, but I supposed English literature. I did not know how many sisters the Crown Prince had, nor how old they were.

So as I lay in the salt spray and watched the black gulls from the Aleutians rising and dipping over the white-tipped, gray, endless waves, I thought about education itself and what we hope through education to do for children, about what I might be able to do for those young Japanese, who were growing up into a world very different from that into which they had been born and who must be bewildered and dismayed.

I thought about the Emperor, who had been such a figure of mystery to us during the war, the symbol of all that was militaristic, a god-king on a white horse. I had read, as everyone has, that people were not allowed to look upon his sacred person and especially not to look down on him from a height, so that when he passed by people were required to go into their houses and close all the doors and shutters. But I had been told also, by people who had lived in Japan, that he was actually a man of

[13]

simple tastes and habits, a scientist by avocation, who disapproved of what the war party did in his name and who had at different times attempted to avert war.

Sometimes I thought how strange it was that I should be there among the dependents and the missionaries and the nuns, sailing into the unknown to take up a fabulous assignment, and my mind went back over the steps that had brought me here.

In the spring of 1946 an American Education Mission composed of twenty-seven distinguished educators headed by Dr. George D. Stoddard visited Japan to survey the educational system and make suggestions for its reform. In the course of a reception at the Imperial Palace, the Emperor suddenly turned to Dr. Stoddard and asked him if he could get an American tutor for his son, the Crown Prince.

It has often been assumed that the American tutor was imposed by the Occupation. Nothing could be further from the fact. The idea proceeded from the Emperor himself; he made the proposal on his own initiative without even consulting the people in charge of the Crown Prince's education, and it was an unprecedented step for him to take. For a long time after my arrival in Japan I did not realize just how extraordinary it was for the Emperor, who traditionally accepted the decisions of the experts about his son without question and even without comment, to take on himself a decision of this kind.

The next day two or three Japanese gentlemen called on Dr. Stoddard at the Imperial Hotel to discuss the terms and arrangements for the American tutor. It was to be a woman, "a Christian but not a fanatic," and not an "old Japan hand," but one who came fresh to the country, without even a knowledge of the Japanese language, since she was to teach by the direct method entirely in English. Her age, they thought, should be about fifty, but Dr. Stoddard persuaded them that she might well be younger. She was to have a house, car, servants, secretary, and a salary of $2,000 a year, and the contract was to be made for one year, renewable by mutual consent.

Dr. Stoddard returned to the United States charged with the task of finding a "schoolmarm" for the Crown Prince. I read about it in the newspapers with interest. I thought that it might improve the lowly position of women in Japan if a woman were elevated to teaching the Crown Prince, not knowing that women

[14]

had been given the vote in the spring of 1946, had flocked to the polls in great numbers and elected thirty-five women to the Diet. That I myself might be the tutor no more occurred to me than that I might fly to the moon and back on Tuesday.

I was at that time working for the American Friends Service Committee, writing reports, articles, and appeals. I am a Quaker, and every Quaker, I think, wants to work at some time for the Service Committee. Because its work is directed not only to the binding up of the wounds of war but to furthering the cause of peace through the healing of tensions and misunderstandings, I had chosen it as my war service to the country. Now the war was over and I was preparing to return to the ordinary work of my life, which was the writing of books for young people. I had a book blocked out and the summer planned.

One morning late in May Samuel Marble, now President of Wilmington College, Ohio, who was then organizing the Committee's relief project for Japan, came in to talk to me about an appeal we were preparing. After we had finished the business in hand he turned to me and said without preamble, "Would you consider having your name suggested as tutor to the Crown Prince of Japan?"

The idea was so extraordinary, so far from any plans I had ever made for myself, and I felt myself so inadequate and inappropriate, a quiet Philadelphia Quaker at the most elaborate and mysterious court in the world, that my instant reaction was to say no. Positively No.

"Wait and think it over, at least over the week-end," he urged.

That evening I told my sister about it as something so fantastic as to be almost amusing. The Highland Scottish element, which we both inherit but which is stronger in her than in me, was in the ascendant that night. Its forebodings, sometimes called second sight, though by no means dependable, are never to be quite ignored, and her swift realization of the seriousness of the proposal was very sobering to me.

In the end my answer was that if Friends thought I could be useful I could not refuse to have my name suggested but that I would not lift a finger to get the job. Clarence E. Pickett, then Executive Secretary of the American Friends Service Committee, wrote exactly that to Dr. Stoddard.

During the days that followed, my mind inevitably dwelt

much on the question. The responsibility, the delicacy of the position, the demand on talents, abilities, and training which I felt I did not have, the giving up of my book, the separation from my sister, the difficulties of life in a land wholly unknown to me and one where I thought the bitter resentments of war and defeat would still be keen: all these considerations weighed on me so that I find written in my diary: "With all my heart I hope it doesn't come."

On the other hand, I wanted deeply to give myself to the cause of peace and reconciliation. That Japan had renounced war in her new constitution was to me immensely significant. Here perhaps was an opportunity to uphold the hands of those who were willing to risk greatly for peace, and to bring before the Emperor's son in his formative years the ideals of liberty and justice and good will upon which peace must be based if it is to endure. So it was that after a week I could write in my diary: "I reach the point of leaving it in God's hands."

Two weeks after the subject had first been broached, I went to Albany for an interview at Dr. Stoddard's request. He was then finishing his work as New York State Superintendent of Education preparatory to assuming the presidency of the University of Illinois.

We talked for most of an afternoon, Dr. Stoddard asking me questions and answering those I asked him. He was in himself very reassuring, a man of stature, moral and intellectual as well as physical, calm, gentle, wise. He told me of the experiences of the Education Mission, of the coöperation which they received from the Japanese, the friendliness, the lack of bitterness, the eagerness for help in building a new Japan. It was the first time I had heard from one who actually had been there the report that often surprises and puzzles as well as impresses Americans. War and the militarists were thoroughly discredited; the Japanese were turning toward democracy, were trying to understand and practise it. It was an extraordinary opportunity to teach the son of the Emperor.

For my part I gave Dr. Stoddard the facts of my life: my Quaker and Scottish background; my education at the Germantown Friends School, Bryn Mawr College, the Drexel Institute School of Library Science; my teaching experience, which was little enough but did include a good deal of private tutoring;

[16]

my marriage to Morgan Vining of the University of North Carolina and his death in an automobile accident four years and eight months later; my eleven books for young people and the travel that had gone into the preparation of some of them; my work for the American Friends Service Committee.

I remember that he said something to this effect: "You would be under great demand for talks and meetings and leadership of all kinds among the Japanese women especially, but you would have to remember always that your work was to teach a small boy English. There is a great deal of drudgery in that. Do you think you have the patience for it?" To which I answered, "I don't know. I've never tried it."

I remember too that I asked whether the teacher would be "a prisoner in the Palace" and was assured that she would have entire freedom as to her life and friends.

Dr. Stoddard told me that he had decided not to make the final choice of the teacher himself, but to send the names of two or three and material about them to the Emperor for his decision. He thought that it would be better for the Japanese to have a part in the responsibility themselves. He asked me to give him the names of some persons who would recommend me. I suggested Rufus M. Jones and two others, and then I went home and told them what I had done.

Rufus Jones, our beloved Quaker philosopher and saint, wrote back to me by return mail: "This news in thy letter of June 7th is perfectly wonderful. I cannot think of anything more exciting and I very greatly hope the selection will come to thee. Of course I will write vigorously to Dr. Stoddard, in fact I am writing just such a letter to him today."

Later I heard from Dr. Stoddard that he had sent my name and one other to the Emperor and I settled down to await the outcome. Life was normal on the surface, with a subcurrent of unspoken possibility. My sister and I went to the cottage which we loved on a hillside in New Hampshire, and I savored with delight every swim in Lake Sunapee, every thrush's song, the sunsets, the high pasture, the northern lights, in case I might not have them soon again.

On the seventh of August a telegram came from Dr. Stoddard asking me to telephone him in Champaign, Illinois. After some delay the call was put through, and Dr. Stoddard's voice came clearly over the miles. He read me the cable he had received:

"'The Imperial Household has decided on Vining (repeat) Vining.'"

There was a little further talk and then he said the words that came back to me as I sat in my deck chair among the missionaries, backed by their various boards, the nuns, strong in the embrace of the Catholic Church, and the dependents supported by the might of the United States Army:

"Well, you're on your own now!"

CHAPTER TWO

IT WAS RAINING when we reached Yokohama at three o'clock on October fifteenth. The harbor looked dingy and war-battered, with burned hulks of ships still riding its gray waters, but on the shore there were substantial buildings and a city's life was obviously going on.

On the *Marine Falcon* excitement reached fever height amid the delays and confusions of disembarking. Those who were going to outlying parts of Japan were taken off first; the rest of us, who were destined for Yokohama or Tokyo, waited. A few husbands were allowed on board and here and there little clusters of families radiated happiness.

I was told that there were two carloads of officials down on the dock to meet me, and for a frantic half hour I was batted like a shuttlecock between officials who urged me to get off the ship immediately and others who said reprovingly that I must wait for my turn like anybody else. Someone told me that the welcoming delegation below had been there since one o'clock.

Part of my time of waiting was taken up with what was for me, unaccustomed to being a public figure, a severe ordeal. A colonel, whom I never saw again, summoned me by loudspeaker to the deserted lounge and threw me to the lions, in the form of some twenty-five American reporters and photographers. Their questions came thick and fast: Where was my house? How big was it? Exactly what would I teach the Prince? How was I to be paid? Didn't I realize that the United States was still at war with Japan? Why had I come at such a time to be an employee of the Japanese Emperor (for whom the speaker had a low regard)?

There was in the attitude of some of the questioners an antagonism that was a surprise and shock to me, for I had never before encountered aggressive rudeness in American men, whom I have always regarded as my kind protectors and rescuers from all difficult situations. Months later I met again the man who harangued me most bitterly and he apologized handsomely, but from that first interview I had acquired a wariness of the press which colored my relations with newspapermen until I was finally reassured by the friendly and courteous representatives whom I later met.

At the end of the interview one of the reporters said to me, "Do you realize, Mrs. Vining, that the Imperial Household especially asked that you give no newspaper interviews at all?"

This was, I later found out, not true, but it added to my distress at the time, for I thought that before I even got off the ship I had unwittingly done the wrong thing.

At about half-past five I finally walked down the gangplank and set foot for the first time on Japanese soil. In the dark and rain and in my weariness the delegation of Japanese and Americans, who had waited patiently so many hours to greet me, were a confused blur.

After the introductions, handshakings, and bows, I found myself in one of the cars, waiting in the dark for the suitcases or some other business. A low and gentle voice spoke beside me. "I am Tané Takahashi," it said. "I am to be your secretary."

She went on to tell me that she had been educated in the United States and was herself a member of the Society of Friends. I could not see her face in the dark, but as she spoke and I felt her serene and perceptive personality I realized that someone had put a great deal of thought and effort into finding just the right person to help me. Someone among the Japanese themselves must sincerely want this undertaking to be a happy one, and if *they* wanted it to work and *I* wanted it to work, then we had a good chance of success. From that moment the burden of uncertainty and anxiety lifted, never to return.

Soon the two Americans from the Civil Information and Education Section of the Occupation joined us and we were on our way to Tokyo. One was Colonel Mark T. Orr, the head of the Education Division, and the other was Mr. Edwin Wigglesworth, one of his assistants. They both explained very carefully that they had no official connection with me but said that they would be glad to help in any way they could. Both had, I learned later, done a good deal of work in preparation for my coming, conferring with the Japanese about my contract, making a special arrangement for the payment of my salary in dollars, and so on.

The road from Yokohama to Tokyo was rough, lined on both sides with miles of devastation that in the dark looked like some bleak, bumpy moor. I saw road signs marked in English "Route 1," which looked incongruous against a background of tiny shops dimly lighted and lettered in Japanese. All the traffic moved along the left side of the road.

When we reached Tokyo my companions pointed out the Imperial Palace, but all I could see through the rain-spattered window were dark sheets of water and great stone ramparts rising mysteriously beyond.

About twenty minutes after we passed the Palace we turned off the wide street into a winding lane with walls and hedges on both sides. Presently we came to a white gate so narrow that the car had to back twice to get through it. At the end of a short driveway was a big fir tree and an open doorway from which light streamed out onto the steps.

People poured out to welcome me. Esther B. Rhoads was there, my friend and fellow member of Germantown Monthly Meeting. For many years a teacher in the Friends Girls School in Tokyo, she had spent the war in the United States and had returned to Japan just a few months before as American Friends Service Committee representative on the newly organized relief agency, Licensed Agencies for Relief in Asia, known familiarly as LARA. Another Friend was there too, Luanna J. Bowles, a member of the Education Division of the Civil Information and Education Section. Bowing on the steps were the household staff that had been selected for me, the cook, Inoue San, tiny, gentle, gray-haired and gray-kimonoed, and her daughter Michiko, a girl of nineteen, pretty, deft and bright. Yukio, the son, had a job in the government but lived in the house as additional protection.

The house, of white concrete and yellow brick, was built in the western style and like all the rest of the western houses in reasonably good repair it had been requisitioned by the Occupation, but through the good offices of Colonel Orr had been released to the Japanese government for my use.

Most of the furniture came from the Akasaka Palace, a miniature Versailles which had been built for the present Emperor's father when he was Crown Prince and now was on the point of being dismantled and turned over to the Diet. There were delicately carved French chairs upholstered in pale rose brocade, sofas to match, and round tables on which stood that evening the orchids and chrysanthemums that the Empress had sent to welcome me. The dining-room had heavy oak furniture belonging to the original owners. All three of the downstairs rooms had large, non-functional fireplaces with marble mantels. French windows faced south on to a terrace and garden.

Upstairs two of the bedrooms had beds bought for the visit of the Prince of Wales in 1924, high-backed and elaborate, of some shining red wood, with gold encrustations. The beds in the other two rooms were of white iron and brass. There was a huge marble-topped chest of drawers in my room, a simple dressing-table, and a tiny stationary wash-stand that barely reached my knees.

The furnishing of the house was not quite finished that first night, but the essentials were there and the other things came later: beautiful firescreens to hide the useless hearths, a black and gold coffee table, a desk and bookcase, currant-colored brocade curtains for some rooms, blue for others. I added gradually my own things and rearranged the furniture. On one of Luanna Bowles's subsequent visits she said to me—and I felt half pleased, half rueful, and wholly amused—"You know, in spite of the furniture from the Akasaka Palace, I'd know this anywhere for a Philadelphia Quaker's house."

She did not elaborate, but I knew what she meant: the kind of books, the *Friends' Intelligencer*, *The Friend* and *The Saturday Review of Literature* instead of *Life* and *Harper's Bazaar*, the potted plants, the few ornaments chosen for association rather than color, the slightly prim arrangement of the furniture, and a certain air of comfort and serenity withal.

Two or three people stayed for dinner that first night, and I remember we had roast beef, an especial gift from the Palace, and stewed prunes that came in someone's relief package, a combination symbolic of my early days in Japan, when war conditions still lingered. Esther Rhoads spent the night, and we talked late.

As I lay in bed waiting for sleep, I heard the sound of wooden clogs in the street outside, a clip-clop that made me realize more keenly than any other one thing that now I was actually in Japan. Clip-clop, clip-clop, lightly yet with a little drag, the wooden *geta* passed along the lane and died away. Later in the night I felt my first earthquake, a tiny tremor from the earth's center like the flicker of a fish's tail—a catfish, the Japanese say, moving its whiskers. In the morning the rain was gone and I woke to a dazzling blue and gold October day. From the flat roof on top of the house I could see Mount Fuji, ethereal in the distance, white-shawled against the blue sky.

That day I went to the Palace for the first time, to sign the contract and to meet some of the people who were to be important in my life in Japan. Tané Takahashi, my secretary and interpreter, went with me and on the way we picked up Mr. Wigglesworth. Tané in the morning light fulfilled the promise of the night before. Small and slender and quiet, she had a humor and a gentle gaiety that gave her a piquant charm. To a loving heart she added clarity of spirit and a rock-like integrity. Her five years in the United States, at Western Maryland College and the Quaker graduate school, Pendle Hill, made her seem sometimes as much American as she was Japanese, and she was the only person in Japan whom I called by her first name alone, without the formal *San*.

It was a twenty-minute drive from our house to the Palace and in the clear light of day I could see the appalling destruction that follows war. As soon as we left the little oasis of trees and gardens in which our house stood, we were in the midst of a flat waste in which squash vines clambered over the foundations of houses that were gone, or piles of twisted iron and broken stone waited to be carted away. Here and there a burned safe stood alone on its concrete base or a stone lantern tilted over what had been a garden. In the midst of the waste people were living, some in the stone storehouses where they used to keep their treasures, some in new little wooden shacks, some in huts made of rusted iron and tin. I was puzzled to see a woman emerging from a hole in the ground, and realized with a pang that there was a low roof over it and that she was living there. For many months I was not able to look at those wasted gardens and make-shift homes without seeing vividly in my mind the planes at night, the fire, the terror, the running people, the loss, and the sorrow.

As we neared the Palace, the buildings of the center of the city stood up for the most part undamaged.

The Imperial Palace occupies a tract of 240 acres right in the center of Tokyo. It is surrounded by a moat and massive stone walls built three centuries ago and pierced at intervals by beautiful old gates in the traditional Japanese style. The Sakashita Mon and the Inoui Mon, on opposite sides of the circle, are the main gates. The Nijūbashi, with the exquisite double bridge overlooked by an ancient, white-walled, black-roofed watch tower, is the one sacred to the Emperor. Other gates are used by different members of the Imperial Family and by employees of the Household. All were guarded then by both Allied soldiers and Japanese policemen.

In the winter twisted pines that overhang the walls are reflected in the still waters of the moat, where wild ducks come to float, or occasionally snow covers the banks and lodges in the pine branches. In the spring, the drooping branches of the willows are like green rain, and there is a froth of cherry blossoms over the top of the walls. In summer all the trees within the walls are richly green and the old stone blocks turn from gray to purple in the misty rain. In September pampas grass grows out of the cracks between the stones, and November brings scarlet to the maples.

Outside the Palace lies Tokyo. On the east are the outer Palace gardens, an open park-like place with more moats and walls and grassy lawns under ancient pine trees, crossed by motor roads. Since the war the young people from the big office buildings near by swarm out in their lunch hour for games of baseball and volley ball, or walk about in the sunshine. A fringe of fishermen lines the moats. The wide space in front of the Nijūbashi, called the Plaza, is the center for labor demonstrations, Allied military parades, and Easter sunrise services.

On the south side of the Palace are the gaunt ruins of Japanese government buildings and the earliest housing centers for Occupationaires, little villages of converted Quonset huts with their names in arches over their gates; Palace Heights, Jefferson Heights. The British Embassy occupies the most attractive site on the west side, overlooking the moat through a screen of

[24]

spectacular cherry plantings. On the northern side is the Yasukuni Shrine, where the souls of dead soldiers are honored. Formerly the center of the ultra-nationalistic cult, it is now shabby but still frequented.

All this on the outside, and on the inside—mystery. The rare American who got through the Sakashita Mon must be invited by the Japanese government and approved by the Occupation; his pass admitted him for a single occasion. I was to possess the only "permanent" pass.

That October day when I entered the Palace for the first time, there were four Allied sentries, two American and two British. When our passes had been inspected we went on to the Japanese policemen beyond the Moat in the arch of the great tile-roofed gate. They were expecting us and waved us through.

We came at once to a large modern building, once white, now darkened and streaked by the protective paint with which all light buildings had been covered during the war to make them less visible from the air. In front of it was a little pond, surrounded by beautiful dwarf pines. This was the Imperial Household Building, the administration center for what had been formerly one of the most important divisions of the government. The Imperial Household employees had numbered about seven thousand, the Minister had had a Cabinet post. Now the employees were reduced to less than one thousand, and the Minister had become the Emperor's Grand Steward.

We swept under a porte-cochère and got out of the car, to be greeted by gentlemen waiting on the steps, an official in the Department of Ceremonies, the secretary of the Grand Steward, and others.

Up two flights of marble steps we went, to the office of the Grand Steward, which looked over the pond and the gate, the Moat and the outer gardens, toward a line of tall office buildings in the distance. I did not know till later that one of these buildings was the headquarters of General MacArthur, nor did I hear till very much later that the affectionate nickname for the General in the Imperial Household was *Ohoribata,* Honorable Across the Moat.

The Grand Steward at that time was Mr., formerly Viscount, Yoshitami Matsudaira. He was rather elderly and spare, scholarly-looking and courteous, a little nervous in his manner.

[25]

He spoke excellent English, having studied at Oxford. The room seemed filled with people, many of whom were there no doubt to take a look at the Crown Prince's tutor.

After we had a cup of tea, the delicious green tea in handleless cups that accompanies any operation, important or trivial, in Japan, the contract was brought out. It was typed on white paper, beautifully lettered by hand on the cover, tied up with purple ribbon and sealed with the imperial sixteen-petaled chrysanthemum. It provided, besides the salary, "all necessary living expenses, including house rent and utilities, motor car, provisions, laundry, payment of employees (domestic servants and secretary) and traveling expenses in Japan," as well as travel from Japan at the expiration of the contract.

Though even in my first hasty reading of it I knew it was a generous contract, designed to provide in every way for my comfort and safety and to protect my interests, I did not realize until I had been there a long time how much more was given to me, the American tutor, than to the Japanese who served the Imperial Family or taught the imperial children in the schools. This is perhaps a good place to say two things. One, that in all my experience in Japan I was never aware of jealousy or resentment on the part of my Japanese colleagues who had less and worked more; and second, that in all their dealings in regard to the contract, financially and otherwise, I found the Japanese not merely prompt and scrupulous but generous as well.

There was a further clause to which I paid scant attention at the time but which as I have studied it later takes on more significance:

"In all respects the scale of living provided by the party of the first part for the party of the second part shall be such as will uphold the propriety of her position as a person whose entrance into the Japanese area has the interest and sanction of the General Headquarters of the Supreme Commander for the Allied Powers."

It had not entered into my thinking that I came as one of the conquerors, but I had, of course, and here it was quietly stated. I thoroughly disliked that position, and the fact that some of the courtesies, some of the consideration, some of the deference that I received so abundantly in Japan came from that basic situation was one of the never entirely conscious burdens that I was thank-

[26]

ful to shed when I returned to the United States and began again to drive my own car and pay my own house rent and utilities.

For my part I was to "perform the following duties:

(a) Tutor the Crown Prince in English once a week and

(b) Perform such teaching duties both in the *Gakushuin* (The School for Boys) and the *Joshi Gakushuin* (The School for Girls) to further the instruction of the Crown Prince or other children of the Imperial Family, such instruction not to exceed eight (8) hours per week in all."

As a matter of fact, I am thankful to say, many more duties came to be added to these, but that was part of the unfolding story of the years.

As I moved forward to the round table on which the contract lay and put my name to it, I was swept by a sense of the strangeness of the destiny that brought me here in this imperial fastness within the Moat, a feeling that became familiar with the years but never faded or lost its keenness.

Later that day I met Mrs. Tsuneo Matsudaira. No relation to the Grand Steward, she was the wife of the former Ambassador to Great Britain and to the United States and mother of the lovely Setsuko, who after her education at the Friends School in Washington, had returned to Japan to marry the Emperor's younger brother, Prince Chichibu. Mrs. Matsudaira, gray-haired, serene, humorous, and wise, truly deserves the title of "a great lady." She was to be of the greatest possible help and support to me, and I was to see her frequently. When I asked her for guidance in the intricacies of court etiquette and procedure, she said simply, "Just be yourself and don't worry," advice which proved not only reassuring but sound. It got me through.

The other caller that day was Mr. R. H. Blyth. He is an Englishman who has found his home, physical, mental, and spiritual, in the East. For years he taught in the University of Seoul in Korea; he married a Japanese girl, and came to Japan, intending to take Japanese citizenship. The war intervened, however, and he was interned. After the war he taught English at the Peers' School, as well as a number of other schools, and had a house on its campus. In the spring of 1946, when the Crown Prince's class began the study of English, he was engaged on the recommendation of Mr. Yamanashi, the President, to tutor the Crown Prince one hour a week.

He is a charming and scholarly man of middle age, a devotee of Zen Buddhism, with a wide knowledge of Japanese life and culture. A kind of modern Lafcadio Hearn, he writes of English literature for the Japanese and of Japanese poetry for the westerner.

He gave me much interesting and helpful information that day about the Crown Prince and the Peers' School, and then he said:

"Tomorrow when you meet the Crown Prince, he will say to you, 'Thank you for coming so far to teach me.'" He paused, and added with a smile, "I have told him that you will answer, 'Thank *you* for welcoming me so kindly.'"

It was a more artificial approach than I had intended, but I promised to try to remember my line in this little dialogue.

CHAPTER THREE

I SAW THE Crown Prince for the first time together with his father and mother. The occasion was without precedent.

It was a beautiful, mild October day, and I had been in Japan not quite forty-eight hours. Mr. Nagamitsu Asano, the round, genial secretary of the Peers' School who did so much to help me that first year, arrived to escort Tané Takahashi and me to the Palace. We left our house at two in order to be at the Imperial Household Building at two-thirty. About halfway there, Tané suddenly cried out in an anguished voice, *"Do shimasho!"* (What shall I do?—the first Japanese words I learned. The next one was *dozo*—please.) The pass had been forgotten!

Back we went to get it, Tané and I abashed, Mr. Asano laughing merrily. Then he explained that we really didn't have to be there until two-fifty; he had made allowance for just such contingencies. So we reached the Palace in good time, and went as we had done the day before to the office of the Grand Steward.

I had brought from Philadelphia some chocolates for the imperial children, and I now produced them. They were taken away to be presented before the audience. While we waited I was introduced to Mrs. Tatsuo Takaki, who, with Mrs. Matsudaira, was to be a beloved friend and mentor. Mrs. Takaki had lived for many years in New York, where at least two of her children had been born. After her husband's death she had returned to Japan and for twenty years she had been a lady-in-waiting and interpreter to the Empress. A woman of quiet and compelling charm and great sweetness, she has made it her particular mission to bridge the gap between Americans and Japanese, and she had among the Occupation a host of admiring friends.

Presently Mrs. Takaki and an elderly, rather severe lady-in-waiting and I went to the audience chamber. As we walked down one long corridor after another, Mrs. Takaki explained that the big room formerly used had been destroyed during the war but that Their Majesties liked the smaller room better.

The famous Phoenix Hall, of which I had seen pictures, was gone, with the rest of the Palace built in 1889. It had not been bombed, it was burned by accident. On the night of the great raid of May 26, 1945, the B-29's had left and the all-clear had sounded, though fires were still raging all over the city. From the blazing War Ministry Building across the Moat, big bundles of flaming papers were caught up by the wind and blown over the walls into the Palace grounds, where they fell onto the Palace itself and set it afire. In spite of all the efforts of the fire department, the buildings were consumed in a very short time. Since then the Emperor and Empress had been living in a small concrete building, originally a library, over the air-raid shelter, deep within the walls and hidden gardens of the inner enclosure. Rooms in the Imperial Household Building had been fixed up as audience chambers, drawing-rooms, and other apartments for their use during the daytime.

It was in one of these rooms that we now sat and waited. The room was spacious and uncluttered, ornamented with beautiful wall-hangings and gold screens.

After a moment or two the door opened and we stood up. The Emperor, the Empress, and the Crown Prince came in. Mrs. Takaki presented me to each in turn. We all shook hands. Their Majesties said that they were so glad that I had come and they had been looking forward to my arrival eagerly.

Now it was the Crown Prince's turn. I waited for the prepared speech. But Prince Akihito had a mind of his own. "Thank you for the candy," he said.

He was twelve years old then, a lovable-looking small boy, round-faced and solemn but with a flicker of humor in his eyes. He wore the dark blue uniform of all Japanese schoolboys, long trousers, a jacket high in the neck and hooked down the front under a line of braid. At the collar was the mark of his school, a small silver cherry blossom. Like all Japanese schoolboys, his head was shaven close to the scalp; his short black fur of hair was glistening and his skull was well shaped, without the bumps and hollows that make this haircut so unbecoming to many boys.

The Emperor waved his hand to indicate a chair to me and we all sat down.

My first impression of the Emperor was that he was a shy and sensitive man and a friendly one. The Empress was a beautiful woman with the rather long, aristocratic face seen in some of the old prints, though unlike them her face lights up with a most charming and infectious smile. She was not wearing the traditional kimono and *obi* (wide brocade sash) but the simpler court dress developed during the war. That day she wore one made of soft gray-green silk; it had a kimono top and a full long skirt, with a narrow belt tied at the waist. She had tiny satin slippers to match. Of a comfortable motherly figure, she still looked much younger than her forty-two or forty-three years.

The audience lasted half an hour, and its atmosphere was unstrained and natural. We chatted easily on a variety of subjects, Their Majesties speaking in Japanese and Mrs. Takaki translating so smoothly, so skilfully that it scarcely seemed to come through a third person. They inquired solicitously about my trip and the conditions of my house. Her Majesty regretted that it was furnished with "odds and ends," and I replied that the furniture was lovely and I thanked her for all that had been done for me.

I said that I had come to Japan with friendship in my heart and in hopes of making some small contribution to the cause of peace among nations; I spoke of the honor and privilege of teaching their son and of my determination to do my best for him. The Emperor replied politely that it was an honor for their son that an American lady of such knowledge and understanding should come to teach him.

The Emperor inquired after Dr. Stoddard and also after Esther Rhoads, of whose work with LARA he was informed. Both Their Majesties thanked me, as an American, for the food that had been sent to Japan by the United States government during the previous summer of severe food shortage. We spoke of the Emperor's trip to Europe as a young man and he regretted that circumstances had prevented his visiting the United States.

The Empress said she would be glad if I could teach the princesses not only English but other things as well, that they had had very little experience. I replied that I should like very much to have them come to my house and show them things

[31]

that American girls enjoyed. Her Majesty said that was exactly what she wanted.

That day, October seventeenth, happened to be a holiday, the harvest festival. I asked the Crown Prince how they celebrated it at his school and he told me, in Japanese, that they had had a sports day, and described one of the games traditional in the Peers' School. Three boys form a horse and a fourth boy, perched on their shoulders, is the rider. Horse and rider then engage another horse and rider in combat, each rider trying to pull the other off his mount. I was interested that the Crown Prince was involved in this kind of rough and tumble and amused later when I heard that he had got thrown. A rather widely circulated account of the Crown Prince in an American magazine asserted that although he had playmates they were never allowed to defeat him in any game. This I found over and over to be untrue. He was often defeated and when he won he won fairly. He took both defeat and victory in good part, though like any other boy he preferred victory.

The audience was brought to a close by Their Majesties' saying that they hoped they would see me often. A great armful of pink and white cosmos was brought in and the Empress gave them to me, saying that she had grown and picked them herself. I expressed my thanks, we all shook hands, and the Imperial Family withdrew.

Mrs. Takaki and I went back to the room where Tané and Mr. Asano were waiting, the car was called, and we left, to the clicking of many cameras.

When we reached home we found Mr. Katsunoshin Yamanashi, the President of the Peers' School, waiting to hear all about the audience. Mr. Asano must have telephoned him, for he had arrived with a vase big enough to hold the imperial cosmos. It was Mr. Yamanashi, incidentally, who had found Tané for me.

He was a small, erect old gentleman with the kind of mellow, strong, kindly face that you sometimes see in old carved ivory. His eyes, which were very keen, had a way of looking off into the distance as if he were scanning the sea for a sail; then suddenly they would veer around at you and you would realize that a very acute judge of human nature had just summed you up.

Forty-seven years before, Mr. Yamanashi had studied in England, and he had a life-long love of the English people, their landscape and their poetry. He was often to surprise me by the variety and aptness of his quotations.

A former admiral, he had been vice-chairman of the Navy Ministry and had attended the Washington Naval Conference of 1926 and the London Conference of 1937. After the latter, his opinions differing from those of the dominating military party, he resigned and was made President of the Peers' School. As the Peers' School was maintained by the Imperial Household, I thought that the fact that a man at odds with the militarists should be appointed to its presidency might be an indication of the Imperial Household's own attitude toward the military policy.

After the purge decrees of the Occupation went forth, by which all career Army and Navy people were forbidden to hold political or educational office or take certain positions in business, Mr. Yamanashi resigned the presidency of the Peers' School.

He listened carefully to my account of the audience, looking pleased, and then he said, "I think everything is going very well and we are not going to have any hitches at all."

CHAPTER FOUR

It was a surprise to me to learn that the Imperial Family did not live together within the Moat. The Emperor and Empress lived in Obunko, the former library over the air-raid shelter. It was small and severely plain, but the Emperor refused to have the Palace rebuilt while so many of the Japanese people were still homeless after the war. The eldest daughter, Princess Shigeko, was married to the son of Prince Higashikuni, who had been the first post-war Prime Minister, and the young couple, with their two children, lived at that time in the house of the princess's father-in-law. The three unmarried princesses lived within the Moat but at some distance from Obunko. Prince Masahito, the younger brother of the Crown Prince, had his own house near the Imperial Household Building, again rather far from his parents. The Crown Prince lived outside the Moat altogether, in a house on the grounds of the Middle School Department of the Peers' School, about a forty-minute drive from the Palace. Once a week he went to the Palace, spending Saturday or Sunday night there, and the whole Imperial Family had dinner together.

To Americans and to many Japanese this seemed a lonely and unnatural way to live. To us the happy, wholesome and normal life of the British royal family, which becomes for the people at large an expression of ideal family life and an example to admire and imitate, seems the pattern for royal household arrangements. Even with two thousand years of an entirely different tradition behind them, many Japanese spoke to me of their regret that the Imperial Family could not share in the new freedom that had come to Japan and enjoy a happy life together.

One wondered, of course, why it could not be, and I heard

many discussions of the question. The usual reason given was that the court officials were still too much bound by the old ways to permit it. "Oh, they are stoneheads," said one Japanese lady with disgusted finality.

It is difficult for Americans to realize to what extent decisions involving his personal life were made not by the Emperor himself but by relatively obscure officials for him. That this seems to have always been the case is borne out by a story which I heard of the present Emperor's grandfather. The Emperor Meiji, who had more personal power than either his son or grandson, objected strongly to the Akasaka Palace when it was being planned as a residence for the then Crown Prince, declaring that such an imitation French affair was unsuitable in Japan. He could express his disapproval beforehand and demonstrate it afterwards by refusing to enter the finished Palace, but he could not prevent its being built. Indeed, even outside of the court, important decisions of policy in Japan are frequently made not by the people at the top but by underlings, and a study of this practice and the philosophy behind it would offer interesting sidelights on some of the more baffling aspects of Japanese history.

The Nippon Times, a newspaper published in English by Japanese, said in an editorial entitled, "The New Tutor to the Crown Prince":

"Every indication the public has been able to receive indicates that the present Emperor and Empress themselves possess most enlightened and democratic inclinations, indeed far more so than most of those who surround them. But it cannot be denied that too many of the officials of the Imperial Household Ministry and members of the court circle are still entangled in the meshes of their own out-worn customs. Undue formality and unsound practices, such as the maintenance of a separate household for the Crown Prince apart from his Imperial Parents, give evidence of the persistence of unnatural and restrictive influences. It is to be hoped that Mrs. Vining, apart from her formal duties of instruction, will be able to exercise her influence to break down these unsound conservative customs and to emancipate the Imperial Family to its rightful position."

"It has never been done before" is, of course, a potent reason for not making changes even in new and democratic countries, and certainly as one reads the history and literature of Japan one sees that from time immemorial the royal princes were taken away from their parents at an early age and set up with establishments of their own. The reason behind that, I had thought, might be a form of the familiar prescription, "Divide and rule," for undoubtedly the members of a family separated from one another and managed in all small details by their chamberlains, advisers and officials, are less likely to get out of control than a united family supporting one another's decisions and desires.

It was to protect the Crown Prince from constant awareness of his rank, the chamberlains told me, that he was kept outside the Moat. Away from the Palace he was also away from the excessive veneration which his parents received from those around them and from the marks of special rank which differentiated him as Crown Prince even from his own brother and sisters. In this way his education could be more "democratic." Any suggestion that there were other ways to accomplish this very desirable end within the framework of a normal family life met the weary answer, "You don't understand."

Prince Akihito's education had already broken away from the pattern of that of his father and grandfather. Both the present Emperor and the Emperor Taisho as children had gone to the *Gakushuin* (Peers' School) through the six grades of Elementary School. After that their education had been continued in something called an "Institute" especially established for them, in which they received instruction with a very small number of selected companions. In 1946, after Prince Akihito had graduated from the Elementary School, it was intended that a similar "Institute" should be established for him. This plan was opposed by the Occupation.* He became therefore against all tradition a regular student of the Middle School, and had in addition some lessons "which were considered especially necessary for him" given by private tutors. These included history, poetry, oriental culture, which was really the teachings of Confucius, archery, and the extra English lessons. This is the only instance of which I have knowledge of the Occupation's interfering in any way with the education of the Crown Prince, and it preceded my arrival.

* *A Short History of the Peers' School*, published for its centenary celebration in 1947. Mimeographed.

This decision was made in 1946 for three years only, the three years corresponding to our years of junior high school. At the end of that period another decision would be made.

The Peers' School itself had undergone changes since the war. Originally designed for princes of the blood, children of court officials and of peers, it did from the first admit a few sons of selected commoners of wealth or power or fame. It was supported by the Imperial Household, the fees were small (twenty-two yen a year), and the advantages many. During the war parts of it were destroyed. The peers themselves were brought to an end by a single sentence in the new Constitution: "Peers and peerage shall not be recognized." In 1946 the Peeresses' School (*Joshi Gakushuin*), which had been a separate institution administered by the Imperial Household for princesses and the daughters of peers, was combined with the Peers' School and both were reorganized as an independent private school without any connection with the Imperial Household, except that the imperial children were to attend it. It was opened to all children who could pass the entrance examinations and pay the not excessive fees. The name, *Gakushuin*, was kept, for though it was called the Peers' School in English, the literal translation of *Gakushuin* is simply Institution for Learning.

The three years of Middle School, corresponding to our junior high school grades, were settled in 1946 at Koganei, about twenty-five miles from the center of Tokyo. The last three years, with the College Department, were on the battered Mejiro campus, near my home. There were at the time of the reorganization 1,860 students in the school, of whom 574 were girls and five were children of the Emperor.

Before my first week in Tokyo was out, I was on my way to Koganei to visit the school there and to meet the Crown Prince's class, which I was to teach once a week.

After about half an hour of driving along wide city streets past areas of devastation, we emerged suddenly into the country. The day was gray and chilly, but there was color in the bamboos, the evergreens, and the occasional vermilion of a *torii* (gate) before a shrine. Sometimes the road wound through a village where the thatch-roofed houses and open-faced shops crowded close together. There was not much in the shops but piles of the giant white radishes called *daikon* and small fat tea-kettles dangling on a string from the ceiling.

We had to creep through the villages because of the life swarming over the road, bicycles, ox-drawn wagons, hand-carts of all kinds, and slow-moving pedestrians. Every woman, it seemed to me, wore the baggy trousers called *mompe* and had a child on her back. Throngs of four- and five-year-olds played in the path of the car. The little girls often wore faded red kimonos, padded so thickly that they were about as broad as they were high. Small boys topped their dark trousers and layers of sweaters with short white pinafores that covered them all round and rose up ruffled over their rotund stomachs in a very engaging way—without in the least detracting from their masculinity.

Beyond the villages were fields, cut up into small strips, to which the farmers often walked long distances several times a day from their homes in the village. Near a temple grove of tall, straight cryptomeria trees we turned to the left, sped between fields of radishes crossed by rows of tea bushes, waited at a railroad crossing for a small and shabby electric train with passengers bulging from every window and door, passed the golf links which had been taken over for the use of the Occupation, and turned finally into a driveway between plain gateposts marked only "Off Limits." A Japanese policeman came out of a sentry box and saluted us.

The driveway curved across a field and through a scarf of woods to a low, wooden building with unpainted walls and a black tiled roof. At the entrance were a number of men formally bowing in welcome.

"You will find our school very simple and shabby," someone had said to me earlier. "You will be shocked, I am afraid. I hope it will not be too uncomfortable for you."

Even though thus warned, I had made allowance for oriental deprecation and was not prepared for the shabby, unheated, primitive place that I found. The building was so close to the ground and the ground so damp and muddy that there was a penetrating chill along the floor. The most depressing thing about it was the dirt. The boys were supposed to clean the classrooms themselves, but there was a fatal shortage of cleaning supplies and implements, of will power, and of adult direction.

When I saw other schools in post-war Tokyo, I decided that

this one was no grimmer than most and better than some. The schools had been badly hit. The precision bombing which could pick out the German Embassy to demolish and leave intact the Allied ones, save structures that would be useful to an occupation while eliminating others near by that had military or ultra-nationalistic significance, had not spared the schools. In many cases, it is true, the Japanese Army invited attack by using the schools as military barracks; in others the children were making parts for munitions during school hours. Both sides, child-loving nations, had valued military advantage above the lives of children.

After I had met the principal of the Middle School, Mr. Iwata, the English teacher, Mr. Kikuchi, several other teachers, and the Crown Prince's chamberlains who were on duty that day, I was presented to the whole school in a brief ceremony.

The boys were marched out of their classrooms and lined up on the playground. The Crown Prince joined them last and stood in the middle of the front row, his invariable position in any school gathering.

Mr. Iwata explained to me through Tané that he would make a speech of welcome and that all I had to do was to bow in return. "But," I said, "I'd like to answer it, and Miss Takahashi can interpret for me."

When he had finished, I thanked him, and then I said:

"I am happy to be here after my long journey. I appreciate deeply the welcome I have received and the thoughtful kindness with which my coming has been prepared for. I think today is a day we should all remember. In myself I am not in the least important, but the fact that I am here this morning is a sign of something very important. That your Emperor asked me to come at this time and my government helped me to do it, is something new in the world and something hopeful.

"The chief reason why I wanted to come is that in her new constitution Japan has renounced war as an instrument of national policy. Other nations must follow. I believe that out of her great suffering and defeat Japan will draw a new strength and a new vision that will enable her to lead the world in ways of peace.

"You are the generation that will have to do it. Your job will be to create a world in which every human being can develop

[39]

the best there is in him, a world in which free men can work together for the good of all. I come to you in friendship and in the hope that I can take a small share in helping your many distinguished teachers to prepare you for your great task."

I doubted as I looked at those childish faces, if it could mean very much to them, and yet I wanted to mark the occasion for them with my sense of its significance. If one or two got anything from it I felt that I would be satisfied—and the teachers could understand. When I left Japan four years later, some of the boys referred in their farewell letters to what I had said that day.

Now, only five years later, as I write these words, I hear our leaders talk of rearming Japan. We have not even waited for these boys to grow up.

Tané translated my little speech to the boys and teachers. Later Mr. Iwata gave a copy of his speech to Tané and she translated it for me.

"Today," he had said, "is such a memorable day for our school because our long awaited teacher, Mrs. Vining, is come. As you all know she has come as a tutor to the Crown Prince at the desire of the Emperor. It is such a great pleasure for all of us to see her looking so fine in spite of her long tiring trip from the United States.

"It has been decided that Mrs. Vining will teach besides the Crown Prince by himself, the whole first year class. Every girl and every boy of Japan must wish to be taught by her. But that is impossible. Only you have received the honor of being taught by Mrs. Vining and to think of it must make your heart beat with joy. You will receive her instruction as the representatives of the millions of other Japanese pupils. It is a great honor and at the same time your responsibility as a result will be great. I sincerely hope that you will show her the good, the diligence, and the intelligence that the Japanese boy has. You must remember well that the eyes of all Japanese boys are watching you. If you are idle or if you lack seriousness, you will disgrace not only the Gakushuin but all the boys in Japan.

"We hear that Mrs. Vining is such an understanding teacher. I imagine that she will teach you with Christian love. You will, I hope, return her love by following her teaching earnestly, faithfully, with respect and adoration."

When I read this speech I wondered, as I was so often to wonder, whether, had the situation been reversed and a Japanese woman had come to teach in an American boys' school, she would have received an introduction so designed to build up the respect and coöperation of the students.

After this little ceremony the boys returned to their classrooms and I visited the English classes. By this time numerous photographers had arrived and pictures were taken at every step.

Although most of the classes in the Gakushuin, as in other schools, were divided into sections of fifty or more each, the Crown Prince's class of seventy-three was divided into three. There were twenty in his section, and they had a sunny room with windows on three sides. Beyond it was a grassy place with some shrubs and trees, and then a high wooden wall enclosing the house in which the Crown Prince lived. There were two or three wooden sentry boxes and the Japanese policemen on guard there often looked in the window with interest as the lessons proceeded.

The walls of the room were of white plaster, scarred and stained. The desks were clamped to the seats. On the side of each desk was a hook for the student's cap and school-bag. A low platform ran across the front of the room for the teacher's desk and chair, and behind it was a blackboard. There were no pictures, no books.

The lesson began that morning with a brisk little ceremony. As Mr. Kikuchi entered, the boys stood stiffly to attention. The "captain" of the class rapped out a command, "Bow," and they all bowed. Another command, and they sat down. I murmured to Tané that they need not do that for me, and they never did. The lesson had to do with pronouns: Taro is my brother. How old is your brother? Each boy recited in turn, and there was a short dictation, using the textbook sentences.

The next day I returned to Koganei, this time with Mr. Blyth to observe his private lesson with the Crown Prince. Mrs. Tsuneo Matsudaira went with us, since she was to attend all my private lessons. She talked as we drove through the dripping countryside of her experience with "those royalties" both in England and Japan, and of various crises during the war which she met with the formula which came to be firmly associated in my

[41]

mind with her imperturbable, indomitable personality: "Well, never mind. I will show you."

We went in past the school building, past the high fence that hid all but the low roof of the Crown Prince's house, and came to a large Japanese building with a dramatic curved roof of cocoa-brown bark. This building had been set up in the Imperial Plaza in 1940 for the ceremonies of the 2,600th anniversary of the founding of the imperial line. Its name, Kokaden, meant Palace of Glorious Light. Later it had been brought to Koganei, and now part of it was used for the Crown Prince's private lessons.

When my car drew up at the side entrance to the Kokaden, a man servant was there to open the car door. There were two men who alternated in this job and I came to know and like them both. They were very earnest and devoted to the Crown Prince, and they gave me a friendly courtesy that touched me. One of them knew a little English and one day he practised it on me. "Hello!" he said triumphantly.

We were escorted to a waiting-room, where we found three gentlemen. Dr., formerly Baron, Shigeto Hozumi was the Crown Prince's Grand Chamberlain. A distinguished lawyer, a Confucian scholar, a connoisseur of Japanese art, literature and drama, reputed to be an outstanding liberal, especially in regard to women's rights, he was then sixty-seven years old and had occupied this position with the Crown Prince since 1945. He was a small, rotund man with a moustache and spectacles, and he had that unmistakable air of the genial, aristocratic, somewhat stuffy, old gentleman of all countries. His English was too good for me ever to make use of Tané's interpretation, but it invariably deserted him when I tried to engage him in any serious and definite talk about the Crown Prince. He spent most of his days at the Crown Prince's house in Koganei, where he had an office of his own, attended the Prince on many occasions, and, in consultation with the five other chamberlains and Mr. Nomura, made the really important decisions in regard to all the affairs of the Prince's daily life.

Mr. Koichi Nomura, who had charge of the academic education of the Prince, was a little younger than Dr. Hozumi, rather tall and pale, with long-fingered, sensitive hands and a sometimes disconcertingly abrupt manner. Though he had grown up in one of the rich old families of western Japan, he was a German scholar of note, had taught German in the College Department of the Gakushuin, and until he took his present post had been president of that department. As I came to know him better I learned what a rarely boyish and innocent spirit he had, what transparent honesty. Both he and Dr. Hozumi had been bombed out during the war and lost all their possessions.

The third man in the waiting-room was Mr. Shiro Sumikura, one of the five chamberlains. All the chamberlains were university graduates, chosen for their intellectual attainments and their character. Before the war they had all come from noble families, but these barriers had been lowered. Two now were of the nobility, three were not. They accompanied the Crown Prince wherever he went, sitting in an ante-room within call when they were not actually in the same room with him. One of them slept in an adjacent room at night, wearing kimono and *hakama* (a pleated, divided skirt that men, and sometimes women too, wear over their kimono on formal occasions) so as to be fully dressed in case of emergency. One of them would sit in the room with the Prince while he ate his meals but did not eat with him. As they were all married men with families of their own they "went up" for two or three days at a time and then "went down" to their own homes. Theirs was a rather curious position without recognized authority yet with immense potentialities for influence. They had not been consulted about the appointment of an American tutor and I was told by the Grand Steward, Viscount Matsudaira in May, 1947, that they were at first very suspicious of me. But they always treated me with courtesy and consideration. Mr. Sumikura, whom I met that October day, had been in the United States before the war as a secretary to Prince Konoye on a trip and he spoke English rather well. He was gentle and sensitive and I came to know him very well and to like and respect him.

The waiting-room was furnished with a sofa, chairs, and a round table covered with a brocade cloth that became very familiar. It was of silk with squares of alternating colors, red, blue, green, yellow, with a sort of fleur-de-lys woven in the center of each square, and it appeared in all imperial waiting-rooms. Sliding windows opened on to a pretty bit of woodland that lay between the school grounds and the golf links.

Japanese tea was brought in. Presently we heard footsteps along the corridor outside and then another chamberlain came to the door, bowed, and said that His Highness was ready. Mrs. Matsudaira, Mr. Blyth and I followed him into a large, handsome room where the Crown Prince was waiting to greet us. He bowed to Mrs. Matsudaira, who bowed very low to him, and shook hands with Mr. Blyth and me. His small hand was cold.

We four sat down at a square table in the center of the room. The chamberlain sat at a small table to one side. There was a blackboard, an electric heater, and some oil paintings.

Mr. Blyth dealt with such sentences as: I am walking to the door. I am opening the door. I am closing the door. Now I am sitting down. Prince Akihito answered the questions correctly; he named various objects in the room; he did everything that was required of him carefully and exactly. I thought he looked rather bored (an expression that I was to know quite well) and once I saw him steal a glance at his wrist watch. Once or twice something amused him and his face lighted with a puckish smile.

At the end of an hour we all said good-by and shook hands again. We returned to the waiting-room, and the chamberlain escorted the Prince back to his house. Tea was again brought to us, English tea this time, to which sugar and boiled milk had already been added, and with it the small, hard, scalloped cookies that like the tablecloth appeared in all imperial waiting-rooms. After a suitable time we left. Dr. Hozumi, Mr. Nomura, and Mr. Sumikura went with us to the car and bowed us off. The policeman saluted.

The Crown Prince had disappeared and the gate to his house was closed. Only the low black roof showed above the top of the wooden fence. "Poor little boy!" I thought.

CHAPTER FIVE

Mrs. Matsudaira and Mr. Sumikura both attended my first private lesson with the Crown Prince, sitting at the little table at one side of the room while the Prince and I sat at the big table in the center. That first day I took a volume of the *Book of Knowledge* and we 'looked at the pictures together and talked about them as far as the Prince's limited vocabulary would go, which was not far.

The theory of teaching English entirely in English is that the student, learning or guessing the new words without interpretation, comes to think of them in English, instead of thinking of them in his own language first and then translating. In the second place, if English is the only language used, then he must plunge in and use it as best he can. The trick is the teaching of new words in such a way that the pupil really understands them and the building up of a new vocabulary through explanations in terms of already familiar words.

It took time, a great many pictures, and considerable agility. Sometimes I drew pictures on the blackboard, often I made use of the *Golden Dictionary*, a simple picture dictionary, and sometimes I demonstrated a word by getting up and acting it.

One quality of the Crown Prince's that very soon became apparent under the stress of this kind of learning was his intellectual honesty. It would save time and often tiresome repetition to pretend to understand, for instance, the distinction between *bring* and *take* before one actually did, but the Crown Prince never took that short cut. Looking a little worried and puzzled, he would admit frankly that he did not understand, and we would go at the problem again from a different angle. Then suddenly his face would clear and a happy look spread over it, and I would know that he had it. If I labored the point any further, to make sure, he would raise his hand impatiently and say, "Yes, yes, yes," in a way so like my own father that I was flooded with reminiscent amusement.

The presence all that autumn and winter of Mrs. Matsudaira and a chamberlain hampered both of us. It makes one feel a little silly to wave one's arms in the air in a swimming motion or to demonstrate the difference between jumping and hopping before two serious, interested, dignified adult spectators, but I learned in time to forget them. The effect on the Crown Prince, I felt, was more serious. Before answering any question he looked hastily at the chamberlain, whether for reassurance or because he felt self-conscious about making mistakes in front of him I did not know. The fact that he was noticeably more relaxed in the presence of those chamberlains who did not speak English suggests that the latter explanation was the right one. But as I saw him oftener outside of lesson hours, I realized that he was turning in everything to the chamberlains for prompting. The simplest question he seemed unable to answer for himself without seeking their help. This dependence upon them seemed to me undesirable and I longed for him to have the experience of doing his work entirely on his own, of daring to make mistakes.

At the same time I realized that I was to him a very tall and possibly rather frightening stranger from America and that perhaps he needed the presence of the familiar attendant. I understood also that the chamberlains must wonder uneasily just what I was going to do to their adored Prince, and I was glad to have them see my methods and my subject matter.

After a month we had a lesson with only Mrs. Matsudaira present, no chamberlain, and I find in my diary for that day: "The best lesson yet." As time went on, the chamberlains gradually ceased to attend the lessons and in April, 1947, for the first time Mrs. Matsudaira was not in the room. After that she attended the lessons only occasionally, in order to report to the Empress about the Prince's progress.

The great problem all the way through was to get reading material that would be simple enough English for the Crown Prince and yet mature enough to engage his interest. I prepared my lessons very carefully, trying to work in each time the words he already knew and to add new words and constructions in a logical way. As he would always answer questions to the best of his ability but never volunteered anything, either question or comment, I spent a good deal of time teaching him how to ask questions in English, and for a part of each hour he had to ask me questions of his own making.

I sought in every way to stimulate his desire to use English as a tool, to be so eager to say something that he would perforce put it into English since there was no other way to get it said. His chief interests at that time, I had learned, were fish, riding, and tennis, which he was just beginning to play.

On a visit to the International Cultural Association Library I had been given a pre-war picture book of Japanese fish, beautifully illustrated by Japanese artists and printed in full color, with a simple text in Spanish. Fortunately my college Spanish was not too rusty, and so I translated the text into simple English, Tané typed it neatly and pasted it over the Spanish, and the Crown Prince and I discussed the life of fish, using the words that were useful also in other contexts: water, river, ocean, swim, live, fresh, salt, warm, cold, deep, shallow, and so on.

Another picture book which I rewrote was Jan and Zhenya Gay's *Shire Colt*. The beauty and integrity of those lithographs of the sturdy colt and its mother, the life of the Cotswold farm, and the universal quality of the colt's adventures in discovering an ever-widening world, make it appealing to any age, and the Prince seemed to enjoy it.

But my most successful venture during those early weeks was my invention of a tennis match played on paper and in English. I made a chart of a tennis court, and cut balls and rackets out of cardboard, and we played tennis in English, scoring, commenting on the game, and in the end walking to the net and shaking hands over it. The Prince had encountered the simple past tense before, but in the tennis match he was served the perfect tense with: You have won the game. I have lost the game. Who has won the game? Who has lost the game?

The lessons tended to follow a general pattern. We would have some free conversation. (*Free* is a technical term, for anything so slow, so labored, so stilted as those early questions and answers is not usually considered free. How are you today? Is your cold better? What day is today? Did you have a good time yesterday? Did you play tennis? Now you ask me some questions.) We would read and talk about what we read. We would do some simple exercises. The Prince always enjoyed the kind in which blanks were left in sentences to be filled in with a choice of words. We would have some dictation, some practice with new words. Sometime during each hour I found some reason for him to get up and walk about, to write on the blackboard or go to the window and look out and tell me what he saw, or some other excuse to ease the stiffness of sitting still so long.

After a while in order to stir up the passivity which tended to leave all decisions, all initiative, to others, I began to say, "What shall we do first, dictation, conversation, reading?" At first he would demur, "You say," but after being prodded, he would generally choose dictation, which he liked least.

People have asked me what I called him. *Denka*—Highness—was what the Japanese called him, both teachers and classmates. In his family and around the court, he was called *Togusama*, Honorable Eastern Prince, and by his father it was shortened to *Toguchan, chan* being the affectionate ending. Prince Akihito was the form considered suitable for foreigners, and that was what I called him, except in the lessons in school.

Before I went for the first time to meet my classes in the Gakushuin, I was asked if I wouldn't like to have a Japanese teacher sitting in the back of the room throughout my lessons to keep order. There had never been a woman teacher beyond the Primary School of Gakushuin before, and furthermore many students were interpreting this new "democrashy" to mean that they could do exactly as they liked, and the teachers were afraid that I would have trouble in controlling my classes. Remembering what fiends we were to the French and German conversation teachers when I was in school, I thought it quite probable that I might have difficulty, but I did not think that having a Japanese teacher as a policeman in the room was a satisfactory solution.

One of the most fertile sources of foreign-teacher-torture, I remembered, was derision in all its varied forms of the way in which they mangled our names in pronouncing them. So I thought that I would eliminate that hazard at any rate by giving all the boys English names. There were other reasons also for the decision. One was that in their English textbooks the names of the children were all Japanese—Taro, Jiro, Yoshiko, Fumiko—

and I thought they ought to learn to pronounce the English names. Then too I wanted to establish during that one hour as much of the atmosphere of an American classroom as possible. In the third place I thought it would be a good experience for the Crown Prince for once in his life to be on exactly the same level as the other boys, with no title and no especial treatment at all.

Accordingly I made out a list of boys' names alphabetically arranged for each section, and I marched into Section A the first morning very calm outwardly but feeling a bit adventurous within.

The boys all stood up. "Good morning, boys," I said. "Good morning, sir," they replied with one voice. I laughed and they laughed. Then I told them that you said Sir to a man but you called a woman by her name. The boys sat down and looked very expectant, their black eyes shining.

"My name is Mrs. Vining," I said, and turned to the boy who sat at the first desk on the right-hand side. "What is your name?" He told me.

"That is your real name," I conceded, "but in this class your name is Adam."

He looked surprised, as well he might.

"Now," I announced, "I am going to give you all English names." I went back to the first boy. "In this class, your name is Adam. Please say Adam. Please say, 'In this class my name is Adam.'"

It took a little while to get the idea over, and in the process we had some practice with pronouns. Your name is Adam. My name is Adam. His name is Adam. I wrote it on the blackboard. Adam wrote it in his notebook. I went on to the next, whose name became Billy.

The second boy caught on more quickly and the third boy jumped up eagerly to get his name. As I worked toward the Prince, who sat in the exact center of the room, I could see the others cutting their eyes around at each other, all agog to see what I was going to do about that situation.

I reached the Prince and said, "In this class your name is Jimmy." There was no particular reason for Jimmy, except that it just happened to be one of my favorite names.

He replied promptly, "No. I am Prince."

[49]

"Yes," I agreed cordially. "You are Prince Akihito. That is your real name. But in this class you have an English name. In this class your name is Jimmy." I waited, a little breathless.

He smiled cheerfully, and the whole class beamed. I realized that he probably had thought I hadn't recognized him, seeing him for the first time among the other boys. Also I think that he had always been identified in his own mind with his princeship and was unable at first to think of himself as a boy among other boys.

The other names went off quickly, and we passed on to the practice of prepositions. Near the end of the hour, Dr. Hozumi, Mr. Kikuchi, and a chamberlain tiptoed in to see how things were going. By that time the boys were answering to their names and the Crown Prince was raising his hand and responding to "Yes, Jimmy?" just like any other schoolboy.

The observers tiptoed out again. When I joined them in the chamberlains' waiting-room for a cup of tea between classes they all appeared pleased.

Afterwards I heard that there was a flurry among some of the boys' parents, who were not pleased, but Mrs. Matsudaira stood up for me loyally and it passed over. I used the same names for about two years. By that time I knew all their real names and could pronounce them reasonably correctly, and as they were growing up rapidly I felt that they were beyond that sort of play and I dropped it. Some of them, however, still sign their letters when they write to me with the names I gave them then.

I told nobody outside our closed circle about all this, for I was in terror that the newspapermen would get hold of it and head-lines would appear in the *Stars and Stripes*: "Tutor Calls Emperor's Son Jimmy." The secret never got out—among westerners. The Japanese knew and, evidently, approved. Only a short time after it was done, a newspaper in Ibaraki Prefecture came out with an editorial about me, in which "Vining Fujin" was urged to take "her Jimmy" with her to school in the United States when it should become possible.

Incidentally, I never had any trouble with discipline.

CHAPTER SIX

I HAD TWO classes a week also in the Joshi Gakushuin, the Girls' School. One was a class of nineteen girls who would graduate in March. They knew a fair amount of English and they were very high-spirited and enterprising for Japanese schoolgirls, who are usually so afraid of doing the wrong thing, of being considered "forward," that they take refuge in giggles. The other, larger, class corresponded to our tenth grade and included Princess Atsuko, the Crown Prince's sixteen-year-old sister. They knew less English and were much more timid. To all of these girls I gave English names. The Princess's name was Patricia.

During the war the school's beautiful, Japanese-style building had been destroyed, and now classes were being carried on in a former cavalry barrack of brick and concrete with rough wooden floors. The assembly hall, where I first met the girls in a ceremony similar to that at Koganei, was formerly a storeroom, bleak and barren. It was rainy that day and the roof leaked dismally. The classrooms at that time made me think of box-stalls, for partitions between rooms and corridors were only waist high. Panes were out of many of the windows, and the rooms were dark and drafty; there was no electric light. The girls had narrow benches and stools to sit on, and by the end of the day their backs were bent and their shoulders drooped. As the autumn wore on, the classrooms became colder, with the peculiar penetrating chill of unheated concrete buildings, so that often it was actually warmer out of doors than it was inside. One December day, when there was ice on the pool in my garden, I had my girls pick up their stools and we moved out of doors into the winter sunshine against the sheltered south front of the building.

The girls wore the clumsy and unbecoming uniform of the Japanese schoolgirl, which consists of a dark blue serge middy

[51]

blouse, short, straight and loose, over a dark blue pleated skirt, with black cotton stockings and black shoes. The girls' shoes tore my heart, they were so shabby, often so ill-fitting. More than one pretty, delicate girl clumped about in boots that were obviously a legacy from an older brother or perhaps a father who was not there to wear them any more.

This uniform tended to take individuality from the students and make them all look alike. When I saw my Senior girls in their kimonos for the first time, I could hardly believe my eyes. The grubs had turned into butterflies, gay, graceful, romantic, pencil-slim and willowy, with their long sleeves flowing and their little white-socked feet carefully toed in.

The first time I saw the tenth grade class, even before she was pointed out to me I recognized Princess Atsuko from her resemblance to the Crown Prince and her look of well-being. She was dressed exactly like the others, but her blue serge was not shabby and she was well shod. She had curly hair and an unusually fair skin, a shy, rather eager smile. She liked science and volley ball and took little interest in clothes.

About thirty-five per cent of the school, students and teachers alike, had been burned out during the war. Some were living in cramped quarters with relatives, some commuting from long distances. I knew of more than one who spent seven hours a day in crowded trains. But I never heard a complaint, and I was constantly impressed by the cheerfulness and zest of the students, the patient courage of the teachers. As one said to me, "It is all hopeful. Every time we get a new thing, that is something better."

During the second week of November my classes, just getting under way, were interrupted while I was given a trip to Kyoto, the capital of Japan from 794 to 1869, which because of its art treasures had been spared bombing. The Imperial Household, on Mr. Yamanashi's suggestion, sent me there so that I might see something of the beauty of Japan and get some understanding of her ancient culture. Though at first I felt the trip to be an interruption to the work which I was eager to do, I never ceased to be thankful for it afterwards. It gave me a perspective that I could not possibly have got from westernized, ruined Tokyo.

Five of us, Mr. Asano, Mr. and Mrs. Blyth, Tané and I, left on November sixth and returned on the eleventh.

I shall never forget the beauty of the ten-hour train ride from Tokyo to Kyoto as Japan unfolded itself before my eyes. It was a rainy day, so that Mount Fuji was blotted out, but the vistas of the sea, with misty islands in the distance, surf creaming over rocks, the golden rice fields half harvested, sheaves hanging on the racks, orange groves on terraces, small sharp mountains with a fringe of bent pines outlined against the mist, thatch-roofed farmhouses, water wheels, men in blue cotton pushing carts, women with towels over their heads and great piles of brush on their backs, white herons in the rushes: one after another the prints I had seen and never quite believed were spread out life-sized before me.

In Kyoto we stayed at a small, delightful Japanese inn, the Tawaraya. I am sorry for people who visit Japan without staying in a really good Japanese inn. The proprietress met us at the station. At the entrance to the inn, which was hidden away on a plain little street lined with wooden walls, all of the maids in kimonos greeted us with deep bows. We took off our shoes at the door and in slippers flapped down the polished wood corridors to our rooms, where we left the slippers in the hall and stepped in on the *tatami* (a thick, springy matting) in our stocking feet.

Tané and I together had a suite of rooms with a little porch and garden and lavatory. In the larger room there was a *toko-noma*, or alcove, with a flower arrangement and a picture scroll, and a long low table, perhaps a foot high, of red lacquer. Around the table were flat cushions covered with brocade. A *hibachi*, or charcoal brazier, with a few sticks of charcoal pro-vided heat on the hypothesis—never yet proved to my satisfaction —that if your hands are warm the rest of you is warm. Sliding paper doors opened on the little porch with a wicker table and chairs, where one could sit and look through glass doors at the tiny garden, whose rocks, moss, ferns, stone lanterns and bam-boos were so arranged as to give the illusion of a large garden with a stream flowing through it.

In the bigger room we sat in the daytime, our meals were served on the red lacquer table, and at night our beds of quilts were spread on the *tatami*. The smaller room was a dressing-room, with a dressing-table that had no legs but a tall thin mir-ror covered by a silk curtain when it was not in use.

The little maids in their bright kimonos came and went on

endless errands for our benefit. Each time they came in they knelt to open the sliding door, rose to step over the threshhold, knelt again to close the door. They knelt, smoothing their kimonos at the knees each time with a swift movement of the hand, to serve our meals. They knelt when they said good-morning or good-night or welcomed us back after an excursion, and placing their two hands, palms down, on the floor in front of them, bowed so low that their foreheads touched the floor.

Now I was plunged into Japanese life: sitting on the *tatami*, eating Japanese food with chopsticks, clumsily but with growing appreciation of this cleanly, economical, ingenious way of dealing with food; sleeping on the floor; surrounded by people speaking Japanese, which to me was unintelligible, flowing, and marked by unexpected cadences and sudden emphases. Tané indefatigably translated for me, but there were long periods when I waited, watching the faces of the speakers, listening for the score of words that I had learned.

Crowds of Japanese newsmen followed me everywhere, and I remember standing before the Shosoin Treasure House in Nara, watching a butterfly sun its wings on a stone and feeling a pang of envy as I nerved myself to turn and face seventeen photographers.

People were intensely curious about the American who had come to teach the Crown Prince, and no doubt anxious, though they covered their anxiety with kindness. Mr. Blyth was in an entirely different category, as Mr. Yamanashi explained to me one afternoon when he came to call. Mr. Blyth had become almost more Japanese than English; he lectured and taught at the Gakushuin and a number of other schools and universities; he had been recommended by Mr. Yamanashi, who had great respect and admiration for him both as a man and as a scholar, to tutor the Crown Prince one hour a week for his accent, though of course actually he brought far more to the Prince than that. But I was the Emperor's own appointee; I had come from the United States for the single purpose of teaching the Crown Prince; and it was recognized that the teaching of English was only a medium for the larger task of opening to the Crown Prince and others the thought and practice of American democracy, which stood in so new and dynamic a relationship to Japan. As Mr. Yamanashi wrote me later: "The problem, educational in broad sense, but with an infinite consequence upon political and diplomatic fields, is really unique in the history of any nation."

It was essential that I have some understanding of the nature of the country to which I had come, and during those few days at Kyoto, it seeméd to me that the whole of Japan's history, folklore, and art beat upon my head like a drenching shower of rain. When I reached saturation point I went to see American missionaries whom I had met on the *Marine Falcon,* Miss Frances Clapp at Doshisha University and Miss Sarah Field at Kobe College, and so got my balance again. Of the Occupation and the haunts of Occupationaires, the Miyako Hotel, Yamanaka's famous shop, the geisha houses and the little streets of curio shops, I saw nothing at all.

One of the most interesting experiences of that trip was a tea ceremony in a house three hundred years old, in which Mr. Shoshitsu Sen, the fourteenth great-grandson of the founder of the tea ceremony, lived and taught his art. It was raining that day. Many of the nicest tea ceremonies I have been to were held on rainy days, and the sound of the rain pattering on the roof and dripping off the bushes in the garden outside, mingled with the sound of the kettle boiling within, is to me the characteristic melody of the tea ceremony.

We walked through a green and dripping garden, splashed our hands from a wooden dipper at a tiny well, and crawled, for the sake of humility, through a door two and one half feet square. If we had had swords we would have left them in the sword rack outside, in the interests of harmony. The *tokonoma* in the tiny tea-room contained a single blossom in an old vase and a scroll with only characters for decoration. The tea master's motions were all prescribed by the rule of centuries and were rather beautiful, controlled yet easy, like some slow dance. The powdered green tea was beaten up into a froth by a fragile whisk cut from a single piece of bamboo. It tasted bitter as one drank it with the proper three and a half sips, but sweet cakes took the taste away. The quiet, the consciousness of being enclosed from the world in this old and peaceful house, produced the effect for which the tea ceremony is intended: harmony, simplicity, self-control.

The Japanese people themselves are divided in their opinions of the tea ceremony. To some it represents a philosophy and a technique of self-control and detachment that, if spread wide, could cure the world's ills. To others it is an out-worn fetish, hollow and time-consuming. For my part I found it at its best beautiful and full of meaning; at its worst, done hastily and perfunctorily at one extreme, or, at the other, with an excessive regard for ritual and appointments, I thought it boring and empty.

At the Kyoto Imperial Palace, which we were shown in great detail, I lost for a time, perhaps in the vast Enthronement Chamber with all its symbolism of majesty, the simple, kindly royal family I knew, and touched for a little the immense shell of formality and mystery which had enclosed the Emperor in pre-war days. It appeared to me a heavy and chilly load to carry, but as Tagore has written, "The sparrow is sorry for the peacock at the burden of his tail."

In the garden of the Katsura Palace in the northern suburbs I began to understand a little the spirit of the Japanese garden: the delicacy, the precision of detail, the emphasis on suggestion instead of statement, the provision for balance rather than symmetry, the love of things-in-themselves, the texture of wood, the solidity of rock.

An old stone lantern beside the inner gate was pointed out to me especially, because in its base was carved a small "Maria." It was astonishing to me to think that into this imperial pleasure garden of the sixteenth century had slipped a representation of the Virgin Mary, but the explanation, which I got more than three years later, was simple enough. The lantern was made by an artist named Oribe, in a time when Christianity was briefly popular, and motifs were taken from it as we today take designs from the tomb of Tutankhamon or the jewelry of the Incas, without embracing their religion.

When we went to Nara, which was the capital of Japan from 710 to 794, an official from the Education Ministry came all the way down from Tokyo to explain the Horyuji Temple to me, to show me how the eighth century wall paintings in its Main Hall were being preserved, how copied with infinite care. Two years later this building was burned, through carelessness with the electrical equipment used in the preserving of it, and the priceless paintings destroyed.

[56]

The abbot of the temple, Abbot Saeki, a distinguished scholar, aged and ascetic, himself took us around. He wore a purple kimono with a brilliant piece of brocade hanging over his shoulders like a stole, and he slid the polished wooden beads of the rosary on his wrist rhythmically through his fingers all the time he talked.

The wealth of ancient and magnificent works of art in the Horyuji is overwhelming, but the thick cloak of dust which the Buddhas wear on their shoulders and the orange peels and bits of paper that litter the paths detract from the atmosphere. At the Chuguji Nunnery near by, which is cared for by women, everything was exquisitely clean, polished, and orderly.

Here is enshrined the Nyoirin Kwannon, the goddess of compassion, in meditative pose with her chin on her hand, the most beautiful, I think, of all the Kwannon. After we had looked long at her, quietly and alone with just our own group, the abbess, who was a princess and looked like one, served us tea. She had the completely shaven head of the Buddhist nun, the naked skull not protected by any draperies or scarves, but even that could not extinguish her beauty. With the tea we were given a sweet typical of that frugal autumn, thin slivers of sweet potato dried in the sun and toasted to a delicate crispness.

At both the Horyuji and the Chuguji one is very much aware of Prince Shotoku, the great figure of the late sixth century, who as Crown Prince and regent gave great impetus to the Buddhism newly introduced into Japan, made an enlightened code of laws for his country, encouraged art and learning, and was in himself brilliant, learned, brave, beloved. He was the founder of the Horyuji; he meditated in the octagonal building called the Hall of Dreams; he is even credited by tradition with having carved the Nyoirin Kwannon. It was never expressed to me in so many words, but always I felt behind the things that people said, Perhaps our Crown Prince will be another Prince Shotoku. I felt behind their eagerness when they greeted me and when they thanked me for having come to teach him, the unspoken plea: Help him to become the kind of man who can lead Japan in her hour of need.

CHAPTER SEVEN

When I returned to Tokyo Viscount Matsudaira gave a luncheon for me, to which a small group from the Occupation were invited as well as a number of Imperial Household officials and their wives. It was a beautiful occasion, and my heart was especially warmed when the Emperor's interpreter, Mr. Hidenari Terasaki, took me aside and whispered, "Everything is *all right*."

Shortly after this I went to my first Occupation party. Mr. George Atcheson was called the American Ambassador, though he was accredited, as were all the diplomatic representatives, to General MacArthur, Supreme Commander for Allied Powers. Mr. Atcheson had recently made a statement about the substantial agreement between the aims of the Allied Occupation and Japan that had been misunderstood and had stirred up a furor of comment and protest in the press. He was the U. S. representative on the Allied Council, where he had to meet the thrusts of both the Russian and Australian representatives. He was a hard-pressed not very happy man, but a man of great courage, kindness and understanding. His rather fragile and very charming wife was the niece of Dr. Frederick de Laguna, a beloved professor of philosophy at Bryn Mawr College in my day.

They lived in an attractive modernistic house that had been requisitioned from one of Japan's *zaibatsu* families. The party that evening was in honor of a visiting senator, and the guests were from the diplomatic group with some Army and Navy people and a few journalists. It was an interesting and stimulating evening and I enjoyed it immensely, though I wrote in my diary afterwards, "I felt jostled by the unseen guests—the personal and national ambitions that were out in full force."

The party was late in breaking up, and it was nearly twelve when I started on the long drive home across the devastated city.

My chauffeur had driven a Japanese Army truck in China during the war and had come to me after a year of working for the Gakushuin. He wore still the soldier's khaki cap laced up the back which had become familiar in war pictures. As I sped along the dark empty streets of the occupied city between the piles of darker ruins, alone in the car behind that army cap, I thought how extraordinary it was that I should have no feeling of uneasiness, not the slightest fear of being shot at from some dark pocket.

Thanksgiving dinner I had in the Dai Iti Hotel with a group of Civil Information and Education people. The Dai Iti was the billet for men and women of rather high rank, military or "assimilated." It was noisy and crowded. Except for the servants, who were all Japanese, no Japanese was allowed in the hotel, a regulation which had been made necessary by the abuse of the guest privilege, but which was very trying to those who had legitimate reasons for wanting to entertain their Japanese friends.

Many of the Americans were indeed the "crusaders" that General MacArthur has called them. Dedicated to the attempt to build a new and democratic Japan upon the ruins of the old empire, they poured their experience, their ideals, their strength into the cause. They worked overtime, they talked and thought of almost nothing else. In their effort to produce a perfect model of democracy they sometimes instituted measures that would be advanced experiments in many of our own states and which were bewildering to the Japanese, who were only learning their democratic ABC's. "But why," they would say, "shouldn't they avoid the mistakes we made?"

People like Luanna Bowles, more realistically but no less devotedly, worked patiently with the officials of the Japanese Education Ministry, trying through persuasion and explanation to make them understand the reasons for decentralization and other measures and through practice and contagion learn to substitute discussion and voting procedures for the old rule by pronouncement. Ethel Weed, then still a WAC lieutenant, was working with women's groups up and down the land, infusing them with her own courage, enthusiasm, and initiative.

I have still the menu of dinner that night. "Thanksgiving Greetings—1946—in the Orient" is the legend on the cover. During dinner somebody told me that the latest rumor about me was that the Crown Prince had had a British tutor with him since birth, that he spoke perfect English but very little Japanese, that nobody knew what I was doing there since there was no need for me to teach him English and I could not possibly teach him Japanese.

Two evenings later Esther Rhoads, Tané and I were dining with Prince Takamatsu, one of the Emperor's three younger brothers. Princess Takamatsu was ill that evening and her sister, a lovely young war widow, took her place as hostess. The Takamatsus were then still living in their "palace," a mansion of large and gracious proportions which later, because of the capital levies that destroyed the fortunes of all the Imperial Family, they had to leave for a cottage on the grounds.

Prince Takamatsu was slender, elegant, and cordial, with a dark, bird-like profile. He spoke English fluently but with a rather pronounced accent. He asked me to give him an hour of practice in conversation once a week and from the first of December until the following July the Crown Prince's uncle was one of my pupils. He and his beautiful and vivacious wife were very active, not to say hard working, in post-war Tokyo, visiting all kinds of good works to encourage them, sponsoring bazaars, going on endless visits of inspection, opening athletic events, entertaining and being entertained by a variety of western visitors.

Prince Takamatsu was not the only new pupil I received that autumn. Mrs. Takaki was the first to speak to me about the Empress's desire to have some English lessons. Though she spoke French well, Her Majesty knew no English, Mrs. Takaki said, and would start from the ABC's. About a week later Mr. Asano called upon me to make the formal request. It was not in the contract, he pointed out, and they wanted to be sure that it would not be too much for me. The lessons, which were to come twice a week, would begin after the first of the New Year, and I would go to the Palace for them. A day or so later Tané went with Mr. Asano to give my formal reply to the Grand Steward. I was of course delighted with the prospect.

On the seventeenth of December I was asked to go to see the Empress, not for a lesson but for an informal visit.

The Empress's study-room was up a flight of marble steps in the Imperial Household Building and past some gold screens into a wing of the building used by Their Majesties. It was a large corner room, furnished with small tables holding flowers, some overstuffed chairs, and a round center table. Two cabinets attracted my attention. One contained shelves filled with tiny rabbits of crystal, ivory, wood, and china, which the Empress had collected because she was born in the Year of the Rabbit. The years in Japan are counted in cycles of twelve named for the signs of the Japanese Zodiac. The Crown Prince was born in the Year of the Cock, which is a good year. I was born in the Year of the Tiger, which is considered very unlucky for girls and frightens away prospective husbands. The other cabinet held a miniature Noh theater perfect in every detail, with pine trees, musicians, and pebbled yard. Beneath the stage were shelves of small and exquisite dolls representing characters in the Noh plays, the maid servant who pleads through two mortal hours in *Yuya* for permission to go home and visit her sick parent, the girl who loved a young priest and turned into a snake to frighten him, the legendary hero who beat his prince in order to preserve his disguise in the face of suspicion, and dozens of others.

The morning sunshine flooded the room.

In a few minutes Her Majesty entered, accompanied by another lady-in-waiting, shook hands with me, and invited me to sit down. We talked for about half an hour, with Mrs. Takaki interpreting. I learned that the Crown Prince had told his mother about the *Golden Dictionary* and that Princess Atsuko was pleased with her English name. I described my trip to Kyoto.

At the end of the time Mrs. Takeya, the lady-in-waiting, brought in a lacquer tray with a little vase on it and placed it on the table before the Empress, who then gave it to me, saying that it was for Christmas. In ordinary households in Japan gifts are presented wrapped up in white paper and tied with red and white string in a special way, accompanied with a little paper symbol, called *noshi*, of the fish that is traditionally a part of every gift. The recipient says thank-you and later opens it in privacy. In the Palace, however, the gift is presented on a lacquer tray, accepted, admired, and thanked for, and then it is taken away and beautifully wrapped and put in one's car.

This was an exquisite little vase of cloisonné in the "mountain, water and peony" pattern. It had a small carved ebony

[61]

stand and a little wooden box lined with white silk in which to keep it.

There was also another part to the gift, which was too heavy to carry in and which appeared later in the car, ten or a dozen cans of peaches, a very welcome, neighborly sort of gift.

The Crown Prince's thirteenth birthday came on the twenty-third of December, but the birthday tea-party to which I was invited took place three days earlier. The twenty-third itself would be spent formally receiving former chamberlains and servants, after which he would go to the Palace for dinner with his family.

After the regular lesson on Friday afternoon, Mrs. Matsudaira and I returned to the sitting-room until the party was ready. Presently we were invited to return to the lesson-room. The square table had been taken away and a larger one substituted, covered with a white damask cloth and set with six places. There was a silver bowl of orchids in the center and at each place a white and gold plate marked with the sixteen-petaled imperial chrysanthemum and laden with a neat pile of sandwiches. The Crown Prince's plate, in the middle of the far side of the table, was covered with a large, pierced silver cover, rather like a cake cooler, as if to protect his sandwiches from the common air.

The guests, besides Mrs. Matsudaira and myself, were Dr. Hozumi, the Crown Prince's Grand Chamberlain, Mr. Nomura, director of his education, and Mr. Sumikura, one of the two English-speaking chamberlains. Prince Akihito came in last and sat between Dr. Hozumi and Mr. Nomura. I was waved into the center seat opposite him. The cover was whisked off the Prince's sandwiches and tea was served by the two familiar footmen. I said Happy Birthday to the Prince and gave him the fountain pen and pencil set I had brought for him. He grinned over it like any other child, returned to it when the conversation grew boring, and said that he would take it to the Palace on his birthday to show his family, especially his younger brother. I had not met the younger prince yet and this was the first time I had heard Prince Akihito speak of him; there was obvious affection in his voice when he said his name.

When the conversation turned to the Crown Prince's dog, Shiro, Mr. Sumikura, to whom I had given a copy of my *Adam of the Road,* a story about a medieval minstrel boy and his dog, pulled out his notebook and read from it a passage which he had copied out, about the highroad and its meaning in the medieval world, saying that he thought it was a beautiful piece of writing. Then he made a little speech, telling me on behalf of all the chamberlains that they appreciated what I was doing for the Crown Prince and my "sincere and eager concern for his welfare." It was a wonderfully kind thing to do for the alien who had come among them, and it made me feel that I was no longer wholly shut out of a very tight little circle. The chamberlains and I usually approached a problem from different angles, sometimes did not recognize the same problems, often differed as to solutions, but we met, then and ever afterwards, on the ground of our common concern for the Prince, and I think we never questioned the sincerity of one another's desire to do the best possible thing for him.

CHAPTER EIGHT

CHRISTMAS IN A non-Christian land is an interesting experience and a poignant one. All the ties of affection are particularly strong. The cards and letters and packages that come from home so far across the seas are especially precious, and the little group that celebrates Christ's birthday in the midst of the indifferent multitudes draws together in awareness of the joy they share. I, at least, felt that I now understood a little the enclosed fellowship of the early Christians.

The celebrations spread over about twelve days as a rule, reminding me of the "twelve days of Christmas" of the old song. It began for me on the fifteenth of December, when Mrs. Kenderdine, my blythe companion on the *Marine Falcon*, and I, with Tané, went to the celebration at Seishin, the convent school of the Sacred Heart. On the boat one of the nuns whom we had known was Mother Britt, the head of the school, and she had invited us to the Christmas play. She was a witty, wise, warmhearted saint and administrator, who could handle with equal aplomb a burglar who got into her office and a G.I. who said admiringly, "Say, you girls are some characters!"

The school, like countless others, had been largely destroyed during the war. As we drove between stone gateposts along the driveway under pine trees, we saw G.I.'s and Japanese youngsters scrambling over ruins where a charred length of fire hose still drooped over broken steps. The building that remained housed chapel, convent, library, and school. Its ten thousand broken windowpanes had been replaced, but the heating system could not be restored because the radiators had all been taken for scrap metal during the war. Though the nuns were then sleeping on tables in the library stacks, the best room in the building had been made into a chapel with altar, candles, statues, and pictures. To a Quaker, it matters not at all how the room is used at other times if only there is a place for Friends to sit together in silence and seek the presence of God, but as I looked at that chapel and reflected how crowded the building was and how much the room was needed for other things, I thought that it was a very effective way of making plain the fact that the worsip of God was the primary purpose in the life of that institution.

The entertainment was given in the icy auditorium. Girls in neat but shabby uniforms and pitiful shoes were lined up on the stage to sing carols. As they sang, slowly and rather cautiously but correctly, I was struck, as I had been struck before, by the way after one had looked at them for a while they ceased to look like Japanese children. One stopped noticing that they all had black hair and brown eyes, and saw instead an engaging nose or a pair of dimples, a tired child or a thoughtful child, an eager or a dreamy one.

After the carols there was an artless little nativity play in English, in which some children accompanied the shepherds to Bethlehem and laid offerings of canned goods before the Babe. It was all very simple and childish until suddenly the shepherds lifted it on to another plane. Coming forward one by one, kneeling and rising again with lovely flowing movements, each recited a part of Crashaw's "Nativity." The stately yet easy seventeenth century cadences of that beautiful poem, spoken by those clear young voices, while the elusive sunshine touched the grim ruins outside, invested the moment with a touch of eternity.

Christmas at the Friends Center came next. From my first Sunday in Tokyo I had been attending the Friends Meeting there. A handful of people, almost all Japanese, gathered every Sunday morning in the only house that was left in the two compounds which before the war had held a meeting house, dwelling house, and dormitory, and the numerous buildings of the Friends Girls School. For Sunday the twenty-second the group of young Friends that was the backbone of the Meeting, had planned a visit to a near-by camp of repatriates whom they had been helping, and I went with them.

The camp, which had formerly been an inn on the main road to Yokohama was now a reception center for repatriates from Manchuria. Most of them stayed for three days and then were moved on, but a few who had no other place to go were allowed to remain. The government provided shelter and tickets for rice, which was served in a dingy little restaurant across the street. Medical students gave their services. A public bath up the street offered reduced prices for baths. There was no water on the second floor of the building and no heat at all.

Two hundred and thirty people were living in twenty rooms. The inn was built around a small open court that was probably once a garden. That day there were piles of refuse on the hard, bare earth, and a ragged little group was hovering around a tiny fire on the edge of one little garbage dump.

On the second floor the Sato family (not their real name), three adults and a child, lived in a room nine feet square. The quilts on which they slept at night were piled up to make a sort of couch; an electric plate, a saucepan, and a little pile of dishes were stacked neatly on the floor. There was no other furniture.

Mr. Sato had been born in Switzerland. Before the war he had been on the staff of the Japanese Embassy in Berlin. At the end of the war he and his mother, his young German wife, and their four-year-old son were sent by the Russians to Manchuria and robbed of their possessions along the way. From Manchuria they were "repatriated" to Japan, which none of them had ever seen before. Young Mrs. Sato, thin, tired, pretty, still managed to look smart in brown slacks and sweater. She and her husband both had small jobs with the Army of Occupation and were struggling to find some other place to live. Mrs. Sato was learning to speak both Japanese and English.

The children of the camp, who numbered between thirty and forty, ranging from babies to boys and girls of thirteen or fourteen, were gathered together in the "nursery" for our "party." They came in with the pathetic docility of undernourished children and sat down close together on the tatami. One little girl with a turned-up nose and the conscious charm of the congenitally frivolous, had curled her stiff black hair, though there was a bad sore on her dirty little neck. One child of two or three cried fretfully in his mother's arms and was comforted then and there with her breast.

Led by a young Japanese kindergarten teacher, the children sang several nursery songs for us. One involved the raising of hands in the air and the rhythmic opening and closing of them, a touching sight, for the hands were so small and cold and dirty and so terribly empty. The young Friends sang "Silent Night" and "O Come All Ye Faithful," and a Japanese children's hymn which says in effect, "God cares even for the sparrows and so He cares for me." Then we gave these bedraggled little sparrows some lollypops which I had, and more substantial food from the American Friends Service Committee was given to the parents, and we went back to the Friends Center for Meeting for Worship.

On the way we saw the struggle to live going on around us. Women did their washing crouching over their wooden tubs in the streets near the faucets where they could get cold water. They had no soap. Others scrubbed the rust off pieces of tin to patch the huts in which they lived. The concrete steps which were all that was left of the Friends Meeting House were used by the neighbors as a place to wash sweet potatoes and spread them out to dry in the sun.

Sweet potatoes were the main item of the Japanese diet that winter, as they had been during the war. The U. S. Army surpluses that were released through the Japanese government to supplement the sweet potato ration were gratefully received but often found difficult to use. Corn meal, for instance, without eggs, milk, fat or salt is a problem. Many people made it into dumplings which they steamed in shallow pans over their little earthernware cooking stoves. That winter when charcoal was so scarce and people had to use wood instead, they cooked in the yard beside the steps because of the smoke. I often saw them struggling in the rain to cook these meagre meals. Once when I was describing their corn meal dumplings to my partner at a diplomatic dinner party, he looked at me curiously and said, "How do you know these things?" "Oh," I answered, "I drive around Tokyo, I see things, and I ask questions."

That Sunday before Christmas sixty people came to Meeting, the largest gathering of Friends in Japan since the war. A little wood fire burned on the hearth in the living-room of the Center, and a Christmas tree, flowers, and illuminations in the windows brightened the shabby room. There was a warm sense of fellowship as some of the members met one another for the first time in years.

On Christmas Eve some American friends came to have din-

[67]

ner with us and to help trim our little tree. While we were at dinner, we heard singing in the distance, faint at first and swelling as it drew nearer. When it came to a halt in our driveway we all jumped up and ran out, to find about a dozen children standing under the fir tree in the frosty dark singing "Silent Night" in Japanese. They were from a mission church near by. We filled their hands with candy, and their thanks and "Merry Christmases" floated back through the dark. On Christmas morning just as the sun was coming up I was awakened by carols sung under my window by my own "family." Three Inoue daughters who lived elsewhere had come to spend Christmas with their mother. Their voices, added to the others, with Tané's lovely soprano, had an almost unearthly sweet and hopeful sound.

The day after Christmas we invited some of our small Japanese friends to see the tree, and included the little Sato boy from the repatriates' inn. Six parents came too. We played games on the roof; we had a candy hunt in the living-room; we looked at the tree and each got something from it. But it was the half-German child who was really fascinated by it. He crept back again and again to stare wide-eyed at it, to touch the balls gently, to move the rabbit in the snow closer to the Santa Claus. We had refreshments in the dining-room, where a red candle burning in the center of the table decoration evoked from Tané's little nephew, Chamo-chan, the solicitous question, "Has the electric light given out?"

We ended the party with Christmas carols. There were four nationalities among us, German, Japanese, English, and American, and we sang our carols in three languages at once. I saw the German girl trying not to cry, and I wondered if it wouldn't have been easier for her to stay in the nine-foot-square room and let her sleeping memories lie.

CHAPTER NINE

JAPANESE SCHOOLS HAVE a winter holiday which begins about the twenty-second of December and lasts till about the middle of January. The imperial children all went to Hayama that year for the vacation, staying as usual in separate houses. I was asked to go down one Friday and give the Crown Prince an English lesson.

Hayama is a summer resort on the shore of Sagami Bay, about two hours by car from Tokyo. From Yokohama on, the road led past rice fields and through villages crowded in among small, sharp hills, now and then beside the sea, where women waded in icy waters getting seaweed, and fishing boats moved in the distance.

Two American soldiers guarded the main gate of the Hayama Palace, which was surrounded by a high wall, but Mrs. Matsudaira, Tané and I went in by a smaller gate, where Japanese policemen, expecting us, saluted vigorously. A short, white-pebbled, carefully raked drive led to the front entrance of the Palace, which was hooded by a low, black-tiled roof and veiled with beautiful plantings of shrubbery. The general effect was similar to the palaces I had seen in Kyoto, of a low, elegant building, walled in wood and paper and glass and roofed with tile, which kept its secrets of hidden inner beauty behind a mask of simplicity.

The door was open, and on the red-carpeted steps waited the same men who brought tea to us at Koganei. A table with the familiar brocade tablecloth stood at one side, with a book spread open on which people coming to pay their respects to the Crown Prince could write their names.

Chamberlains were there to greet us, and we were led to a charming room, half Japanese, with its beautiful scroll and ornament in the *tokonoma*, and half western, with its chairs and table and rug. It was warmed by a *hibachi* of a type found only in imperial palaces, a sort of bronze cauldron with little bandy legs and curved feet and over it a high, rounded bronze cage.

Vaguely I had had some idea that since this was a holiday lesson perhaps the Prince and I might take a walk in the grounds or along the shore, and he might show me things in which he was interested. But this was not to be.

First we had lunch, Mrs. Matsudaira and I in one waiting-room, and Tané, in spite of my protests, by herself in another waiting-room. The Prince lunched somewhere else, by himself. After lunch Mrs. Matsudaira and I were led along corridors and up a flight of stairs to a large sunny room which had, I think, the most beautiful view in Japan. In the foreground were the pine trees of the imperial grounds, beyond was a curve of beach and the brilliantly blue waters of Sagami Bay; far away, misty purple in the distance, the mountainous ridge of the Izu Peninsula ran down into the sea, and over it floated in the sky the snow-covered, blue-ribbed cone of Mount Fuji.

In this room Prince Akihito waited for me. He looked listless, I thought, and he had little to say, either in English or in Japanese to be interpreted. I had brought with me a game of jackstraws, and the Prince worked out quite a complicated score in English, while Mrs. Matsudaira and a chamberlain looked on.

I asked what he did to amuse himself and whether he played with his brother. But Prince Masahito, it seemed, had had a cold, and Prince Akihito had been able to go only once to his house to see him. He had collected some sea urchins; he had been walking with the chamberlains. It sounded to me like a very dull vacation for a thirteen-year-old boy, and I said so emphatically to the chamberlains and Mrs. Matsudaira.

The following week we went again, in the afternoon. This time when I went into the upstairs room, all of the imperial children were there, lined up in a row to shake hands and say "How do you do?" in English. Three of them I now met for the first time: Princess Kazuko, the eldest unmarried daughter, who was a student at the Joshi Gakushuin, but not in either of my classes, Prince Masahito, the Crown Prince's younger brother, and Princess Takako, the youngest, who was not quite eight years old. Princess Kazuko and Princess Atsuko had shed their school uniforms and wore pretty blue tweed suits; Princess Takako, with her short black hair cut straight across her forehead, her shy smile and her dimples, looked enchanting in a yellow wool dress. Prince Masahito was small for his eleven years but quick, lively, eager, and full of fun: a very winning child. All five of them seemed happy to be together, and the girls evidently regarded the occasion as an adventure. From time to time they were swept by gales of giggles.

This was to be not a lesson but a "social hour." The chamberlains were not present, and Mrs. Matsudaira interpreted whenever the imperial English broke down, as it frequently did. The Crown Prince drew me to the window to see spread out on the steps below some shells and sea urchins that he had found. A chamberlain obligingly brought out the new puppy, Aka, a fluffy ball of red-brown fur, and walked him up and down the path.

I had brought a game of anagrams, Wanda Gag's *Millions of Cats,* and a photograph of my own West Highland white terrier, Hamish, whom I had left at home in America. We had tea and sandwiches and little cakes; there was no cover over the Crown Prince's sandwiches this time, and indeed it never appeared after that first birthday party.

I did not see the Crown Prince again for several weeks, for after his return to Koganei he came down with a feverish cold, and before he was well I was laid low by a sharp attack of influenza myself. I could not have been better cared for. General MacArthur's physician, Colonel D. B. Kendrick, prescribed for me; my own household nursed me devotedly; the Empress sent orchids; and one morning I was aroused out of a feverish doze by the strains of "Londonderry Air" sung by lovely fresh young voices in the living-room downstairs. "Home on the Range," in Japanese, came next, and then, softly, "Ave Maria." My class of senior girls had had a free period, and they had walked a mile and a half from the school to bring me chrysanthemums and to sing to me.

After the Crown Prince and I were both well again, a second private lesson each week was added to the schedule, to my great satisfaction. Now I saw him three times each week, once in the classroom with the other boys and twice alone, or rather, with Mrs. Matsudaira and a chamberlain.

[71]

I thought that he led a very dull and restricted life, and I longed to set him free, to give him a chance to develop enthusiasms and interests. Even the few steps from his house to the school and from his house to the Kokaden he did not take alone, but always was accompanied by a chamberlain. After weeks of suggestion on my part, progress was made to the point that although the chamberlain still accompanied him to the school building, they parted and went inside by different doors! What was still sadder, he did not even seem to feel the need of greater freedom. When Mrs. Matsudaira, who understood and sympathized with my concern, told him that he should come to his lessons alone, his answer was "Why?"

The weather that winter was cold and sunny. We had one five-inch snow that lingered on the ground in patches for about a week, but little rain or sleet. The schools were bitterly cold and there were many absences among the children. Three boys in the Crown Prince's class dropped out with tuberculosis. Milk that winter was available only from the drugstore and on a doctor's prescription, for sick babies, but I was able to get powdered milk for them from LARA. Transportation was hideous. Trains and street-cars were cold, dirty, and often windowless as well as jammed to the roof. People climbed in through the windows after the aisles and steps were filled. Cloth of all kinds was so scarce that even the worn green plush upholstery had been cut off by passengers and taken home to patch clothes. It was not unusual for people to have their ribs broken in the crush, and I myself saw a pencil that had been splintered in a man's breast pocket. One of my pupils wrote, "My foot are stepped on, my hair are drew, my hands are caught. I feel like canned sardine."

Most of my pupils spent from two to five hours a day in these trains. They sat all day in icy schoolrooms. At Koganei, which was several degrees colder than Tokyo, the temperature was often in the low twenties and the boys would put their feet on the lower bars of their desks to get them off the cold floor. Some of them wore overcoats in class but most wore only their thin wool uniforms with sweaters underneath. Many of the uniforms were shabby and ill-fitting, obviously outgrown or not yet grown into; most were neatly patched at seat and knee and elbow.

The Girls' School had been greatly improved during the winter vacation by building up the partitions along the halls and by

[72]

painting the plaster walls. The missing panes in the windows had been replaced, but the windows were small and not very much sunshine came in to take the edge off the penetrating chill.

I wore a topcoat and often gloves to teach in, and wool stockings, but even so I got chilblains. The students' hands, including the imperial children's, were red and puffy with chilblains. Yet somehow they all managed to keep cheerful, to put their minds on their work and to study hard.

As the winter went on, it became obvious to me that the Crown Prince was happiest and most himself when he was with the other boys. I saw him in the classroom between classes, always in a knot of other boys, laughing, alert, and interested. Sometimes I would see him racing down the corridor to the room where they played ping-pong. There were three tables, and he awaited his turn to play, like anybody else, roaming the aisles between tables, picking up the balls that went astray and tossing them back, commenting on the game. The boys called him *Denka*—Highness—and outside the school they bowed to him and kept their distance, but in the school building and on the playground he was one of them, and the difference in his demeanor and his whole expression showed how that normal and happy relationship fed and watered his soul.

For this reason and to increase the opportunities for contact outside the schoolroom, I was eager to have two of his classmates join one of his private lessons each week, and when the new term began in April this was done. I chose the boys myself in consultation with the chamberlains and English teacher and, privately, with the Prince, and each term new ones were selected. I was always interested in the Prince's comments on his classmates, for he had a keen sense of character and he sometimes suggested boys whom I would not myself have thought of; in one case it was because he thought it would help the boy. The basis for choice was, first, character and personality, and second, at least a moderate ability in English. I liked to have one whose English was a little better than the Prince's and one whose English was not quite so good. The Prince himself stoutly resisted anyone who could speak very much better than he!

That first winter especially, people outside our immediate circle were interested in what I was teaching the Crown Prince and had large ideas of what I might accomplish. One February afternoon the Women's Committee of the United Christian Church gave a tea for me and presented me with a beautiful piece of handwoven tapestry in a design of mandarin ducks. This was an expression of the hope which many Christians felt and which others put to me in far more blunt terms, that I should convert the Crown Prince to Christianity.

There were also other misconceptions of the purpose of my work there. A prominent editor, for instance, asked me if there was any resistance to my democratization of the Imperial Family.

This was not what I had been invited for. I had been asked simply to teach the Crown Prince English. But early in my stay in Japan, Grand Steward Matsudaira said to me, "We want you to open windows on to a wider world for our Crown Prince." It seemed to me then that through the medium of English I could present to him the ideals of the western world and help him to understand the essential spirit of that democracy which Japan was embracing with a hasty and bewildered sort of zeal in reaction from her great disillusionment with military dictatorship.

I never tried to indoctrinate him with any specific dogma. I tried only to expose him to the best that I knew. Religion, I have always felt, must be caught before it can be taught, and democracy is learned at least as much through living and doing as through an intellectual understanding of its theory. There were some to whom this point of view was a great disappointment. I reminded them that the Crown Prince's English at that time encompassed no more than a simple discussion of the pictures in the d'Aulaires' *Abraham Lincoln* and a folk story, "The Monkey Wants Its Tail," which appeared in an American first grade reader, and recommended patience to them.

Much earlier I had realized that I must clarify my own ideas of the essentials of democracy, not only for the sake of the Crown Prince but for others who asked me. The first essential, I thought, was respect for the worth and dignity of the individual. The second I found best expressed by William Penn when he said, "That government is free to the people under it where the laws rule and the people are a party to those laws."

As a Quaker, I believe in regard to the first, that humanism is not enough, that the individual's worth and dignity derive from the light of the divine within his soul, and that when George

Fox, the first Quaker, told his young followers to "walk cheerfully over the earth answering that of God in every man," the kind of *answer* he had in mind was social justice for everyone and a peaceful environment in which each soul can live out its fullest potentialities. So it was natural that my aspirations for the Crown Prince should take the form of a prayer, which I wrote during that first winter and which was a comfort to me when there seemed so little that I could do for him but to pray. It went like this:

"Heavenly Father, bless this child to whom some day will come great responsibility. Grant him free and happy growth to his fullest capacities of mind, body, and spirit. May he learn to know and trust Thy light within his own heart and come to respect its presence in his fellow men. Endow his teachers and chamberlains with wisdom and courage and grant that we may serve singleheartedly his best development, putting aside all selfish interests and desires. For His sake who gathered the children about Him, Amen."

CHAPTER TEN

THE WINTER, FORTUNATELY, was short. Plum blossoms came early, bringing with their fragrance the message of courage in adversity. One of the prettiest sights in Japan is a gray, thatch-roofed farmhouse surrounded by its tight hedge of evergreens, with a burst, a veritable explosion, of white or rosy plum blossoms against the gray and the glossy green.

Early in March, when red camellias were beginning to bloom in the garden, a long deferred event took place: the princesses came to my house for the first time. What hesitations and consultations went on within the Moat I did not know, but I was aware that there was some doubt about it and that if the visit was not a success it would not be repeated. Mrs. Matsudaira, who regularly steered me through new ventures, came to see me beforehand and every detail was most carefully planned.

Because of the narrowness of the gate and the length of the princesses' pre-war Packard, it was decided that they should leave the car at the turn of the lane and walk in "like ordinary people." We watched from the window for their approach, Mrs. Matsudaira, Tané and I. Policemen in plain clothes were drifting up and down the lane, and a few passers-by, drawn by the air of expectancy, paused to see what was going on. Presently we heard the subdued slam of the car door and then a little procession came into sight between the walls and hedges; the three princesses in single file, followed by Mrs. Takaki and Miss Hana Natori, the princesses' wise and devoted governess. Princess Kazuko, as the eldest, came first, smiling, her head a little on one side, then Princess Atsuko with her curly hair in pigtails, and last little Princess Takako trying to look very serious and grown-up. They all wore pretty, light wool suits; later they would come straight from school in their uniforms.

Michiko San, our little maid, who looked her best in a dark red kimono and peach-colored *obi*, opened the door and bowed very low. The princesses came in, bowed to Michiko San, shook hands with me, saying, "Good afternoon, Mrs. Vining," and bowed to Mrs. Matsudaira and Tané.

We had the "lesson" in the study upstairs. The study was the largest and in some ways the pleasantest room in the house, with windows on two sides, looking into the big fir tree and over the garden. Floods of sunshine, and books, flowers and pictures mitigated the formality of the fine, damask-covered carved chairs and sofa from the Akasaka Palace.

Because an English lesson for three pretty, shy, and speechless princesses whose ages were eighteen, sixteen, and eight, with an audience of three adults, was sure to produce stiffness and self-consciousness, I set them to making a scrapbook, to be given to a children's hospital, and taught them to ask for the scissors, offer one another the paste, and discuss the pictures in English, while the three ladies hovered over them watching and helping.

We had tea brought up to the study. The sandwiches and cakes and tea we served that day were the first food that the princesses had ever eaten that was not prepared by the imperial cooks. The conversation in both Japanese and English ranged over books and national customs, and though the grownups did most of the talking, the three girls listened attentively, laughed at our jokes, and occasionally stole glances of private amusement at one another.

The experiment was evidently considered a success. Her Majesty was pleased and told me so when I went to the Palace for her next lesson. In fact, with a lovely spontaneity she took the orchids from the vase in front of the screen when I said good-by and gave them to me.

In the middle of March all lessons were interrupted by the ending of the school year. Examinations were followed by graduation exercises, and then there was a holiday of two or three weeks before the new school year began in April.

The Crown Prince made a trip to Kyoto and Nara during the holidays, his first such trip. I was delighted that he was to get out and see new places and meet new people.

I too had holidays and I accepted an invitation to go to Osaka and give some talks there. In December I had spoken to some five hundred English teachers in Yokohama at the request of the education officer on the military government team there, and my talk on purposes of education and the problems of the English teacher, translated by Tané, had been printed and widely circulated by the Japanese. I could not possibly accept all the invitations to speak that I received, but I usually tried to fill some of the requests during holidays. This time I had also a very kind invitation from Mr. Mikimoto, the "Pearl King," who had developed a scientific method of pearl culture and whose pearl farm was one of the sights of Japan.

Tané and I, through some not quite legal kindness on the part of Occupationaires, managed both to get on the train reserved for the Occupation and so we traveled in comfort. We went by day to Nagoya, spent the night there, and went on the next morning to Yamada, where we were met by Mr. Yoshitaka Mikimoto, the grandson of the Pearl King, a tall and slender and gentle young man of twenty-seven or twenty-eight. He had a car and he took us first to the Shrines of Ise.

These, I had understood, were the center of Shintoism and of the Emperor cult. Here the imperial messengers came to report to the imperial ancestors, who were gods, any important events; here a new prime minister came to tell of his appointment.

I knew little about Shintoism, only that it was the indigenous Japanese religion, a form of nature worship in which the forces of nature were not so much feared for their power as appreciated for their beauty and bounty. State Shintoism was a modern perversion by which the ultra-nationalists had introduced a cult of state worship and made of the Emperor an instrument, sacred in the eyes of the people, which they could use to arouse a willingness to make sacrifices and to sanction their plans of conquest.

Now the Occupation had banished State Shintoism from the schools and had cut off government financial support for the shrines. The Emperor with his Rescript of January 1, 1946, had dissociated himself from his supposed divinity in these words:

"The ties between us and our people have always stood upon mutual trust and affection. They do not depend upon mere legends and myths. They are not predicated upon the false conception that the Emperor is divine and that the Japanese

[78]

people are superior to other races and fated to rule the world."

It is beyond question that the present Emperor never considered himself divine. I think that this Rescript was possibly issued more to reassure westerners than to inform the Japanese.

People had told me that even in the days of Emperor worship the Japanese did not mean the same thing by it that we do. They have, for instance, no word for God that means what we mean by God, who is to us the creator and the source of love and truth. Their word is *kami*, which means simply superior or upper. There are literally millions of gods in Japan, all the deities of Buddhism and the manifold deities of Shintoism, the gods of the sea and mountains, of thunder and wind, of rice, of especial trees, of waterfalls, of useful things. On a certain day of the year, for instance, dressmakers' needles lie idle, so that the god of the needle may be thanked and honored. Heroes are deified; ancestors, even quite recent ones, become gods. Why not the Emperor?

The word worship, too, has a different meaning. Worship is a formal act of profound respect. It is rendered to living people as well as to the shrines and images of the gods. When a Christian teacher said to me that she went to a place which the Crown Prince would pass in order to "worship" him, I was shocked, but when one of my own pupils wrote to me that her mother would like an appointment to come and worship *me*, I began to have some inkling of the meaning the Japanese attach to the word translated as worship.

Many Japanese, moreover, are agnostics. They honor their ancestors, are married by Shinto rites, bow at the shrines when it is the thing to do, and are buried with Buddhist services, without any but the vaguest religious sentiments.

What has changed the Japanese attitude to the Emperor more than the Imperial Rescript of 1946 is the way that he has come out among the people. Whereas formerly they were literally not allowed to look on his face, now they can press close to him in crowds as he goes about over Japan, visiting schools, factories, museums, hospitals, coal mines, and a multitude of other institutions. He appears at department store exhibits in Tokyo and at baseball games. On New Year's Day the people go into the Palace by the thousands to sign their names as evidence of respect and affection, and the Emperor comes out on the roof of the Imperial Household Building to wave his hat at them. They have learned to love and respect him not for his divinity but for his own character.

All this came to me gradually. At that time I was grateful for the opportunity to see the Ise Shrines, in the hope that it might bring to me greater understanding.

We saw the Outer Shrine first, which is dedicated to the gods of production, and then drove about four miles along a winding road lined with cherry trees (not yet in bloom) to the Inner Shrine, which was dedicated to Amaterasu-Omikami, the Sun Goddess, who according to myth was the imperial ancestress.

The thing that strikes one first, after one passes under the great wooden *torii*, is the trees, huge cryptomeria and camphor trees, standing as they have stood for centuries. Through the grounds of the Inner Shrine runs a little river, the Isuzu, whose water is wonderfully clear and pure, where people purify themselves by washing their hands and rinsing their mouths before going to the shrine. All Shinto shrines provide water for the purification that is so essential a part of the religion, but only Ise has a sparkling river. The shafts of sunlight through the trees glancing off the limpid water, the stillness, the knowledge of centuries of dedication, gave the place an unearthly quality and laid a finger of awe upon one's heart. "Be still, my heart," wrote Tagore. "These great trees are prayers."

The priests who conducted us wore white silk kimonos and purple *hakamas*, a costume beautiful and dramatic among the trees. They were themselves, however, incongruously worldly and ordinary, with trim little moustaches and neat spectacles.

The buildings of the shrine are made of Japanese cypress, unpainted and unvarnished. The shape is the same as that which appears in the smallest fox shrine, an archaic form with beams that cross on the roof, which evidently prevailed in Japan before the Buddhist influence brought in a new style of architecture in the sixth century.

We walked along an avenue through the trees, passed under more towering *torii*, and came to a wooden fence and gate. There believers bowed, clapped their hands, and uttered a silent prayer. Beyond the fence was a yard, covered with white pebbles all the same size and brought from some very special place. Beyond a second gate was the shrine, the small wooden building sacred to Amaterasu-Omikami, which housed the Mirror, one of the three sacred treasures of the regalia of Japan. The public must stop at the first gate. The Crown Prince could—and indeed a few days before had done so—bow before the second gate. Only the Emperor might go to the shrine itself.

Besides the various buildings that held treasures and records, there was a hall where sacred dances were performed. Mr. Mikimoto had arranged for a performance for my benefit. We left our shoes at the door and went in and sat down on flat cushions on the *tatami*. The room was large and square with sliding doors open to the sun-splashed trees outside. About a third of it was occupied by a raised platform where there was a simple altar and two rows of musicians and dancers.

The musicians, who wore ancient costumes of green, played the weirdest music I had ever heard, on instruments that I had never before seen: a bamboo flute, a lute, a set of pipes that had to be dried out from time to time over a small charcoal brazier especially for the purpose, two flageolets, two drums of unusual shape, and a pair of wooden clappers. Sometimes the music made me think of a saxophone, sometimes of the Scotch bag-pipes, sometimes of Ravel's "Bolero," though it was like none of these. It was primitive and it was also extremely sophisticated. None of the discords was unintended and the effect on the raw nerves was entirely calculated.

The girl dancers wore ancient court costumes, with white kimono tops embroidered in colors, and red trousers about three times as long as their legs, so that they shuffled along in them with trouser-trains dragging behind, a form of the more familiar *hakama* (divided skirt) called the *nagabakama*. Their long black hair tied in three places, hung down their backs and they wore a sort of tiara with red flowers shooting out from their foreheads.

Part of the dance was the bringing of food offerings to the altar. A priest in a scarlet and white costume with a magnificent headdress then came and chanted a prayer. Four young men in pale blue robes with black headgear did a slow and stately dance in the course of which they wriggled one arm and shoulder out of the pale blue, divulging brilliant scarlet and white kimono sleeves underneath, which they waved in wonderful patterns of color and rhythm. It was all done with great reverence, and I wondered what it meant to a Japanese, to whom the words of

[81]

the prayer were as unintelligible as they were to me, for the language was archaic.

After a delightful two days spent with the Mikimotos, we set out for Osaka, where my work was laid out for me. I made five speeches in two days, with a heavy schedule besides of press conferences, presentations, thank-you meetings, and "messages."

We were too early for the cherry blossoms in the west, but shortly after our return to Tokyo they burst out everywhere, foaming masses of pink blossom overhanging the stone walls of the Palace, softening the bleak, barrack-like buildings of schools, making tunnels of bloom down avenues everywhere, flinging their beauty against the blue sky. Personally I like the plum blossoms better, but they do not evoke the excitement, the festivities, or the holidays that the cherry blossoms do. Everybody turns out to enjoy the cherries, from charming family parties, sitting on red blankets on the grass and tying poems on the trees, to troops of young men noisy with *saké*. The beauty of the cherry is evanescent; it comes in a sudden glory, it falls without withering in a shower of petals; it is beautiful, the Japanese say, even in death. In poems written before the war it was often made the symbol of the young soldier, but that idea has gone into retirement now.

The most beautiful cherry blossoms that I saw were those within the Moat. One Thursday afternoon after her English lesson the Empress took me walking with her to see the cherry blossoms and then to go to Kuretakeryo, where the princesses lived, to have tea and see their dolls.

This was the first time that I had seen anything of the Palace grounds but the Imperial Household Building. We started out in procession, a guard preceding us about fifty feet ahead, then the Empress, then I, then Mrs. Takaki and Mrs. Takeko Hoshina, the chief lady-in-waiting, a charming person with whom I always felt ties of understanding and friendship even though we said little to one another. Her Majesty looked lovely in a pale gray kimono with cherry blossoms on it, and Mrs. Hoshina wore a long-skirted purple crepe dress with a jewelled clasp at throat and waist, an 1890 style which has been for years the prescribed costume for ladies-in-waiting. Shorter skirts are not suitable for deep bowing.

We walked up a little hill called Momijiyama along a winding path through woods now rosy and pale green with the promise of spring, and from the top of it looked down on an inner moat and a froth of cherry blossoms fuller and fresher than any others I had seen. Wild ducks were swimming on the Moat, and it would have seemed scarcely believable that this wild and romantic bit of woodland was in the heart of one of the biggest and busiest cities of the world, had it not been for the white tower of the Diet Building rising in the distance above the clouds of pink and white blossom.

We had about a twenty-minute stroll through the trees, down a path bordered with violets, across the driveway that I knew, over a little bridge, and through an opening in another enormous stone wall, and up a hill to the princesses' house, Kuretakeryo, which means Bamboo Dormitory. Here we found the three princesses standing in the open doorway, with Miss Natori a little to one side. They wore flame-colored kimonos with flowers embroidered on the sleeves, and *hakamas* of leaf-brown silk so stiff that it crackled and stood out. They looked perfectly entrancing in these lovely costumes and I wished that they might wear them all the time. They bowed to the Empress and then shook hands with me.

I was taken into the big room where the dolls had been set up, while Tané, who had arrived earlier by car, had a brief audience, her first, with Her Majesty in another room.

In ordinary families the Doll Festival is celebrated on March third. Every little girl at birth is given a full set of the special dolls for this day and usually acquires others by gift or inheritance as time goes on. On the third of March tiers of shelves are set up and covered with a red baize cloth in a room which for the time is given over entirely to the dolls. On the top shelf go the Emperor and Empress dolls, seated, in ancient costume of scarlet and green and gold, with a gold screen behind them and a miniature standing lantern on each side. Below them come the three beautiful ladies-in-waiting, the arrogant and important ministers of the right and left, usually with beards, the three servants in white costumes, laughing, crying, and frowning, the five musicians with their instruments, and the old man with a rake and the old woman with a broom, peasants in country clothes. On the lowest shelves are all kinds of tiny lacquer furniture and appointments, little chests filled with clothing, racks on which to hang the minute kimonos, boxes of wigs, mirrors, games, fans, coaches for the dolls to ride in, and the miniature trays of food for the dolls to enjoy.

The princesses celebrated the Doll Festival about a month later than ordinary folk, more or less by the old lunar calendar. Their dolls, too, were different. Though the Emperor and Empress dolls occupied the top shelf in the traditional way, below them, instead of the usual figures, was a whole series of the so-called "Court" dolls, fat and chunky and stylized, which were once peculiar to the court, though now anybody may have them. Each one stood on its own little platform with a small flowering tree of some kind and some other adjunct, such as a dog or a barrow of flowers, a fish or a crane. Some of them represented characters in Japanese fairy tales, like Urashima Taro with the turtle on which he rode to meet the princess in the depths of the sea, or Kintaro, the strong boy, with his bow and arrow.

When the Empress returned we had tea sitting at a table with a white damask cloth and eating the kind of dainties that are prepared for the dolls on miniature trays with tiny bowls and dishes. Lacquer boxes in layers were brought in with fascinating little cakes like flowers, and of course there was plenty of tea. Mrs. Takaki, Mrs. Hoshina, and Miss Natori brought in the delicious dishes but did not sit down with us, though they joined helpfully in the conversation. After tea the princesses played some pieces on the upright piano in the corner and sang a Japanese song.

The Empress was so gay and laughing, enjoying her daughters' dolls and their accomplishments with a charming mixture of affection and detachment, that it was difficult to realize what a wholly unprecedented occasion this was. Hitherto her contacts with all outside the closest family circle had been marked by the greatest stiffness and formality. I felt then, as I was so often to feel, what a remarkable triumph of personality it was that she could keep her freshness and spontaneity throughout the years of rigid ceremonial.

On the way home in the car I told Tané about what I had seen and done and she told me about her part of the party. After the audience she had been taken to a sitting-room where she had tea with a lady-in-waiting. The lady-in-waiting had told her that a few days earlier the Emperor had said at lunch, "If ever anything I did has been a success, it was asking Mrs. Vining to come here."

CHAPTER ELEVEN

No ONE IN Japan after the war could fail to be aware of General MacArthur or to look forward with lively interest and curiosity to an opportunity to meet him. Though he was not then the controversial figure that he has since become, he was the object of much speculation and discussion, of criticism and admiration. The newspapermen had dubbed him the new Mikado. Many people resented his "aloofness."

Living among the Japanese as I did, I saw him through their eyes. It was well known that his life was austere and his schedule rigid; that he went every day including Sunday to his office in the Dai Ichi Building; that he did not leave Tokyo except to meet visiting dignitaries at Haneda Airport; that he seldom or never appeared at even the most formal diplomatic parties; that he did not drink; that his hours off duty were reserved for his wife and the little boy whom they both adored. It was a regime that the Japanese understood and respected; it indicated to them a sacrificial devotion to duty that was comparable to their ideal of the *samurai*, the austere warrior.

Beyond that, they knew him as their friend, a stern friend, perhaps, as befitted one who had been first a conqueror, but also an understanding friend. The magnanimity of his policies, which they had not expected, they regarded with gratitude and humility. To many of them, who had suffered in silence under the grip of the Japanese military, he was also a liberator. To others who already were fearing the Communist menace, he was a protector. The fact that the Emperor liked and respected him was well known to all, and they were proud of the good feeling that existed between the two. Every day at the hours when he was expected to go in or out of the Dai Ichi Building, people lined up along the pavement to see him pass. In the newspapers he was often referred to as *Magensui,* an affectionate abbreviation that might be translated as General M. A Japanese picture book for children showed him first, head uncovered and bowed, with four officers standing at attention behind him, engaged in silent prayer for the peace of the world. On the next page he was at home with his pipe and a book, while a portrait of George Washington on the wall looked down approvingly. Another captioned "Kindness," showed him inviting a Japanese to ride in the elevator with him. His daily trip to the Dai Ichi was followed by a picture of a ship at Yokohama unloading food for the Japanese, and in the next a delegation of Japanese children arrived to say thank-you with a bunch of flowers. The final picture showed him standing with Mount Fuji in the background and gray pigeons hovering about, with the comment that he did not like to wear military decorations but instead looked toward peace in the world as his greatest happiness. This picture book appeared in Tokyo bookstores and the edition was quickly exhausted.

The Japanese furthermore depended on his authority. During the autumn and early winter of 1946-47 there had been much labor unrest, with many demonstrations by workers in the Imperial Plaza. I used to see the flag-waving and hear the shouting when I drove downtown and I noticed that in a time when cloth was so scarce that it was hard to get even enough for small patches there seemed to be an unlimited supply of red cotton for banners. The labor union movement, starting from scratch after the war, had grown rapidly, with encouragement and guidance from the Occupation. It was a desirable and indeed necessary development, but it came, as many reforms did, too quickly for the Japanese people to assimilate it comfortably. There was a good deal of social indigestion aggravated by the Communists behind the scenes. The unions, instead of confining themselves to the legitimate objectives of higher wages and better working conditions, wanted to take political action against the conservative government headed by Mr. Shigeru Yoshida, and, some said, to set up a dictatorship of the proletariat. By January they had decided upon a general strike that would include a million and a half government workers of all kinds, teachers, communications workers and so on, and would paralyze the nation. Government leaders and the Central Labor Relations

Board worked frantically to avert it, but the labor leaders went ahead like desperate men in a Greek tragedy doomed to action that would destroy themselves along with their enemies.

The strike was called for February first. On the afternoon of January thirty-first, General MacArthur stepped in and stopped the strike with a message of which the following was a part.

"I will not permit the use of so deadly a social weapon in the present improverished and emaciated condition of Japan. . . . It is with the greatest reluctance that I have deemed it necessary to intervene to this extent in the issues now pending. I have done so only to forestall the fatal impact upon an already gravely threatened public welfare. Japanese society today operates under the limitations of war defeat and Allied occupation. Its cities are laid waste, its industries are almost at a standstill and the great masses of its people are on little more than a starvation diet."

This action had brought relief to everyone, including labor itself, and the country at large was fervent in its gratitude to General MacArthur. Labor carried its grievance to the polls in the spring election and the Yoshida government lost out. It was succeeded by a coalition in which the Social Democrats had the largest representation.

The elections, incidentally, were held throughout April, and I followed them with considerable interest. First the village headmen, mayors of towns and governors of prefectures, all of whom had been appointed in the old days, were for the first time elected by popular vote. Then came the members of the House of Councilors (the upper house of the Diet) and finally the local ward officers. Electioneering was vigorous and noisy. Owing to the paper shortage there was little printed matter, but instead an immense amount of shouting on street corners and from the few trucks then available. Some politicians recognized the new order of things by haranguing the housewives as they stood in line waiting for the ration. I went with Tané when she voted at the public elementary school in our neighborhood, in order to see how it was conducted.

The school was a gaunt wooden building with many windows missing, which stood on a hillside overlooking a district of small factories that had been completely destroyed. As I did not want to look like a foreign inspector, I did not go in with her, but sat on a stone wall in the yard and watched the people coming and going. It was all very quiet and orderly, mostly families coming together. One young father enjoyed sliding down the sliding board with the baby between his knees while Mother went in and voted. After about ten minutes Tané came out, reporting that the voting booths were primitive but afforded privacy. "Nobody tried to intimidate you?" I asked. She laughed. "Nobody paid any attention to me."

The elections were over and the Social Democrats had entered on their six-week struggle to form a cabinet when I was invited by the MacArthurs to luncheon. After nearly seven months in Japan I was to meet the General.

The American Embassy was lovely in the spring rain, and with the honor guards presenting arms and the cars sweeping around the drive and depositing their loads, there was a general air of excitement and festivity. The twenty guests included Mr. and Mrs. Pennink, the Netherlands Minister and his wife, Sir William Webb, President of the War Crimes Tribunal, and Lady Webb, Brigadier Quillian, the prosecuting attorney from New Zealand, and his wife, and a selection of one- and two-star American generals and wives, and a WAC colonel.

The procedure of the MacArthur luncheons has often been described. We were welcomed by Mrs. MacArthur in the drawing-room. Everybody likes Mrs. MacArthur; there is no controversy about her. Small, slender, pretty, vivacious, simple, and warmly friendly, she wins everyone. The General came in last, kissed his wife, and greeted the guests in turn, a number of whom were, like me, meeting him for the first time. He gave me a firm handshake and a long, searching, but kindly look.

I saw a fine-looking man with an old-fashioned courtesy rather like that of my father and his friends, no "swashbuckler." He had a look of almost youthful freshness amazing in a man of sixty-seven, and I was further impressed by the stamp of courage and high purpose upon his features.

We lingered rather long over lunch, which was delicious. As we rose from the table, Sir William Webb came to say that he had seen me at the War Crimes Tribunal one day and what had I thought of it? He went on to ask me if I had a good pupil, but as I was launching into praise of the Crown Prince he sud-

[89]

denly faded away and General MacArthur was there, putting the same question to me.

I told him that I thought the Prince was very promising, that he had brains and even better he had character. He then asked me if "they" gave me a fair chance, and I said that they did, that I was happy to say that I was now teaching the Crown Prince without anybody else in the room.

The General then spoke of the Emperor with real friendliness. "He is a genuinely simple and direct man, and a democratic one."

After a little further talk he invited me to come to see him in his office the following week.

That was on Saturday. The following Thursday I went to see General MacArthur by appointment at six o'clock in the evening, his regular, if somewhat unusual, time for such appointments. His office was on the sixth floor of the Dai Ichi Insurance Building. From the reception room, where his aide, Colonel Lawrence E. Bunker, had his desk, there was a spectacularly lovely view over the moat, walls, and pines of the outer Palace gardens to the great walled enclosure of the Palace itself. Colonel Bunker I already knew, a charming, hard-working, always equable person, well liked by both Americans and Japanese.

He took me into the General's office, which was an inside one without the view. Shaking hands with me, General MacArthur said gallantly, "It's very seldom that I have so lovely a visitor." As I had seen his previous caller on the way in and he had a paunch, boiled gooseberry eyes, and a grizzled look, I felt that the General was perhaps not overstating the case too much.

For the first part of the hour we talked about the work that I was doing. I was impressed by the kind of questions he asked and even more by the delicacy which prompted him to preface almost every one of them with: "Tell me, Mrs. Vining, if you can and if you would like to . . ." None of the questions was one which I was not glad to answer.

He wanted to know about the Crown Prince, his character, his studies, and the arrangements of his life. He wanted to know about my reactions to the situation, and some of his questions were rather illuminating for they showed so clearly that the Emperor's request for an American teacher had come as a surprise to the Occupation and that their first reaction had been one of doubt.

I told him of the kindness and consideration with which my coming had been prepared by the Japanese, and the courtesy and coöperation that I was receiving. I told him of the Crown Prince's class at school and about my giving English names to the boys. He wanted to know the Prince's name, and when I told him Jimmy, he said, "That's a good name." (Which I duly reported to the chamberlains, who seemed relieved and pleased, as if they had feared that the name was not quite dignified enough.) He had had reports on all my speeches and encouraged me to do as much of such work as I could stand.

From the subject of the worth and dignity of the individual soul, which was, essentially, the burden of all the talks I made in Japan, we drifted into a discussion of religion. From Christianity we went on to Buddhism, and from there to Kipling's *Kim.* He had read it when he was a young man and had been carried away by it. Having a holiday in India, he got a lama and together, like Kim and his *guru,* they went down the high road, seeking truth and understanding of the mind of India.

When I rose to go the General asked me how long I was going to stay in Japan. I replied that nothing had been said to me yet officially, but that unofficially I had been told by the chamberlains that they wanted me to extend the contract for another year from October.

"And do you want to?"

I said yes, that I felt I had only made a beginning.

He nodded. "Good. I hoped you would stay."

CHAPTER TWELVE

ONE OF THE first of the educational reforms instituted by the Occupation was the abolition of the old textbooks with their ultra-nationalistic propaganda and the writing of new ones by Japanese educators under American supervision. It was an essential step but the first results were disappointing. The new textbooks were sterilized, no doubt, but dull and commonplace in subject matter and because of the paper shortage, unattractive in appearance, meagre little pamphlets printed on coarse gray paper.

The former practice of issuing entirely different texts for boys and girls, emphasizing the superiority of the one and the subservience of the other, had been discontinued, but distinctions still lingered on. In the English text which my boys were using I found this page: "What are these boys doing? They are sailing a boat. They are driving a motor car. They are carrying a big box." All were activities to give a boy an impression of power and importance as compared with the girls on the page, who were mending their stockings, sweeping the street, feeding the rabbit—not the horse or the dog, but the timid and lowly rabbit!

I wanted something better for my students, and with money that had been given me for "teaching aids," supplemented by some of the proceeds from an article that I had written for *Harper's Bazaar*, I bought American textbooks for all of my classes.

The book I got for the boys was a Macmillan first grade reader called *We Grow Up*, a book with a variety of simple stories of nature, family life, community work and play, folklore, and so on, in which the values of friendliness, coöperation, initiative, freedom and responsibility are implicit. There was great excitement when these attractive new books with their cloth bindings, white paper, and bright pictures were given out.

The boys in the spring looked less tired, less pale than they had in winter, though they were still very thin. "Since defeated the war, Japan has suffered from food," one of them wrote in the diary that they all kept in English during one week of the vacation.

One public-spirited lad wrote: "I went on Dr. Kobayashi to inject to keep off the eruptive typhus. It was a painful injection, but I beared it for the public health." Another boy had changed from a sallow, languid, indifferent child to a vigorous lad with a look of purpose in his eyes and his work improved proportionately. I learned that his family had moved from the air-raid shelter, in which they had been living ever since they were bombed out of their house, into a wooden barrack. "Now I feel like studying!" the boy said.

In the private lessons with the Crown Prince I used a book about turtles and stories from school readers. We had an increasing amount of free conversation. His spring holiday had done him a great deal of good. I thought he came back from it looking happy and stimulated, although a year or so later he told me, "I could not really enjoy it. There were so many people, and only to look at me."

He was able now to tell me in fair detail about his experiences, and when he did not know a necessary word he began to find circumlocutions for it. Though at first he spoke always of "the Emperor," now he began to say more naturally "my father." His admiration and love for his father were evident.

In speaking of trips and traveling one day I opened the subject of traveling beyond Japan. "Some day you will visit many countries," I said. "What countries would you like best to see?" He answered, after some thought and with rather an impish look, "England."

I agreed that England was beautiful and said that I loved England, as I do. I told him a little about the England I knew. He said he would also like to visit America and I asked him what he would like to see there. He listed mountains, farms, cities, rivers, wild animals, fish, and Indians. When I asked if he would like to see American schools he replied, "A little." He was also interested in visiting France and Italy but did not want to go to China at all.

I told this story afterwards because his honesty pleased me,

[93]

but the time came when I wished that I had not, for the Japanese newspapers picked it up and repeated it ad nauseam with embellishments and distortions and to my last day in Japan I was trying to clarify what the Prince actually had said about preferring England to America. As he grew older and more fluent in English, he said that he wanted to visit both England and the United States, but that as Europe was the fountainhead of American culture he wished to go there first.

His interests in those days were almost entirely confined to fish and I felt that they needed broadening. The mechanics that fascinate so many boys had no appeal for him at all, and I was no one to turn his attention in that direction, but I tried constantly to arouse his awareness of people, through stories, history, and observation. One day, I asked him to notice the different kinds of people he saw as he drove from Koganei to the Palace and report to me at the next lesson. He came up with quite a good list: boys, children, babies, pupils, men, women, storekeepers, Americans, Australians, farmers, workmen—and gentlemen.

One of the private lessons each week now included two of his classmates, and I started this series of lessons with a game. It was called "Cargoes," and it involved a map of the world with the shipping lanes, a stack of "Cargo cards," and four ships. The ships stopped at a port to unload a cargo of rice or pig iron and take on a cargo of coffee or sewing machines. They ran into fog and had to turn back or a favoring wind sent them forward. There was a good deal of vocabulary practice in the conversation about the game. Incidentally, although the track on the map led to Yokohama no cargo was provided for Japan. At that time there was a rather widespread feeling of despair in Japan that she had nothing the world wanted and that her trade was forever gone, a feeling which this aspect of the game would only emphasize. Accordingly I doctored one of the cards and provided Yokohama with an export of pearls, wishing that I might as easily settle the actual situation, for Japan must have trade and markets if she is to buy the necessary food to feed her people.

In the Joshi Gakushuin, now that the Senior girls had graduated, I had two classes corresponding to our eleventh and twelfth grades. Princess Kazuko was in the latter, Princess Atsuko in the former. For those classes also I had got American texts, a Macmillan reader called *Wide Wings* and one by Rowe Petersen, *If I Were Going*. These provided a basis for simple conversation, and I gave the girls also from time to time poems to memorize.

Because it is difficult to teach three girls of such different ages, I recommended a change in the Tuesday afternoon arrangements, and in May this went into effect. One Tuesday the two elder princesses came, and on the next, the youngest princess and the Crown Prince's younger brother, Prince Masahito.

The first time the little ones came—Tané and I referred to them in private as the "princelings"—it was another breaking of precedent. Mrs. Matsudaira therefore was one of the four adults who accompanied them, the others being Miss Natori and two chamberlains.

The children, who were obviously happy to be together, had a little while in the garden looking at the tadpoles and goldfish in the pool, and then we went inside. Prince Masahito was introduced to the western custom of ladies first and was made to stand back and let Princess Takako precede him, to the amusement of all. It took a year or more of reminders before the habit was established, and then it held only for my house, and the interior of my house at that. Beyond the doorstep was Japan, and the prince went first.

On that first day I shepherded the princelings to the study upstairs, leaving the four grownups to be entertained by Tané in the parlor. This was, however, the first time that Prince Masahito had ever been alone in the room with a teacher; even in school there was a chamberlain in the room. Presently there was a knock at the door and Mrs. Matsudaira and the two chamberlains tiptoed in, "just to peek." They stayed a little while and watched our work, and then slipped away. A little later they came back again for reassurance. But the next time the younger prince came to my house, he was accompanied by only one chamberlain, who looked in upon the lesson only once. After that we had no visitors during the lesson.

Besides the lessons that spring there were various informal meetings with the Imperial Family. The Crown Prince went to a Boy Scout rally and I was with him there. One day I was invited to a picnic at one of the imperial duck preserves, with the princesses and Prince Masahito. Twice the Empress decided to have a tea-party instead of a regular lesson.

To the second of these parties all of the imperial children came, including the Crown Prince and the eldest princess, now "Mrs." Higashikuni, whom I met that afternoon for the first time. She was the bright and charming young mother of two small children, and she was adjusting to the changes in her life with skill and good humor. The tea-house was a small Japanese building deep within the woods of which I had had just a glimpse behind high walls.

Suddenly there was a stirring in the background, a perceptible excitement in the atmosphere, as of an electric charge, and Mrs. Matsudaira said in a stage whisper: "The Emperor is coming!" We all stood up and His Majesty came in. He shook hands with me and sat down on the chair beside me.

Always when I met the Emperor of Japan—and this was the second of many meetings—there was this dramatic contrast between the excitement and awe of the people around him and the simple, human, friendly personality of the Emperor himself. His character was unfolded to me gradually as the years went on, and I came to have, besides affection for him, a real respect and admiration for his goodness, for his self-sacrificing devotion to his people, his humility (that rare quality) and his genuine love of peace.

The story was told—and I have reason to believe that it is true —that when he first met General MacArthur, the Emperor said to the General: "You may do what you like with me, you may kill me if you wish. But don't let my people starve." Certain it is that on my first audience with Their Majesties they thanked me for the food that the United States was sending to Japan.

That he opposed the war to the best of his ability is well known and well authenticated. Even before the war under the old Constitution the Emperor considered himself a constitutional monarch and felt obliged to accept the decisions of his ministers. I have been told by several people of a meeting early in September, 1941, in which the Cabinet informed the Emperor of its unanimous decision to go to war with the United States if the negotiations in Washington proved unsuccessful. They were not asking for his advice, they were asking for his approval. Instead of giving it, he expressed his opposition by reciting a poem by the Emperor Meiji, which has always been taken as a great expression of the desire for peace.

"Surely in this world men are brothers all
    One family!
Then why do winds and waves on all the seas
    Rage stormily?"

According to one account, the Emperor recited this twice, with feeling, and then turned and left the room. The ministers there assembled were deeply moved by the Emperor's action and went away shaken in their purpose, but when their colleagues and subordinates who had not been there, got at them, they stiffened again in their determination to make war.

People have often asked, Why, if the Emperor could stop the war, couldn't he have prevented it in the beginning? This question was brought out by Sir William Webb, President of the War Crimes Tribunal, at the time of the trials. I think the answer is that the Cabinet ministers were unanimous in their determination to make war and as constitutional monarch the Emperor believed that he could not oppose more explicitly than he did a unanimous decision. At the time of the surrender, however, the Supreme War Council was divided; half wanted to surrender, half to commit national suicide in a fight to the finish. In this case the Emperor felt himself free to insist upon surrender.

But I have got a long way from a sunny afternoon in a green, overgrown garden deep within the Moat. After we had had ice-cream and cake, the ladies-in-waiting and even Mrs. Matsudaira and Mrs. Takaki withdrew and for a little while I was completely alone with the Imperial Family. There was not enough English among us for very much conversation, though I think the Emperor understood English even if he did not speak it. I told them of a recent trip I had made to Nikko. They were always interested in my reactions to the Japanese scene. I think most Japanese enjoy seeing Japan through alien eyes; certainly Lafcadio Hearn has many more Japanese than western readers. One of the things that I had seen in Nikko was the Tamozawa Palace, once a favorite villa of the Emperor Taisho, for a brief time during the war the home of Prince Akihito, and now the property of the prefecture. In its lovely but neglected garden I

[97]

had seen drifts of bluets, the little wild flowers that we call "Quaker ladies" in Philadelphia, and it had amused me to reflect that more than one Quaker lady had got into the Palace.

When the ladies-in-waiting came back, we all went for a walk along the stream and over stepping stones to a little waterfall, perhaps twenty feet high, which I had heard gurgling from the tea-house. There were pheasants in the trees and other birds, and now and then the Crown Prince took hold of my arm to attract my attention. Occasionally I got a glimpse of striped trousers among the underbrush and knew that the chamberlains were unobtrusively on duty.

At the entrance to Obunko, which I now saw for the first time, the Imperial Family said good-by.

During the spring, too, more occasions arose in which I had a chance to talk about the Crown Prince with those who were responsible for the arrangements of his life and his welfare. The English-speaking chamberlains came several times to my house, and though in our conversations we touched for the most part only on superficial matters, nevertheless I began to feel more identified with the group and to have a fuller understanding of the complications of the life of an imperial prince. Mr. Sumikura I had known from the beginning, now I came also to know Mr. Jiro Shimizu. Mr. Shimizu was an earnest Christian; his father had been president of one of the important Christian schools in Tokyo. He himself had been for a number of years a teacher in the Gakushuin. During the war he volunteered to resign, lest the fact of his Christianity be an embarrassment to the school, but his resignation had not been accepted. After the war, not many months before I myself came to Tokyo, he was made a chamberlain to the Crown Prince. He was a very fine, sincere, serious man of high ideals, and I was always glad for a talk with him.

The rainy season began toward the end of May and lasted until about the first of July. It rained almost every day, and when it did not rain the sky was darkly overcast and the air wet and heavy. The water reached the top of the garden pool and I expected the goldfish to float out onto the grass at any minute.

During this period the wheat was harvested and the rice planted. Pathetic little patches of wheat were cultivated in the suburbs of Tokyo, in little gardens, in burned-over lots, even in patches between the sidewalk and the street. So much effort for so little result! People cut it by hand and spread it out on the pavement to dry, then threshed it with a primitive wooden flail. They winnowed it by pouring it from one basket to another and letting the wind blow the chaff away. Some people had a simple wooden machine turned by a crank, but often I saw old women, afraid of losing any precious grain, sitting by the hour rubbing it between their fingers.

Food was dreadfully scarce that summer. The rice ration was three weeks late and prices on the black market were skyrocketing. Where a little rice had been spilled in the gutter outside a food store I saw a woman picking up the grains one by one with a pair of tweezers. Not a bit of fruit was to be bought in Tokyo and meat seemed non-existent.

On the twenty-third of June the first meeting of the Diet was held under the new Constitution. As Prince Takamatsu was to be there, he did not have his English lesson that day, and so I was free to join the crowd of some five hundred Occupationaires in the galleries of the Chamber of the Upper House.

Both houses were assembled for the opening ceremony, and the Emperor entered at eleven, preceded by Mr. Tsuneo Matsudaira, the newly elected President of the House of Councilors, and followed by Prince Takamatsu and various court officials.

Behind the Speaker's desk there was a flight of steps leading up to a sort of stage where stood the Emperor's gold lacquer chair, or perhaps throne is the word. Mr. Matsudaira led him to this, while Prince Takamatsu remained standing on the platform below.

Everybody stood up upon the Emperor's entrance and remained standing through the brief ceremony, with the exception of a very few American officers who with ostentatious rudeness remained seated throughout.

For the first time in the short history of the Diet, which dates only from 1889, the Emperor came as the "guest" of the Diet instead of Supreme Ruler, and several small details symbolized the change. Instead of a military uniform he wore morning clothes. Most of the members of the Diet, after their initial bow, straightened up and looked at him, instead of remaining bent over so that they could not see his face. Most significant of all, when the Speaker of the House of Representatives opened the ceremony with a brief address, he spoke to the Diet with his back to the Emperor.

When the Speaker had finished and stepped aside, the Emperor unfurled a large scroll and read his brief Rescript, in which he spoke of the Diet as the "highest organ of state power" and urged the Japanese people to unite in surmounting the economic crisis. It was significant that in referring to himself he used the ordinary word for I (*watakushi*) instead of the old imperial we (*chin*).

At the end of the reading of the Rescript Mr. Matsudaira received it from the Emperor's hands and the ceremony, which had lasted just nine minutes, was over. The whole thing was serious, dignified, and very impressive.

The spring term in the schools was now drawing near its close. My last class would be held on the ninth of July; after that there would be examinations and a six-week vacation. Ever since I had been there I had been under pressure from newspapers and magazines, both American and Japanese, to allow photographers to come into my class with the Crown Prince and take pictures of it. I had consistently refused, because when I had so little time with the boys I felt I could not afford to give whole hours to the business of picture-taking. As the final lesson of a term is generally a total loss anyhow, I decided that the photographers might as well come then and get it over with. It was arranged accordingly, through the Civil Information and Education Section, that no more than six were to be admitted, three Americans and three Japanese, and I planned a spelling bee.

When I arrived at Koganei they were there ahead of me, not six but forty, including the small son of one who had been brought along to see the fun. Klieg lights and cameras were set up all over the small classroom and desks pushed aside. I cleared our visitors out while I got the class started, but some of the energetic Japanese went around outside the building and shot pictures through the windows, to the boys' delight.

I had to line up my two teams for the spelling bee, the Reds and the Blues, in and out among the lights and camera tripods. Some of the boys I could not see at all and some of them could not hear the words I gave out, for the whirring of the moving picture cameras. But the boys were all wonderful. They watched for their turns and they shouted the answers, and kept their inevitable whispering and giggling down to a minimum. Sometimes there was a pause while one of the photographers darted out to rearrange the position of the Crown Prince, who gave me a rueful and amused glance that sweetened the whole, noisy, confused hour for me. It was a blistering hot day and the Klieg lights raised the temperature of the small and crowded room another twenty degrees.

Finally, five minutes before the end of the hour, they folded their tents like the whirlwind and noisily stamped away. I told the boys to go back to their seats, and one Japanese movie man rushed back into the room, stuck his camera into the Prince's face, and let it run. I drove him off and returned to my desk. Then I saw one of my best boys at the back of the room looking embarrassed and apparently talking to himself. I investigated and found a girl reporter crouched down behind his desk asking him questions. I ran her off. Before I could draw breath, a tall American, breezy, handsome, and exasperatingly cool-looking, stuck his head in at the door and asked cheerily, "May I listen?"

I had often told my pupils that polite people softened the monosyllables Yes and No with a name, Yes, Mrs. Vining, or a further word or two, Yes, I think so, or No, I'd rather not. Now I looked at that nice Associated Press correspondent Tom Lambert and I said, "No." Just, "No."

CHAPTER THIRTEEN

EACH SUMMER THAT I was in Japan the Imperial Household took a cottage for me in Karuizawa for the summer holidays. Karuizawa, about ninety miles northwest of Tokyo, stood on a high plateau in the shadow of Mount Asama, an active volcano, and it is said to have been before the war the most popular summer resort in the Orient.

Our house was a comfortable, rambling one on a hill above the village, surrounded by huge, fragrant balsam trees, through which we got glimpses of distant mountains. Little orange and black and white birds flashed in and out of the balsams by the terrace and sometimes perched on our chairs and tables, cuckoos called in the early mornings, and bush-warblers sang all day long. In an earlier house on the site of this one, Rabindranath Tagore had stayed when he visited Japan years ago; many of the poems in his volume, *Stray Birds,* were said to have been written there and are full of the atmosphere of that quiet, fragrant retreat.

Esther Rhoads and the LARA staff had a cottage near by and together we had a house party for ten members of the little meditation group that had been meeting at my house two Sunday afternoons a month since January. I prepared for a strenuous program in the autumn. Near the end of August the princesses came.

The three princesses and Miss Natori were spending the holidays at Nasu in the mountains about seventy-five miles to the east of Karuizawa. Because it was well understood that they would grow up to marry commoners and enter upon a life very different from that of the imperial princesses of the past, Miss Natori was wisely preparing them for the change that lay ahead. This summer they were living not in the imperial villa at Nasu but in a rented house behind the inn, helping with the housework and learning the ways of ordinary folk. One of the educational features of the summer was a visit of the two older girls to us in Karuizawa.

Tané and I had many conferences beforehand with the local police. We checked and rechecked our food supplies and our menus. Our elderly cook, little Inoue San, had not come with us because she feared the altitude and dampness, and in her place we had Masako San, Michiko San's elder sister, a fine, dependable girl, though inexperienced. We made plans for walks and picnics.

The weather had been abnormally dry throughout the month, but on the day that the princesses were to arrive, the drought broke, and the rain poured down. My heart sank.

About five o'clock we heard the long melodious toot of the imperial car at the foot of our hill. Masako San and Michiko San ran down with big umbrellas, Tané and I went out on the terrace. In a moment the little procession came into sight among the balsam trees: the two princesses in white linen suits, big straw hats, and white slippers, followed by Miss Natori and Mrs. Takaki; the chauffeur and a man from the Imperial Household carried the suitcases, while two policemen flitted about in the rear.

They had had a good trip, our guests told us, and the rain had not started until they were almost there. Tea and a bath and rest occupied the time until seven o'clock dinner. After dinner we played games and I taught them "Snap," that noisy game of my childhood—I wonder if children play it now—in which the players turn over a pack of cards simultaneously and when matching cards appear, the one who first shouts "Snap!" gets the pile.

It was cloudy but not actually raining when we gathered for breakfast at eight. At the end of breakfast it was our custom, since we were throughout a Christian household, to have a family Bible-reading. Inoue San and Michiko San and any others who were around came into the dining-room and sat down at the table with us. I read a passage from the New Testament in English, Tané read the same thing in Japanese, we had a few moments of Quaker silence, and then, after some discussion of the day's plans, we went about our business. In Japan servants are very much a part of the family; their service is more a matter of personal devotion than the mere carrying out of a job. In a household in which two languages were spoken this little morning ceremony served to bridge the gap and to establish the unity of the family group.

Mrs. Takaki, who had visited us earlier in the summer, had told Miss Natori of our custom and she had especially asked that we make no changes in it for the princesses. They, in fact, had come provided with Bibles of their own, the simple paper-backed Japanese translation which the American Bible Society had sent to Japan in quantity after the war.

This morning, we moved our chairs a little to make room and Masako San and Michiko San came in and sat down at the table with the princesses—and one more precedent was shattered. I read the parable of the Good Samaritan.

There were far-reaching consequences to this episode. The princesses liked it. They were impressed by the fact that our two young maids joined us. They were interested in the Bible story. There were conferences in the Imperial Household, and in the end, Mrs. Tamaki Uemura, a distinguished Japanese woman minister, a Presbyterian known to many Presbyterians in the United States, was asked to teach the Bible once a week to the three princesses and later to give a lecture on it once a week to the Empress.

One of the things that the princesses had wanted to do was to walk in the "Machi"—the shopping street—of Karuizawa like anybody else. As we set off, the two princesses, Mrs. Takaki, Miss Natori, Tané and I, followed by the man from the Imperial Household, and the two white-clad policemen, I feared that we would attract considerable attention, but nobody seemed to notice the procession. We did the Machi rather thoroughly, walked through the garden of the villa which the Empress Dowager had had the summer before, and went on to the reservoir. By the time we turned back the mist had thickened into a gentle rain and we put up our umbrellas.

The Japanese have an appreciation of rain that we in western countries do not share. The sound of rain softly falling, the brightness of green leaves newly washed by rain, the gleam of a wet rock: all these give them an aesthetic pleasure, which they savor for its own sake. I was deeply grateful for the Japanese finer feelings as we plodded along the dripping lanes.

It was still raining in the afternoon when we went out for a ride in two cars, the princesses' and mine. The country was veiled in mists that moved and shifted and the colors were lovely in the rain.

It was cold enough for a fire in the fireplace that evening, and I introduced the princesses to toasted marshmallows. Later they wanted to play Snap again. We went to bed rather early in anticipation of an early start next morning. I was to return with them to Nasu.

After we were all in bed, there was a shout from the bottom of the hill that Mrs. Takaki was wanted on the telephone. She put on her raincoat over her nightgown and paddled through the dripping woods down the hill and up the next one to the nearest telephone. A chamberlain was on the telephone with a message from the Crown Prince. He wanted me to come to his house at Nasu for tea on Saturday but he wasn't going to invite his sisters and was that all right?

The Imperial Family had not spent the whole summer together at Nasu, but had gathered at the end of the summer from scattered places. The Emperor and Empress had been in Tokyo and Hayama. Although the Crown Prince and Prince Masahito were both at Numazu they did not stay in the same house, but in two different imperial villas some distance apart. I had recommended strongly, to the Grand Steward, to the chamberlains and to Mr. Yamanashi, that since the princes lived in separate places during the winter they at least spend the summer holidays together, but I had only succeeded in "causing a sensation," as one of the chamberlains wrote me in a warning letter. The reason given, that the "buildings and equipments" of each house were suitable for one small boy but not for two, was so patently not the real reason that I could only drop the matter and hope that the way would open in the future for something better.

On Friday morning we had breakfast at six and started at seven for Nasu. So early a start was necessary because we were going to make a detour to Mashiko to see the potteries there. Mr. Shoji Hamada was a well-known artist whose work had been widely exhibited in Japan and about whom I had heard from connoisseurs in the United States; his house at Mashiko was a veritable folk art museum. Tané and I had been there earlier, and our account of it had so interested members of the Imperial Family that it was decided that the princesses were to see it.

It was a beautiful morning after the rain, and everything sparkled. We had no large cities to go through, just miles of peaceful farming country with thatch-roofed houses amid the rice fields and dramatic mountains against the horizon. Every farmhouse was surrounded by trees and many of them had a crepe myrtle in full bloom.

At Mr. Hamada's we ate our picnic lunch, and saw the process of pottery-making from the primitive wheel to the opening of a kiln. He talked with so much interest and authority about his own pottery and the other kilns in the village, whose smoke went up in several places, that we were late in getting under way again.

At Nasu Tané and I went to the inn, where a room had been engaged for us, and then I bathed and dressed in a great hurry, for I was to have dinner with the Imperial Family.

The Emperor and Empress were staying in the Gohontei, the imperial villa itself; the two princes came from a smaller house up the hill where for this short visit, and perhaps as a sop to me, they were actually together, and the princesses came from their house behind the inn.

The villa was built in the western style, with much paneling and a great many rather small rooms. I went up a long flight of stairs carpeted in red and found the Imperial Family lined up in the order of ascending importance, with Princess Takako first, the Crown Prince next to the Empress, who wore a long, flowered dress with a diamond brooch in the shape of the imperial chrysanthemum, and the Emperor last of all.

At dinner I sat on the Emperor's right. It was the first time I had seen the Crown Prince in six weeks—and at thirteen even six weeks make a difference. He looked taller and thinner, more muscular and very sunburned. He seemed perceptibly more mature and self-confident.

He told me about the summer. The Gakushuin had a summer dormitory at Numazu and for the first time since the war about twenty boys had gone there for a "swimming party." Prince Akihito had been with them during part of each day for swimming, fishing, and excursions. He told me also that the brook trout which we were eating he and Prince Masahito had caught that day at a fish hatchery near by.

After dinner we had coffee in the drawing-room and then the princesses proposed the new game they had learned—Snap! —which Princess Takako was especially keen to try. As long as I live I shall not forget that evening. It was so like an evening with any friendly happy family with children from eighteen to eight, with the emphasis naturally on the eldest boy and the girl who was the "baby" and family pet, and yet—it was the Emperor of Japan whose cards I pounced upon, exclaiming, "Snap!"

Stories of the chasm between the Emperor and the common people before the end of the war kept coming to my mind. From different people I had heard a number of them. An American woman whose husband had been in the consular service before the war told me of the New Year's reception to which all of the diplomatic people were invited and how she had practised before-hand and the instructions she had received, to go so many steps and curtsey, so many more and curtsey again, to back from the imperial presence, but never, never to raise her eyes or look upon the imperial countenance. Another friend of mine, a Japanese in the diplomatic service, told me that he had returned to Tokyo after an absence, heard something going on in the street outside his hotel, and walking to the window had raised the shade and looked out to see what it was. The Emperor was passing below! He hastily pulled the shade down again, but almost immediately two policemen were pounding on his door, demanding that he go with them to the police station. "I had to talk fast," he said, "but I satisfied them at last." Even the Crown Prince in those days was not for the common gaze. A young dressmaker told me that she had studied in a school of dressmaking situated on the railroad near one of the big stations. Occasionally the Crown Prince would be brought in the train along this line. When they came into the station all the shades in his private car would be drawn so that nobody could see him from the station platform. As the dressmaking school lay just beyond the point where the shades on the train were drawn, the curtains in the dressmaking school itself were all pulled down when the train approached. At the moment of its passing, all the students rose and bowed low. My little friend admitted that she used to peek, but she got only a very fleeting glimpse of a small boy and his dignified attendants.

Each morning that they were at Nasu that summer of 1947, the Emperor and his two sons went riding before breakfast. A little after seven, Tané and I, in our second storey front rooms at the inn heard the sound of horses' hooves and hurried out on the little balcony to look.

The inn stood on a hillside, and spread out before it was a vast plain, beyond which ranks of mountains loomed up through the morning mist. Down below our balcony, half hidden now and then by the twisted pines of the inn garden, came a little cavalcade: a groom first, then the Emperor on a white horse, followed by the Crown Prince on another white horse, Prince Masahito on a bay and several more grooms. It was a beautiful sight, the mounted figures against the vast panorama of plain and mountains. There is always something very appealing about the sight of a father riding with his sons, and this had drama besides. When they had passed, I turned to Tané and said, "Well, now you have looked from above on your Emperor."

She answered with her eyes shining: "Mah! Things are different! This is real! This is *nice!* Before, when the Emperor went out, it was just as if the country was in mourning."

Later in the morning the Empress had an English lesson; after that a picnic lunch was planned, and the whole family assembled at the main villa. It was raining when we started off, in procession, each with an umbrella—"bat umbrellas," as the Japanese call our black ones, in distinction to their big yellow paper ones. A guard preceded the Emperor, who was followed by the Empress and the imperial children in the order of their rank, the Crown Prince first, then Prince Masahito, and the princesses according to age. I followed and after me came the ladies-in-waiting, Tané, chamberlains and court officials, the Governor of Tochigi Prefecture, and others. The order was changed from time to time as one or another of the Imperial Family wanted to speak to me, but that was the general pattern.

We followed a steep woodsy path along a rushing mountain brook that gurgled over rocks and among ferns, until we came out at last on an open shelf, where there was a pavilion called Ōmeitei, from which the view of mountains and valley was spectacular.

Here we had lunch—delicious cold trout, potato salad, rice, sliced tomatoes, watermelon ice and sliced watermelon.

Lunch was served on two levels. On the upper platform I sat at the table with Their Majesties and the Crown Prince, the other imperial children were at another table and there was a third table for the ladies-in-waiting and Miss Natori; the rest of the company were downstairs.

After lunch the rain stopped; the distant mountains burst out of the clouds again, and the plain, patterned with fields and roads and woods, was splashed with patches of sunlight. As we looked a rainbow spread its vivid arch over the vast valley. We walked up the hill above the Ōmeitei. The wild flowers of Nasu are famous, and the Emperor is especially fond of them. We discussed the Japanese and English names as we found them. There were pearly everlasting, Queen Anne's lace, evening primroses, bush clover, wild pinks, and a blue bellflower, *kikyo* in Japanese, whose English name I did not know.

When the party broke up, Mrs. Takaki, Tané and I went to the Crown Prince's tea-party at the smaller villa high up on the hillside. Mr. Yasuhide Toda, who was on duty that day, was the Crown Prince's newest chamberlain, a tall, athletic, and attractive man of about thirty, whose boyish, big-brotherly manner with the two princes was most refreshing. He had formerly been one of the Emperor's chamberlains and had been wounded in the struggle at the time of the Surrender, when some of the Palace Guard, rebelling, had tried to capture the record of the Emperor's broadcast and so prevent the surrender message from reaching the people.

We had hot chocolate with French pastries for tea and conversation in both Japanese and English. Now I heard more about the holidays and Numazu, and especially about a visit to a place called Toro, where remains of Stone and Bronze Age settlements had recently been discovered, to the great excitement of the archaeologists. The Crown Prince told me about the artifacts that he had seen there, and talked very well about the various migrations of people who made up the Japanese race. His interest in the origins of his people was entirely objective and had no trace of the myths of divine origin that used to fill the history books in Japan.

After tea the two princes showed me the house, which, though

[109]

furnished with western chairs and tables, was Japanese in its construction. A passageway with a highly polished wooden floor ran around the outside of it, with sliding paper doors to the rooms on one side, and sliding glass doors to the garden on the other, so that any room at any time could be opened up to take in the world out of doors. We went up on the roof to look at the view, which in the afternoon light was lovelier than ever, with cloud shadows trailing over the plain, and the seven mountains behind our hill looming up very high and mysterious.

Dinner was at the princesses' house. They had planned to have just Mrs. Takaki, Tané and me, but when the boys heard about it they clamored to be included too—in spite of not having invited their sisters to their party.

A man from the Imperial Household came to escort Tané and me along a winding path from the inn to the princesses' house. This house was wholly Japanese, and the princesses slept on *futon* (quilts) on the *tatami*. These are big and heavy to handle; every evening at bedtime they are brought out from their cupboard and put down on the floor, and a mosquito net like a cage covering most of the room is hung by hooks from the ceiling. Every morning the whole affair is folded up and put away, and the room is empty and ready for any kind of use during the day. It is a wonderful way to save space, and to make a small house serve many purposes—developed during centuries of living in a crowded land. It was part of the princesses' education that summer to take out and put away their own *futon*, and they came to know well what it felt like to come in late and tired, and have to make their heavy beds themselves.

Before dinner we went into the garden to watch the evening primroses open. The blossoms were as big as small saucers and they opened up suddenly with a pop. One of the prettiest sights I saw in all this visit was Princess Takako, small and slender in her summer cotton dress with her black hair gleaming, crouched before a primrose, blowing on it to make it open faster, while a full moon rose behind her in the sky over the distant mountains.

The whole side of the house was open to the garden and the mountains, as we sat on cushions around a low table and ate the delicious dinner, parts of which—the trout and the eggplant—the princesses had prepared themselves. I found myself feeling a bit confused as I ate poached eggs with chopsticks and a big peach with a knife and fork.

After dinner we played "Hide and Seek." The cry for "In Free" in Japanese is *Boken,* and our shouts must have been heard down the hill at the inn. It was a swift game, in and out among the Japanese rooms in our stocking feet, with all the lights turned out, and I thought of the children all over America playing games in summer evenings after dinner, and begging for just one more, as the Crown Prince did, when the grownups said it was time to stop. "No, two more," said Prince Masahito, and so Mr. Toda granted two more, and then we all said good-night and the princes brought Tané and me back to the inn in their car.

The next morning was clear and sparkling—"real Nasu weather," Mrs. Takaki said, just as we say "a real New Hampshire day." Every pine stood out clearly on the near-by mountains, and distant peaks appeared that had not shown before.

After breakfast we went to the imperial villa to say good-by. I was with Their Majesties for forty minutes, first in the Emperor's study, then in the tower, where His Majesty took me to see the view, then back in the study again, where I was given a length of silk printed with a design of the wild flowers of Nasu especially made for the Imperial Family, and a can of particularly fine tea.

The last thing I saw when I went down the stairs was the Empress smiling at me over the banisters.

CHAPTER FOURTEEN

WHILE I WAS in Karuizawa in 1947, George Atcheson was killed in an airplane crash in the Pacific on his way to an important meeting in Washington. He and Mrs. Atcheson had been very kind to me; I had enjoyed going to their house; and I missed their friendship sorely all the rest of my time in Tokyo. His death was a serious public loss, for his knowledge of the East and his temperate judgment would have been increasingly useful.

I might easily have been on that same plane myself. In June Mrs. Ogden Reid had visited Tokyo and had asked me to return to the United States in the autumn to speak on Japan at the *New York Herald Tribune* Forum. The Imperial Household had granted me leave of absence for the purpose and General MacArthur had suggested that I do some further speaking while I was in America. He suggested also that I go in August on the staff plane and have a little vacation beforehand. I had decided, however, not to go until September, because there was work that I wanted to do in Japan before I left and because Karuizawa was a good place in which to prepare speeches.

Three days after my visit to Nasu I was back in Tokyo, caught up in preparations for my trip.

A new contract was signed, like the first one but with the following changes: the salary was increased from two thousand dollars to three thousand dollars, and the duties which I should perform now included the extra time with the Crown Prince, two hours a week with the Empress, and an addition of two hours a week to the work with the other imperial children.

Before I left for the United States I had luncheon with the Crown Prince at his house in Koganei. It was the first time that I had seen the inside of his house, often as I had passed by the high wooden fence. It was a simple, one-storey, wooden house. He did not like this house. He missed the beautiful one in the Akasaka Palace grounds which had been his home from the age of three, when he was taken from his parents, until at eleven he was evacuated from Tokyo to escape the air raids. The incendiary bombs which destroyed the home that he had loved brought the war personally to the Crown Prince, and his confinement in this uninteresting and makeshift house must have kept the wound from ever quite healing.

The following day I had a farewell luncheon with Their Majesties and Princess Kazuka and Prince Masahito in the pavilion deep in the Palace grounds called Kaintei. This was a small stone and timber house in the English style, with several spacious rooms and a terrace overlooking a pool overhung with willow and weeping cherry, where blue kingfishers came to pause on brown rocks and butterflies lit on an old stone lantern.

Lunch was delicious, with the chef's Paris-acquired skill apparent in all the dishes, but the dessert was the big triumph: the platter contained an eagle, carved out of ice, descending to feed an eaglet, presumably with the balls of vanilla ice-cream surrounding it. I took the thing as a masterpiece of art for art's sake, to the disappointment of Akiyama San, the chief chef, who got hold of Tané later and explained the symbolism to her. The eagle represented me, the American tutor, bringing refreshment to the eaglet, the Crown Prince of Japan.

After lunch we all walked over to Obunko, where Their Majesties now lived. No other foreigner and only the Japanese directly connected with the court have seen this house. It was a one-storey concrete building with rooms, not many, opening off both sides of a narrow central corridor. Beyond the terrace is what was once a nine-hole golf course and now has been allowed to run wild. There are majestic trees here and there and among the trees are planted the wild flowers that the Emperor loves. Nearer the house daffodils and narcissus have spread and naturalized, till they are a glory of blossom in the spring. In the early autumn pink and white and dark crimson cosmos make a sea of color in the foreground.

The Emperor's study was the study of any gentleman of scholarly tastes, with bookshelves along the walls, fine rugs on the floor, a big flat-topped desk with the usual photographs and

[113]

knickknacks, easy chairs, ornaments, and three marble busts, the same that might have been found in countless libraries throughout England and America in the late nineteenth or early twentieth century: Lincoln, Darwin, and Napoleon.

The bust of Napoleon, I learned a year or so later, was there because it was almost the only thing the Emperor had bought for himself and he treasured it accordingly. When as the twenty-one-year-old Crown Prince he had visited Paris, he had gone shopping for souvenirs, and Napoleon remained to remind him of that experience. Darwin was the natural expression of his interest in biology, and Lincoln represented a deep and lifelong enthusiasm. When in the previous winter I had shown a picture of Lincoln as a young man to my class at school, the Crown Prince had been the only one in his section to recognize it. Lincoln was for him part of the family background.

It had been arranged that I was to go to the United States in a staff plane with General and Mrs. Eichelberger, who were going home on leave, and some others who were on a mission to Washington. The plane was a C-54, similar to General MacArthur's *Bataan,* and the General's own pilot, Major (now Colonel) Anthony Storey, was to fly it. As the Crown Prince had never seen a big airplane I suggested that he and Prince Masahito come down to the airport and go over the plane, and this, after many consultations, was decided upon. The flight was postponed a day by a typhoon named, by the G.I.'s in the weather station down the Pacific, "Kathleen," which raged two nights and a day and brought destructive floods to the eastern prefectures. When I drove to Yokohama before daylight on the morning of September fifteenth low places in the highway were covered with water hub deep, and I wondered whether the princes would get there or not. They did, though, arriving with an enormous bouquet of orchids and ferns for me. Major Storey took them all over the plane, showing them the control-room and explaining the instruments. They took turns sitting in the pilot's seat, and they saw the living quarters of the plane, the tables, the comfortable chairs, the two double-decker berths, and the tiny galley.

The great of the Occupation had come to see the Eichelbergers off and the scene on the field was full of the chatter and bustle of departure. It was my first flight and I was in that exalted state of terror and delight best expressed in the nursery rhyme about the man who "jumped so high he touched the sky and never came down till the Fourth of July." I remember only fragments: how the wet asphalt gleamed under the gray, rain-filled sky; how the General's face lighted up when he shook hands with my little princes and how calm and poised Prince Akihito was, how eager Prince Masahito; I remember Esther Rhoads's warm and strong presence; and my thankfulness that Mrs. Eichelberger, so charming, friendly, and feminine, was to be with me on the long trip; and I remember Tané's farewell hug. My ever efficient and helpful secretary and interpreter during the past eleven months of constant association had become a beloved little sister to me.

General Robert L. Eichelberger was a big, genial, honest, simple man, as easy, as they say admiringly in the South, as an old shoe. His magnificent courage, his directness, his concern for his men, and his approachability had endeared him to people of all kinds and nationalities, down to the humblest of Japanese ricksha men. His wife, whom he still called "Miss Em," from their courting days in Asheville, North Carolina, was the little tug in charge of the big liner, and together they were a delight-ful pair. I was fortunate to have the trip home with them.

The ten weeks that I spent away from Japan that autumn were strenuous.

The subject of the *Herald Tribune* Forum was "Modern Man: Slave or Sovereign?" Ambassador John G. Winant made the opening address the first night, and his theme was "Peace is a personal caring as well as a collective action." Secretary of Defense James Forrestal spoke on "Keeping America Strong." Carl Sandburg read his poem, "Man Will Yet Win." Mrs. Ogden Reid, the originator and driving force of the Forum, was the delightful chairman. My contribution on "Young People of New Japan" came rather curiously under the heading of "Outposts of American Democracy," which included also Alaska and Hawaii.

I cannot forget Mr. Winant's obvious suffering and struggle as he paused from time to time in his fine address, almost unable to continue. In a few weeks he committed suicide, overwhelmed, apparently, by the world's troubles and divisions, and less than two years after that Mr. Forrestal followed him. They were two

[115]

men whom our country could ill spare, and their tragic deaths have cast in restrospect an ominous shadow on that evening, whose mood at the time was one of hope and determination.

After the Forum I went about the United States during October and November speaking on the new education in Japan to some twenty thousand people altogether, and answering questions. The questions were the same wherever I went. How old is the Crown Prince? What is he like? How did you get the job? (This question appeared thousands of times, and how utterly weary I became of answering it!) Did you meet General MacArthur? What kind of man is the Emperor? Are the Japanese sincere in their coöperation or are they fooling us? Will democracy last in Japan?

The last question would take a book to answer, with a history of Japan and of the liberal movements that have arisen and been suppressed at intervals since the Meiji Restoration, a discussion of the Japanese mind and character, an analysis of what we really mean by democracy, and some probing as to what the questioner's point of view is, for any answer must take into account what he expects. If he thinks the past can be swept away like the writing on a slate and an entirely new structure be erected in two or three years, then he will suffer disappointment. If he holds the traditional view that East is East and the Orient is inscrutable and unchangeable, then he might be surprised and pleased and a little incredulous. It would take also a look into the clouded future, for Japan does not exist in a vacuum, and what happens in the world outside will inevitably shape the course of democratic development in Japan. But people wanted a clear, positive, and quotable answer in a single short sentence, and this was difficult if not impossible to give.

About the sincerity and genuineness of Japanese friendliness I had no doubt or qualifications. I based my answer not only on the courtesy and consideration I myself had everywhere received, but on the attitude of people in the remotest villages toward Americans. And I cited the evidence of the children. Wherever Americans went, the children crowded about, shy, curious, friendly, smiling. Children reflect what they hear at home. If there were hatred and bitterness and talk of revenge in the family circle, the children would not swarm with obvious delight about the foreigner. They could be taught to chorus, as they did,

"Harro!" and "Goodo-by!" but they could not be taught to hide shrinking and fear and distaste if they had learned them at home.

For the question of democracy, I said, the Japanese loved and trusted General MacArthur; they were trying to understand and to practise democracy. We could not expect that the ultimate result would be a carbon copy of the American brand of democracy; it could live only if it were a Japanese product, expressing the deepest needs and aspirations of the Japanese people. Furthermore, I warned, "It cannot be done overnight. Growth is slow and only that growth that comes from within is sure and permanent. It is no use for us to think it can proceed automatically, without nourishment and without help or that it will not be affected by the storms in the world outside."

I tried to explain the economic problem, which is so acute as to seem at times almost insoluble. Japan is a mountainous country, only sixteen per cent arable. It is enormously over-populated. In Japan there are 3,400 people to each square mile of cropland, in comparison to 1,620 in Great Britain, 1,400 in China, 570 in India, 290 in Russia, and 270 in the United States.* To feed her people Japan must import food. To pay for the food she must export manufactured goods. To manufacture the goods she must also import raw materials. She must have trade and markets. She must find either some way to limit her population or some other lands to which it can migrate.

"Democracy," I said, "does not flourish on hunger. It does not flourish on patronage and subsidies; it grows where people can be self-supporting and self-respecting. The other countries of the world must put their minds on Japan's economic problem and upon her necessities of life. They must help her to earn her own living. This is not sentimentality; it is the most elementary common sense. It is an essential step toward peace."

I found people in all parts of the country interested and sympathetic and remarkably free from hatred, in view of the fact that we were only two years away from a war fought with an unparalleled intensity of bitterness. It was all very encouraging, and yet somehow I found myself weighed down with foreboding. I would wake up early in the morning in Chicago or Greenville

* Figures from *The United States and Japan* by Edwin O. Reischauer (Harvard University Press, 1950).

or Pasadena, my heart heavy with dread and a deep and formless conviction that the world was drifting blindly to its destruction.

After all the speaking was over and before I left by Pan American plane for Japan, my sister joined me on the West Coast and we had four days together in peace and quiet in a little inn on a hillside near Carmel. Then the motors roared in my ears for long hours, until at length in the early morning of November thirtieth, I saw the top of Mount Fuji ghostly in the moonlight and, through a hole in the clouds below, the street lights of Tokyo.

I slept all that day while my welcome raged around me. Tané stood guard, receiving telephone calls and callers. The next day I saw the Empress, who spoke to me for a few minutes at the Joshi Gakushuin, where she was attending a school entertainment in which Princess Takako took part. A day or so later I saw the Crown Prince in school.

Everyone wanted to hear about my experiences in the United States, especially the questions that were asked about Japan, and I spent the next week telling the story over and over. The day I spoke to a group of chamberlains and teachers in the Kokaden, the Crown Prince had a bad cold. As he had been present when I spoke to the school, I was surprised that he wanted to come and hear me say the same thing all over again; and I urged him to go home and to bed. He insisted on coming, however, and it is true that the talk I made to the group of men around the long table in the Kokaden was different from what I said to the boys in the classrooms, and it was part of Prince Akihito's developing maturity and initiative that he should consider this as part of his business as Crown Prince and stick to his intention to be there.

After the Emperor's return from Kyushu, where he had been making one of the inspection trips inaugurated since the war, I was invited to dine with the Imperial Family.

It was the first time I had gone to the Palace at night, and there was a new American guard at the gate who did not know whether he ought to let me in or not. He tried telephoning a number of people, none of whom could be reached at the dinner hour, while I sat in the car fuming, getting later and later for my imperial engagement. At length one of Prince Masahito's chamberlains came along on a bicycle on his way home and stopped to find out what was happening. He very kindly went back and telephoned to Kaintei to explain that I was detained, while I tried to compose myself. The word finally came that my pass was genuine and I was allowed to go on.

The Japanese guards were ready and waiting for me, and the great nail-studded wooden doors of the big tile-roofed gate, which are usually closed after dark, were standing open. The car swept through, past the Imperial Household Building, where a dim light burned in a few of the windows, along the driveway between the rows of bare trees. Another guard was standing at the gateway to the side driveway and waved me on with his flashlight. It was getting darker all the time as I moved farther into the depths of the Palace enclosure between walls and under black over-arching trees. A final guard and a last gateway, and I was on the winding lane that led through the woods to Kaintei. There I found lighted windows and men hastening to open the car door and lead me into the house.

At dinner I sat beside the Emperor, with Mrs. Matsudaira to interpret for me. His Majesty thanked me for my labors in the United States, and the imperial children, with much giggling and conferring in Japanese, thought of things to say to me in English.

There were two bits of by-play during the evening that amused us all. I had been told to dress warmly, for the Kaintei, even with the electric heaters in the dining-room and the drawing-room, was chilly. Prince Akihito, accustomed as he was to the Spartan conditions at Koganei, found the rooms too warm, and at intervals he would turn off the electric heater. Whereupon his father would lean down and patiently turn it on again. When his mother remonstrated, so Mrs. Matsudaira told me afterwards, telling him that I was an American and used to a warmer house, he replied that I went out to the school at Koganei, which was cold, and that I didn't mind a bit.

The other was the Christmas gift that Prince Masahito had made for me. He had asked Mrs. Matsudaira beforehand what she thought would be the appropriate time to present it, and she had suggested after dinner in the drawing-room. He had it wrapped up in a little red *furoshiki*—the square of silk with which the Japanese enfold all packages, even though they may be further wrapped in paper and ribbon—and he kept it with him throughout the period of conversation in the drawing-room beforehand, and had it in his lap during dinner. Occasionally he opened a corner of it and stole a look at it. We were all elaborately unaware of its presence, though Mrs. Matsudaira commented afterwards with a chuckle that he must have been afraid someone would get it if he put it down! After dinner, after we had had our coffee sitting around in a circle in the drawing-room, Prince Masahito presented his gift. "This is for you," he said. He was small for his twelve years, and wearing the short trousers of the elementary schoolboy he looked about eight, and very appealing, as he sat eagerly on the edge of his chair, his eyes shining, and watched me open the present. The other children too, all sat up and looked on with interest. Her Majesty's eyes were very tender.

First there was a card, a block print of birds, clouds, and (I think) a hilltop, which the little prince himself had made in school. Next came a small hexagonal box, which he had covered with alternating segments of purple and yellow and blue paper, a very neat job. Inside the box were shells from his own collection, some from the Ryukyus which had been given to him, some that he had picked up himself on the beach at Hayama. This is still one of my most cherished treasures among the other treasures of imperial gifts. Another is the calendar which Princess Takako made me that same Christmas. Each month had a different picture, drawn with crayon by the young artist: a crane and turtle for January, rabbits and a full moon for June, cosmos for October, and a tall thin Santa Claus for December. The pages for the months were perforated by the sewing machine so that they could be torn off, and the top was neatly bound in crimson brocade. It must have taken those small fingers many hours to make.

The Crown Prince gave me his present, a nest of pretty lacquer boxes, the next day at his birthday tea-party, which was much like the previous year's occasion, except that Mr. Blyth was also there, and there was no silver cage over the Crown Prince's sandwiches. I gave him my birthday present, a can of American tennis balls and two books: *Let's Go Outdoors* and *Let's Go to the Seashore.* I had made the choice the subject of an English lesson beforehand, and these were the things that he decided on. Candy and an American birthday cake with candles he turned down.

CHAPTER FIFTEEN

THE CROWN PRINCE went to Chiba during the winter vacation. Chiba Prefecture occupies the long peninsula that guards Tokyo Bay on the southeast. For seven days he went the rounds of temples, schools and colleges, fish hatchery, lotus farm, weather station, archaeological museum; he climbed a mountain; he saw a performance of a badger dance by elementary school girls, and watched a swimming exhibition—out of doors in January!—in which hardy boys took part. Wherever he went the crowds gathered, in some places got between him and the view that he had been brought to see. He was learning fast that an imperial prince belongs not to himself but to the public, and that the privacy and freedom which his humblest subject takes for granted is a precious possession denied to him. It was a difficult discipline after all the years of being protected from the public gaze. But he did spend two nights in a private house where he could get up in the morning and go for a walk along the seashore followed only by some of his own retinue, who numbered seventeen in all.

The trip did him good, and I rejoiced, when I met him again after the holidays, in the animation and interest with which he told me about his experiences. He made some poems, he told me about things he saw. The two best, he said, were one about the swimming and one on the view from the mountains.

One of the books that we read together that term was Robert Lawson's *They Were Strong and Good*. A book for all ages, it expressed through pictures and simple narrative the essence of our American character. It was the story of the author's parents and grandparents and the racial strains and varying experiences that were woven into the fabric of their lives. "They were not great or famous," says Robert Lawson, "but they were strong

[121]

and good." I used that book with almost all my pupils, for it had something to say to every age, and just the other day I heard that the Crown Prince had given his copy of it to his little sister, Princess Takako.

A part of each hour was taken up with conversations about some person or subject, decided on beforehand. When I asked the Crown Prince to tell me a story of Japanese history, he produced the legend of the Emperor Nintoku of the fourth century, who looked out from his palace on the hill in what is now Osaka and saw the village fires were burning low, a sign of hard times, and ordered accordingly that the taxes be remitted until prosperity returned. A happy epilogue describes his rejoicing in the smoke once more going up from each household enclosure and uttering the sentiment that the people's prosperity was his prosperity.

The Prince also told me about Noguchi, the Japanese scientist, and I told him about Vachel Lindsay and his adventures wandering through America reciting his poems in farms and villages in return for food and lodging. The English textbook which was used in school by the Japanese English teacher contained a brief story about Alexander Graham Bell, and because I tried to fit my work in as closely as possible with the rest of the English work, I amplified the story a bit and we discussed it. The textbook account said that nobody paid any attention to the telephone when it was shown "at an exposition" until "a famous man" took an interest in it. I told the Prince a little about the Exposition, which was the Philadelphia Centennial of 1876, and about my mother's girlhood memories of it. The "famous man," I explained, was the Emperor Pedro of Brazil—and found out to my amazement that he knew all about the Emperor of Brazil. It seemed that when he was eight or nine years old, a man had come to the Akasaka Palace with a *kamishibai*, a "paper drama" in which a series of pictures is displayed in a box on a stand, and a narrator tells the story that goes with them. This *kamishibai* man had told the story of the Emperor of Brazil's visit to the Centennial and the Prince had remembered it.

Sometimes we talked about current events, and I learned that the Crown Prince read the newspapers more or less regularly, sometimes one, sometimes four. We talked about the death of Gandhi, which shocked the world that January, and about what

Gandhi had stood for. The Japanese people generally admired Gandhi and his assassination brought to them a felt loss.

In the lessons which the other two boys shared with the Crown Prince we used a little book by Lois Fisher, *You and the United Nations,* which was designed by means of cartoon and diagrams and a simple text to make both the philosophy and the organization of the United Nations clear to American children of about the sixth grade level. We read it together, did exercises based on the new words and constructions, and discussed, insofar as we were able, the ideas contained in it. Sometimes I had them make sentences using the new words that came up in the lesson, such as promote, contented, freedom of the press, unemployment, permanent, organization. The Prince's sentences always interested me, for they were never merely perfunctory devices for working the word in, but they showed thought and sometimes shed light on what he was thinking about. "I am sorry that there is unemployment in Japan," was one of his sentences. "Democracy is the best organization of government," was another, the word assigned being not democracy but organization.

All through those winter months a discussion was continuing about plans for the future living arrangements of the two princes. In March Prince Masahito would graduate from Elementary School and in April would enter the Middle School at Koganei. It seemed to me obvious that he ought to move into the Crown Prince's house on the school grounds, so that the two brothers, who were very congenial and very fond of each other, could at last be together. I was bitterly disappointed when I heard that Prince Masahito's chamberlains were looking for another house, a separate house, for him in the neighborhood of Koganei, and I carried my protests down every avenue that was open to me. Though the chamberlains were unfailingly courteous to me, I was aware that my popularity with them reached its lowest ebb.

It was all to no avail. Prince Masahito, it was explained to me, was younger and less strong than Prince Akihito. He was subject to colds, and over-fatigue frequently brought on a slight temperature. His ardor and his determination to keep up with his big brother made it difficult to prevent him from doing too much when he was with the Crown Prince. The doctors advised against their living together and most of the chamberlains were opposed. I could entirely understand their point of view and sympathized with it in some ways, though I thought that the doctors—five of them between the two princes—could safeguard the younger prince and that it would help to develop the Crown Prince's initiative and sense of responsibility to have a younger brother with him for whom he must take some thought. Happiness, I ventured to say, had much to do with health, and I was sure both boys would be happier together than living alone, each with his retinue of grownups. But the pursuit of happiness is an American rather than a Japanese concept. In the end, as a suitable house near Koganei could not be found, it was decided that Prince Masahito should stay where he was, within the Moat, but that occasionally he might spend the night with the Crown Prince.

Toward the end of January I got my own car. The one I had been using was a pre-war Plymouth that had been confiscated by the Japanese in Singapore, used throughout the war, and confiscated at the end of it by the Occupation. When the question of a car for me came up, the Imperial Household, having been required to yield up a number of its own vehicles to the Occupation, had none to spare for me, and so the Civil Property Custodian released this one for my use. The Imperial Household spent a good deal of money reconditioning it, and it looked very handsome with its new cream-colored paint, but its inner workings were old and tired and new parts unobtainable. Cars in the United States were still in very short supply, but through a friend I managed to get one of the Chevrolets sold for export; it was shipped to me by freighter and arrived at length in January, 1948. With transportation charges it cost me my entire salary for the first year, but it was well worth it.

I had hoped that the new car would work a change in the attitude of my chauffeur, who was the only member of my staff who did not give me devoted service, but it was not the car he disliked so much as the job itself. The pay was small and he felt stirring within him the potentialities as a businessman which ultimately brought him success. Several months later he was replaced by Takenaka San, a handsome, gentle boy in his early twenties, an excellent driver and a joy to have about the house, for he was willing to pitch in and help in any crisis. He had been at Koganei, driving not the Crown Prince, for he was too young for that, but one of the cars that followed the Crown Prince's car. The Prince knew him and liked him, and when someone had wanted to transfer him to work at the Palace itself, the Prince had refused to let him go. When Prince Akihito was told of my need, however, he said, "Oh, if it is for Mrs. Vining, of course it's all right," and so I got Takenaka San in a way as a gift from my favorite pupil.

One day toward the end of January I went duck-netting with the two princes. Duck-netting is a sport developed in the court and used for the entertainment of foreign visitors. It always puzzles as well as enchants the foreigner and usually disturbs him because it is not sport as he understands it to catch a wild animal that has so little chance to escape. He feels a little ashamed of himself for engaging in it even while he enjoys it. Some of the American officers who were invited to take part in this traditional sport eased their consciences by concentrating on the excellent and abundant *saké* provided at the luncheon and by falling into the canals with the ducks afterwards.

From the Japanese point of view it was not so much a sport as an entertainment, and one designed to make all the guests comfortable and happy. All ages could take part and though not everyone might excel, still everyone could acquit himself reasonably well and be sure of not coming home empty-handed and chagrined. The setting was beautiful and the whole ritual so well planned and directed that nobody who followed the leads offered could do the wrong thing or make himself ridiculous. As for the ducks, they had, it is true, little or no chance to escape after their greed had once committed them to venturing into danger, but it was a comparatively easy death, without any chance of being wounded and not found, as there is in western duck-hunting.

We assembled at the pavilion in the Koshigaya preserve, about an hour from Tokyo. Each of us was given a white celluloid tag with a number on it, which indicated the place which we were to keep throughout the day. "You must be very quiet," we were told, "so as not to frighten the ducks away. Do not speak above a whisper." Finally we were handed large nets with long wooden handles. We carried them over our shoulders and why we did not inadvertently brain one another with these weapons, I don't know.

[125]

In the center of the preserve, hidden from sight by dense bamboo thickets, was the pond to which the ducks came by the tens of thousands, attracted by tame white decoy ducks and by the grain that was provided. From this pond radiated narrow canals like the spokes of a wheel. The general idea was to approach these canals one after another, hide until ducks swam into them, then jump out and catch the ducks before they had a chance to get away.

In silence, our nets over our shoulders, we walked along the grassy lane that was like a rim to the wheel, the huntsmen first, the Crown Prince next, followed by Prince Masahito. Then I came with Tané beside me, then Dr. Hozumi, short, rotund and genial, and after him Mrs. Matsudaira and Mrs. Takaki, with chamberlains and officials.

At the first opening in the bamboo thicket, we saw a mound, which hid the canal. Obeying the motions of the huntsmen, we lined up quietly in the order of our celluloid numbers, in two ranks of four, and waited in breathless silence until the chief huntsman gave the signal.

Immediately, without a word, we all ran around the ends of the mound and took our stand on the raised banks of the canal in the same order that we held outside. Down in the water below us—not more than two feet wide, if that much—swam five wild ducks in line. When they saw us looming suddenly above them, they decided that it was time to leave, and the only way out was up.

As they rose, we swung at the nearest with our nets. There was a moment's wild clashing of nets. I felt a live weight in my net and instinctively twisted it, to imprison the bird, and swung it back out of the way of the others. For a second I felt sick over the wild, free creature struggling there, then a huntsman took my net quietly away from me, removed the duck, and returned the net. He quickly tucked the duck's neck under its wing and hid it under a big bamboo basket upturned on the grass. Whether the duck died immediately and painlessly, as someone there kindly assured me it did, or slowly suffocated, as Dr. Oliver Austin, the ornithologist in the Natural Resources Section, later told me, at any rate its end was veiled from the hunter with a thoughtful regard for his sensibilities.

When I emerged from my own personal hunt I found that the

Crown Prince had also got a duck, and that three more were being put under the basket. This canal was now exhausted, and we went on, again in silence, to the next canal, where we did it all over again.

There was a fascination about it: the moment of breathless silence waiting for the signal, the swift, silent rush around the ends of the bunker, and the wild flourishing of nets. Sometimes a duck escaped between two nets that clashed and a third person swung high and scooped him out of the air. There was certainly an element of skill. It was not by chance that the Crown Prince got more than any of the rest of us.

After lunch I retired on my laurels, having caught four ducks to show that I could, and one of the chamberlains took my place, while I followed with my camera, taking pictures. When we had completed the rounds and the Crown Prince had raised his bag to seventeen, we returned to the pavilion by another way, streaming across the wide open field, a little weary and dis-heveled now, the huntsmen carrying our nets. At tables on the lawn in front of the pavilion, our scores were added up and the ducks were brought for us to see. There were two kinds, mal-lards and teal. They were beautiful lying there limp and heavy, with their bright irridescent feathers gleaming. Hot green tea for us all, and the day was over. Everyone got the ducks he had caught himself to take home. The Crown Prince's were dis-tributed among his imperial relatives.

Toward the end of February, the Empress had her English lesson at her dwelling-house Obunko, for the first time. The reason for its being there instead of the Imperial Household Building was rather interesting.

Ever since the end of the war, when the Imperial Household staff was cut down so drastically and the number of gardeners was reduced to a fraction of the former list, groups of volunteers had been coming to the Palace to work in the grounds. The girls of *Jiyu Gakuen*, Mrs. Motoko Hani's Freedom School, had first conceived the idea and had done the earliest service, but since then literally thousands of people had come from all over Japan to give from three to ten days' work to the Emperor. They slept in dormitories within the Moat, but they brought their own rice, paid all their own expenses and gave their service. Their reward, besides the fun of the trip, the tour of the Palace grounds, and sightseeing in Tokyo, was the personal thanks of Their Majesties, who made a point of seeing and talking with each group that came. I have seen them out in the rain, carrying umbrellas and stepping carefully over the wet grass, bowing to a line of countrywomen in cotton kimonos and *mompes* each with a fresh blue and white towel tied around her head. This day, however, Her Majesty had a slight cold, and the Emperor did not want her to risk going out of doors in the chilly weather to stand and speak to the volunteer workers, yet he did not think she ought to go out in the car to the Imperial Household Building, and not speak to them. So he suggested that she have me come to Obunko instead.

The room in which the Empress had her lesson was a square room near the entrance, with a plain, bright, deep-piled carpet on the floor, furnished with a center table and four chairs, a gorgeous lacquer cabinet with one or two fine ornaments on it, a dwarf pine tree in a pot on a stand, some gold screens, and a couple of oil paintings. One, I remember, was a picture of some goats in a grassy field, with the sun shining through big trees. Two small gas heaters were burning and the sun streaming through the two windows made the room delightfully warm.

From this day on, the lessons were held at Obunko whenever it was more convenient to the Empress to have them there.

The Emperor and Empress spent part of March in Hayama, and I went down at the Empress's request for an English lesson, continuing a very pleasant custom that had been started in January. As it was the spring vacation, the Crown Prince was there too, and I had lunch with the Emperor and Empress and the Crown Prince, Mrs. Hoshina and Mrs. Takaki.

The Emperor and the Crown Prince had been out in the boat together that morning collecting specimens. The Emperor has made a special study for years of hydrozoa, which I understand are obscure forms of life on the threshold between vegetable and animal, and his collections in Sagami Bay contained a number of organisms not hitherto recognized or named. He had a laboratory in the Palace grounds in Tokyo, where he worked regularly two or three days each week with Dr. Hattori, a noted biologist.

The Emperor is no dilettante, but an authentic scientist. A year later his book was published, *Opisthobranchia of the Sagami*

Bay Region. The publication of a book by the Emperor, with his name on the title page, was a tremendous breaking with precedent, something that would have been totally impossible before the war, when even his interest in science was discouraged by the military as unsuitable. It is a very handsome volume, with plates that are beautiful even to the ignorant, and scientists in various parts of the world have reviewed it with real respect. The Crown Prince shares his father's interest in biology and it was good that day to see them together.

So the winter of 1948 passed. For me within my circle of school and Palace it was a happy and protected and intensely interesting time. But it was also a little like being inside a snug warm room while a storm rose outside and the wind began to howl ominously. That was the winter when the Communists took over Czechoslovakia, and tensions that resulted in the blockade of Berlin and the air lift developed. Every day four out of the seven columns on the first page of the *Nippon Times* dealt with the impending conflict between Russia and the free world. Communists in Japan were gathering strength and people were beginning to fear them. At western dinner parties there was a good deal of sombre talk about the possibility of war between Russia and the United States. Correspondents who came back from Shanghai reported how things were going there, and it was no surprise to us in Tokyo when finally communism triumphed throughout China.

CHAPTER SIXTEEN

WHILE THE CROWN PRINCE was away on his spring trip, Tané and I spent several days in Gotemba at the foot of Mount Fuji. A charming cottage on a hillside looking toward the Hakone Mountains in one direction and Fuji in the other had been lent to us by friends.

Prince Chichibu, the Emperor's next younger brother, and his lovely wife, who was Mrs. Matsudaira's daughter, had lived in Gotemba since before the war. In the high, pure mountain air Prince Chichibu, who had had tuberculosis, was able to be up and about and lead a fairly active life, though he had always to be careful.

The house in which they lived was a century-and-a-half-old farmhouse, which had been modernized without destroying its charm. It was a large house with a thatched roof and wonderful old beams blackened by age and rich pine smoke. A big fireplace with a sort of inglenook had been added to the living-room, which had comfortable furniture, a few harmonizing Japanese ornaments, and a beautiful picture of the Matterhorn, which the Prince had climbed in the days when he was known as the "mountain-climbing Prince." The rest of the rooms were Japanese, with *tatami* on the floor.

The place, with its wheat fields and vegetable garden, its tea-bushes and fruit trees, cow, goats, sheep, and chickens, was practically self-sustaining, and both Prince and Princess Chichibu did a good deal of the work themselves. The life that they led in Gotemba seemed an idyllic one, and they appeared to be very happy in it.

When Tané and I were in Gotemba in April we were invited to have lunch with the Chichibus. Prince Chichibu at that time looked actually more robust than any of his brothers.

Thanks to his student days in Cambridge before the war, he spoke English very well and he was a most cordial and kindly host. Princess Chichibu had some of her mother's serene dignity and a beauty and charm that are quite her own. She likes to recall her schooldays in Washington and on a previous visit she showed us an old catalogue of the Friends School, all she has left of it now, for her memory books and photograph albums of those days were burned in the war.

After lunch we went into one of the *tatami* rooms, where the Prince showed us how to card and spin wool. The year before they had undertaken to raise nine thousand silkworms from egg to cocoon, in order to encourage the villagers to revive the silk industry that perished during the war. This year, instead of silkworms they were concentrating on the wool from their own sheep. It takes a good deal of strength and skill to card wool, I discovered as I awkwardly handled the spiked carders and succeeded in transferring only part of a wad of wiry wool from one paddle to the other.

As the day was cold, we sat *"in kotatsu"* in the Japanese room. *Kotatsu* is a peculiarly Japanese arrangement for keeping warm, and I suppose the nearest thing to it in western custom might be the "bundling" of colonial days. There was a low table in the center of the room, and underneath it a deep box set into the floor, with a tiny charcoal fire burning in the bottom of it. We sat on cushions, and lowered our feet under the table into the box. A silk-covered quilt was spread over the top of the table and was tucked in around us, so that all the heat from the charcoal was contained in the box, where it felt inexpressibly warm and comfortable to our feet and legs.

Sitting there we looked at albums of trips that the Prince and Princess had made, and talked about places that we knew. Then the Prince showed me the schedule for the Crown Prince's spring trip to Wakayama.

Prince Chichibu had an uncle's concern for his nephew. He wanted to talk about him with me. "Did you read in the newspaper," he asked me, "that when the Crown Prince got off the train a drunken man came up and spoke blasphemously to him?"

I replied that I had seen nothing in the paper about it but I had heard rumors and wondered exactly what he had said.

The Prince told me in Japanese, which I did not understand,

and explained that it was a very rude variety of Japanese and meant, "You're just Hirohito's brat." He thought it would not upset him too much and that he would not attach undue importance to it, but it did seem to me as if the Crown Prince had enough to adjust to at fourteen without that kind of thing. When I saw Prince Akihito the following week and he told me about his trip he made no mention of the incident.

Prince Chichibu wanted to know, as so many did, what questions about Japan people in America had asked me when I was home, and whether any of them had given me advice about teaching the Crown Prince. I said they were interested and wanted information but had no advice to offer, and I told him of a little episode in the Prince's class at school that had particularly interested people at home.

In teaching the boys new words and constructions, I had to build on the old ones, and there were times when I had to be sure that a key word or phrase was correctly understood. Such a phrase was "Let's go!" and so I had got the Japanese of it from Tané before I taught it by demonstration in English. To make sure that they knew what it meant, I asked what it was in Japanese. One small boy very confidently raised his hand, and when I called on him told me something I did not recognize at all. He seemed so sure of himself—and I was so unsure of my Japanese—that I could not say he was wrong. I only said it was not the word that I knew. Whereupon the Crown Prince, looking amused, rose and told me the words I had been expecting, *"Iki masho!"* Afterwards the first boy sought out Tané between classes, and told her that he had given the correct words, but that he had used the boys' phrase, and the Crown Prince, realizing that I would be expecting it in the form that women would use, had told me that.

Returning to the matter of advice in teaching, I said that I would be very glad to have some from Prince Chichibu. He had no advice, he said, but suggested that it would be a good thing if I could find American boys to play naturally with the Crown Prince.

I thought this was a very valuable suggestion, and promised to keep my eyes open for the right boys. As things were arranged at that time there seemed little likelihood of the occasion being anything but a stiff and rather awkward one, with the Prince's

English still so limited, the setting so very formal, and the pre-ponderance of grown-up men in striped trousers and morning-coats who appeared at any social function, but I hoped that the way would open for something easier and I kept the idea turning in my mind.

Another informal suggestion of Prince Chichibu's bore fruit more quickly. The Church of the Brethren Service Committee, which worked closely with the American Friends Service Committee, was sending at intervals all that year shipments of cattle and very fine goats to Japan as a gift. Volunteers came with the goats to take care of them on the freighters, and these young men usually got to see a little of Japan. Sometimes one of the features was a meal at my house, but one group, which took some goats to Gotemba in May, was lucky enough to be introduced to the Chichibus. Among the group was a young man named Al Brauer, whose hobby was ventriloquism. He took out his dummy—but you must never say dummy, you must say ventriloqual figure—whose name was Bill, and performed for Prince and Princess Chichibu, and Prince Chichibu said he wished his nephew the Crown Prince and the boys at the Gakushuin could see it. "How can I show it to him?" asked Al Brauer, and Prince Chichibu said, "Get Mrs. Vining to arrange it."

So I took Al Brauer to school with me one day, and he and his ventriloqual figure performed for all three of my classes, in English of course, and never, I think, did my boys have an English lesson that they enjoyed as much as that one!

Long before I had an opportunity to introduce American boys to the Crown Prince, I took a little English girl into the Palace. Mrs. Watts, who was the daughter of a former Danish Minister to Japan, had been born in Tokyo, and had known Mrs. Takaki all her life. Her husband was a Secretary at the British Embassy, and they were a delightful young couple, embodying the best of two fine traditions. Their small daughter Tina was seven years old, blue-eyed, fair-haired, with the transparent white skin, quick color and delicate features of English children, thin as a rail and quick as mercury, eager and responsive. In order to communicate with her younger brother John, who spoke only one language, she had learned a little Japanese.

May third was a new holiday, "Constitution Day," and the

princesses gave a belated Doll Festival party. I picked up Tina at the British Embassy, very bright-eyed and excited in a scarlet taffeta frock with her pass clutched in her hands. The rain was pouring down and the Imperial Household Building looked rather gaunt and grim with its wartime protective paint beginning to wear off in streaks. As we swung around it to the side door and the waiting-room, Tina, obviously anxious to be impressed by the imperial splendor, said brightly, "It's a *very* fine palace, isn't it?"

After a little while in the waiting-room, we were told to go on to the house where the princesses lived. Into the car again, over an inner moat, up a hill between enormous seventeenth century stone ramparts, and through a simple gateway to the princesses' simple house. "It's a very *small* palace, isn't it?" escaped from Tina in a small voice.

We were led into the room where the Empress and the three princesses were waiting to receive us, and Tina went through the ordeal of introduction and curtseys with a natural charm that made me wish her parents could have been there to see her.

It was all very gay and Japanese. The three princesses were wearing scarlet and white kimonos, embroidered with garlands of flowers, and the stiff, leaf-brown silk *hakamas* that were the specialty of the court. Her Majesty wore a madonna blue kimono with silver threads woven through it. Tiers of shelves occupied all one side of the room and the princesses had set up a bewildering and fascinating array of dolls, animals, toys, and flowers. The cumulative effect was too brilliant and intricate for Tina, who turned in relief to a western rag doll that Princess Takako brought out, and proceeded to undress it.

Presently Prince Masahito came to join the party, and games were produced. The grownups disappeared, and the three children and I sat down at the table for a combined lesson and play. At Princess Takako's suggestion we had Snap first, followed by a game of divided animals, on the principle of Authors, which provided a certain amount of practice in English conversation—though "Please hand me the tail of the lion" is of limited use in ordinary social intercourse.

There was an amount of giggling and self-consciousness that puzzled me until I discovered what the children already had seen: behind the screen at the far end of the room but perfectly visible in a big mirror, sat the Empress, Princess Kazuko, Princess Atsuko, and Mrs. Takaki, all in a row, watching and smiling. So I asked the princesses if they would come and help us play. The Empress decided to join in too, and after that everything went very merrily. Seven-year-old Tina was of the age where you really can't keep your end up in a game unless you peek into other people's hands a little, which she did in the most open and engaging way. Her Majesty gave to her the lovely tenderness which the Japanese women have for small children, with the air of amusement which is so definitely a part of her own charm.

To my surprise the Crown Prince dropped in at teatime. He found the games childish and suggested Contract Bridge, which was promptly vetoed. Tina begged for another game of Snap, and that was played until tea came in. The Crown Prince ate six cakes, which seemed to cheer him up, and after tea he plunged into English conversation with great verve, addressing an unusual number of spontaneous remarks to Tina and to me. His manner with Tina was very charming. She was the only western little girl he had ever met, and he was obviously interested and pleased by her.

On Sunday afternoon, the sixteenth of May, the Crown Prince came to my house for tea. It was the first time in the nineteen months that I had been in Japan, though a date had been arranged the previous March and then canceled. Prince Masahito came too, but as he had been coming regularly twice a month for more than a year it was no novelty to him.

Mrs. Matsudaira, as was her kind custom when any precedent was to be broken, was on hand early. "I am so sorry it's raining," I mourned. "We can't go into the garden or up on the roof."

"Well, never mind," she answered comfortably, in the formula with which she had met so many real disasters.

The two princes, with two chamberlains and a doctor, came in two long black cars, which filled our narrow winding lane. Eighteen policemen and plain clothesmen guarded the premises and came into the kitchen at intervals for tea.

It was on the whole a stiff affair, and I cannot imagine that the two rather speechless small boys enjoyed it very much. I could not see any reason why they should, except that the sandwiches, cake and candy that went with the tea were good. Our sandwiches, which were made with homemade bread and a variety of fillings and spreads from the PX snack bar, became rather famous in imperial circles, and word was brought to me in a roundabout way that the imperial chefs were filled with curiosity as to just what was the magic ingredient. After tea I took my guests up to the study, and showed some of my color photographs, which aroused a degree of enthusiasm that I had not expected.

But, I told myself, when the day was over and I found myself curiously tired, it was the first time, it was a beginning. Next time—if there was a next time—I would see to it that the boys had some fun.

CHAPTER SEVENTEEN

WASHINGTON HEIGHTS WAS a housing project for Occupation-aires, a jerry-built community erected in a few months upon the former Yoyogi Military Parade Ground. It looked like an American company town with rows of box-like stucco houses set at careful angles to insure play space and clothes-drying areas, and scrubby little transplanted trees and sparse bushes struggling for life. There was a commissary, a PX, a gas station, a movie house, a chapel center, a club, and a school, and the people who lived there need never know they were in Japan, except for the profusion of Japanese servants, who were Americanizing them-selves as rapidly as possible.

The school was very bright and cheerful, well equipped and well run, and with its rows of orange school buses, which collected children from American houses all over Tokyo, it looked like any one of countless elementary schools in the United States. When I visited it I was impressed by the zest with which teachers and children worked together with no apparent discipline but self-discipline, yet without confusion or waste energy. In June I took the Crown Prince and five of his classmates to visit it.

Two boys went from each section, and except for the Crown Prince they were elected by the boys themselves. The teachers had asked me to appoint the five boys, as was customary in such cases, but I seized the opportunity to give them a little practice in democratic procedures.

I began by putting on the blackboard the words representative, nominate, vote, elect, ballot, and teller, which I told them to look up in their dictionaries. Then I told them what they were to elect and had them discuss desirable qualities in their representatives, which also I wrote upon the blackboard. The boys

[137]

who were chosen must be able, they decided, to speak and understand English; they must be interested in the American school and able to show their interest; they must be polite, saving their comments in Japanese for a later time; and they must be able to observe carefully and to report to the class afterwards. Then we had nominations and took the vote. The boy the Crown Prince nominated was not elected. He was a good boy, but his English was really not at that time quite adequate. It interested me that the rest of his section did not feel that they must vote for the Prince's choice. In all three sections the boys elected were among those I should have considered myself, if I had done the appointing.

All six boys were excused from classes for the occasion, and we met at Harajuku Station a little after nine one sunny morning. Besides the six boys and Tané and myself, the party included Mr. Nomura, Mr. Sumikura, the bright-eyed Zen Buddhist chamberlain, Dr. Sato, the senior doctor, Mr. Kikuchi, and Viscount Mōri, who was a friend of teachers in both schools and had been one link in the arrangements.

In three cars we proceeded through the monotonous streets of Washington Heights. Word of the imperial visitor had somehow got around among the Japanese servants, many of whom were out bowing. A few extra policemen were on duty, but the Americans appeared oblivious.

Bill Carty of the Paramount News just happened to come out of his house at the moment when the three cars passed. A very quick-witted young man, he took in the situation at a glance, and I have never seen anyone move faster. He jumped into his blue jeep, turned it around on two wheels, and whizzing past us was on the school steps in time to photograph our arrival.

Miss Marjorie Fox, the blond young acting principal, a very able and attractive girl, was at the door to meet us. She took us first to the teachers' room, where we all sat down and she explained to us very simply and slowly the history and organization of the school. The boys all listened intently and understood practically everything that was said, more, in fact, than the grownups did.

The school was accustomed to entertaining Japanese visitors, mostly teachers who came to see in practice some of the new methods which they had previously encountered only in theory, and the children went ahead with their work without paying any attention to them.

We visited a sixth grade studying South America, listened to a singing lesson in the library, where a group was learning a Japanese song, and passed on to the fourth grade, which was doing a unit on Japan under the imaginative leadership of Miss Fern White. Here we stayed for half an hour, and there was quite an interchange between the American children and the Japanese boys.

The American children were making reports on silkworm culture when we came in. After they had finished those, they showed us the costumes and properties of the play, *Momotaro*, which they had presented a few days before. *Momotaro* is one of the oldest of Japanese folk tales, and concerns a boy who was found as a baby bobbing down the river inside a peach and was brought up by the old man and old woman who found him and who finally, with the help of a dog, a monkey and a pheasant, rescued Japan from the inroads of a pack of devils from another island.

The next day, when the Crown Prince had his regular lesson alone with me, I asked him what had interested him most at the American school. He answered promptly, "The classrooms." To my "Why?" he replied, "Because the children were so free." After a thoughtful pause, he asked, "Why are they so free?"

I struggled to find simple words. "Because they are going to be free when they grow up," I said, "and they must learn how to be free now. They must learn how to work together, and how to be free without disturbing or hurting other people. The time to learn that is when they are in school."

A little later he said, "Which is better, the American way or the Japanese way?"

I never liked to make a direct comparison, and I tried to side step. "Which do you think?" I asked.

The Prince laughed, and countered quickly, "No, I asked you."

So I answered honestly, "There are many fine things about Japanese schools, but I think the American way is better. If people are going to be free when they grow up, they must learn how when they are young."

He nodded thoughtfully, then asked me about English and French schools. I told him that I had never visited English or French schools and had only read about them, but that I thought they studied more Latin, more mathematics, and so forth, but did not have so much practice in doing things as American schools did.

While the Crown Prince and I were having this conversation, Tané was talking it all over with Mr. Sumikura. He told her that the men who visited the school with the boys had been much impressed by the kindness and courtesy and friendliness which they had met there, both from teachers and pupils. I in my turn was impressed by the fact that it was the spirit of the school that had struck them so much more than the equipment. It would have been so easy and natural for them to say in effect, Yes, of course you can have a good school when you have such superior equipment, but there was nothing of that kind.

At various times later we discussed the question of freedom and discipline. They could not understand why the informality and spontaneity in the classrooms did not deteriorate into disorder. There was one aspect of the Japanese schools that never ceased to trouble me. In all the American schools that I had ever known, the students could be depended on, if a teacher was called from the room, to carry on quietly by themselves. If they did not work, they at least played without disturbing other people. In a Japanese school, on the contrary, if a teacher is called out, pandemonium promptly ensues, and neighboring classes can scarcely hear themselves think. As long as the teacher is present, however, rigid decorum prevails, and it is a rare student who speaks without being called upon or who asks a question or volunteers an opinion of his own.

Our visit to the American school was returned the following September, when six children and four teachers from both Washington Heights and the still larger development called Grant Heights came to Koganei. Dr. Yoshinari Abe, the white-haired, genial president of the Gakushuin, who had succeeded Mr. Yamanashi, came to Koganei to meet them. Two of the children were girls and four were boys.

Mr. Miyamoto, one of the English teachers, told them about the Gakushuin, its history, and its various parts, the Elementary

School at Yotsuya, the High School at Mejiro, the Girls' School at Toyama, and the Middle School at Koganei.

They visited my English class first. I was teaching the Crown Prince's section at that time. I had divided the class into pairs, and each pair in turn delivered a conversation on the subject of the Olympic Games. I called on the Crown Prince and his partner while the visitors were in the room and they acquitted themselves well.

They went next to the calligraphy class, where the boys were practising difficult characters with brush and *sumi* (charcoal ink) while the teacher lectured on the order of the strokes and the meaning and philosophy of the character, and then to a geography class which was studying the Kanto region, in which Tokyo is situated. They visited also the Kokaden, on the steps of which a drawing class was making sketches of the trees and the playground and the fence around the Crown Prince's house. The gate was opened for the visitors and they looked in. From there they went to a gym class in which the Crown Prince took part. But the high point of the day turned out to be the chestnut grove, where they were turned loose and allowed to gather all the chestnuts that they wanted. The gardener had made some simple bamboo tongs with which to pick up the burrs, and one small boy climbed up into a tree to shake the boughs. They collected burrs to take back to school to show the others, and they stuffed their own pockets with nuts.

"Here," said one youngster, presenting his rear elevation to Tané, "you put 'em in. It's too tight for me." So she poked and pushed until she squeezed the fat brown nuts into two very small hip pockets. She told me about it later with amusement.

As time went on there were still other exchanges between the two schools, a baseball game at Grant Heights in which each team was composed of both Japanese and Americans, so that there should be no possibility of international rivalry, followed by a feast in the lunch-room. The Crown Prince did not attend this event, but Prince Masahito went to another one with a group from his class, and played in a lively game of dodgeball and afterwards conquered a nourishing sandwich of staggering proportions and a mug of hot chocolate.

Further pleasant relations developed when the mothers of the Japanese boys gave a party for the American mothers and this

[141]

was returned. More than one young woman from Grant Heights spoke to me of her disappointment that she had so few opportunities to meet Japanese people and her pleasure in the occasional contacts that she had.

CHAPTER EIGHTEEN

In April, 1948, the Crown Prince had entered upon the third and final year of Middle School, and already the question of the next stage for him was looming up. Some of his councilors and chamberlains were in favor of taking him out of school and having him taught entirely by private tutors; others wanted him to go through the whole course of Gakushuin and graduate from the High School with his class.

The argument of the conservative group was based not merely on tradition and the precedent set by his father and grandfather, but also on the character of high school education in Japan. Since the objective of most of the boys would be to "climb up into" Tokyo University and the competition was intense, the work of the last three years of school was usually aimed at the memorizing of enough material to meet the requirements of the examiners. The Crown Prince, his advisers felt, would need broader and more liberal instruction than this kind of cramming for examinations. Part of the effort of the Education Division of the Occupation had been directed toward changing this condition in Japanese high schools, but evidently the results were not yet such as to create confidence. This group among the councilors pointed out triumphantly that Princess Elizabeth had been taught by private tutors instead of going to school.

The other group insisted that the advantages of the Prince's being with other boys outweighed all the disadvantages.

I was of course eager for the Crown Prince to continue in school and I gave my opinion in season and out.

There were five on the advisory council: Dr. Hozumi and Mr. Nomura, ex officio; Dr. Yoshinari Abe, a fearless and distinguished scholar, former Education Minister, and for many years director of the Imperial Museum; Dr. Chuji Tsuboi, who, though youngest of the group, was a world authority on geophysics and professor at the University of Tokyo; and Dr. Shinzo Koizumi, writer and former President of Keio University. They met regularly once a month, and Mr. Yamanashi, though "purged," occasionally met with them.

Early in March of 1948 I met Dr. Koizumi for the first time when he came to my house to call.

I had heard something of his history beforehand. A tall and athletic man, a famous tennis player, he had been in his younger days so handsome that people turned in the street to look at him. He had studied in Berlin and Cambridge, had taught economics at Keio University, the first great liberal university in Japan, had become its President, and as its representative had attended the Harvard Tercentenary in 1936. He had written widely on economic subjects and was known as a liberal, an anti-Communist, and a man of deep and wide culture. During the war his only son, a rarely fine and promising boy, had been killed; his house had been bombed and burned, and he had escaped by jumping out of a second-storey window. His injuries had been so severe that for nearly two years he had been in bed, and was only now beginning to get about with a cane. He had resigned the presidency of Keio and was intending to devote himself to writing. He was an immensely respected and popular figure among the Japanese people and anything he wrote was eagerly read.

Though I knew that he still bore the scars of his burns and injuries, I had not been prepared for the extent of them. At first sight one's heart is smitten with compassion and with horror that in a civilized world man can inflict such agony on his fellow man. After talking with him for only a little while, one forgets the scars, so completely does he rise above them himself, so triumphant is his personality. Until the end of the war people with physical defects were not permitted even to come into the presence of members of the Imperial Family, which made Dr. Koizumi's appointment as adviser to the Crown Prince even more remarkable; a tribute to him and an indication of the changes that were taking place.

About a month later the whole advisory council, except for Dr. Abe, who was away, visited one of my private lessons with the Crown Prince. They came without warning, filed in silently, and sat down in a row along the wall. The Crown Prince was just finishing the task he had prepared, which was to tell me something about a Japanese naturalist. I asked him a few questions, and then we went on to the subject of Audubon. I had brought *Boy of the Woods,* and though it was too long and the English too difficult for him to read in its entirety, I used the pictures and the text as a springboard from which to launch stories and conversation about Audubon's life. The emphasis was on Audubon's perseverance and devotion to his calling, his imperviousness to conventional criticism but willingness to be helped by those who knew, with explanations of pioneer life in America. I linked him with Daniel Boone, whom we had already talked about, and Sir Walter Scott (for whom Audubon had a passionate admiration) who was next on my list. The Prince looked interested, to my relief. He was very transparent in those days. I could always tell from his expression whether I was getting my effect or boring him completely.

In June I was asked to meet with the council for the first time. That the suggestion came from the chamberlains pleased me. It had worried me a little that I should have been in Japan for more than a year and a half before I was asked to appear before the Crown Prince's council either to be officially inspected or to be given directions or advice by them, though of course I was in constant touch with Dr. Hozumi and Mr. Nomura and frequently saw Dr. Abe and Mr. Yamanashi. It was part of the separation and specialization of the Japanese way. The council did not see me on the one hand, nor on the other hand did the Emperor see the council. All communication was carried on through intermediaries.

This occasion was a luncheon at Koganei, in the Kokaden after my morning classes at school. During lunch the conversation was entirely on general subjects; after lunch we returned to the familiar sitting-room and I was asked to give my "opinion" about the Crown Prince, Tané interpreting for me.

As I looked about the circle of distinguished men, brilliant and scholarly men of affairs, I felt, not for the first time, my inadequacy. I felt too their bigness of attitude in being willing to give the time to hear the views of a woman, an American, who had come from the country with which Japan had so recently been at war and who, they must surely feel, could have very little real understanding of what is suitable for royalty. But I recognized that we were all seeking to prepare a boy whom we all loved to take a responsible place in a changing and uncertain world, and that as a woman and an American I could perhaps contribute a point of view centered upon the boy himself rather than his position.

After thanking them for giving me this opportunity, I spoke of Prince Akihito himself and his splendid innate qualities: his intelligence, his honesty and directness, his sense of responsibility. I said I thought the chief aim of his education should be to give his natural potentialities a chance to develop freely to their fullest capacity. I spoke of the British royal family and their happy and united home life, and what that had meant in the development of the little princesses, as well as what it meant to the British people to have before them an example of family life at its best. Since the Crown Prince could not have the advantages of this kind of life, I felt that it was important for him to have a normal school life, to be as much with the other boys as possible, sharing all of their school experiences. The danger of being a "special student" taking just a few classes was that he would not be part of the group but would be always on the outside.

The discussion that followed wandered off a bit to the question of freedom and discipline in the American school, and the maintenance of respect for the teacher. The point was made that outward forms of respect when carefully engaged in, produce corresponding inward attitudes, a Confucian doctrine that may have a sound psychological basis. My own theory, of course, was precisely the opposite, that the inward attitude comes first; the spirit determines the outward expression and the ultimate form; that really significant and lasting changes of behavior must start from within. It was a discussion repeated many times over while I was in Japan, with the Japanese invariably supporting the outward forms approach and I the inner spirit. But perhaps in the end we might agree that both are necessary.

Nothing was said at that meeting which had not been said before as I had met with individuals among them, but I was happy to have had the opportunity to see them all together, and I appreciated the attention which they gave me and the assurance that they approved of what I was doing with the Crown

Prince and wished me to extend my efforts rather than hold back in any way.

As far back as February I had been told that the Imperial Household wished me to renew my contract for another year from October, 1948. The official request came in May, and with it the suggestion that I have my *Oneisama*—Honorable Elder Sister—join me. My sister and I were all that was left of our immediate family and we were very close. We began at once to plan for her coming in the fall.

The spring of 1948 brought a change in the personnel of the Imperial Household. Viscount Matsudaira had been in failing health since the previous December and in June he resigned his post as Grand Steward. He had been connected with the Imperial Household all his life in one capacity or another, ever since he had been a childhood playmate of the Emperor Taisho. His point of view was inevitably tinged with the traditions of the past. In his place the Diet appointed Mr. Michiji Tajima, a man who came in from the outside world of banking and education. He had been one of the famous group known as "Dr. Nitobe's boys." Dr. Inazo Nitobe was a Friend, a well-known and beloved educator, and a man of wide spiritual influence, whose pathway is marked by the outstanding men who are proud to number themselves among his disciples. Everybody spoke well of Mr. Tajima, and the appointment was a very popular one.

With him came Mr. Takanobu Mitani, who replaced Mr. Mosujiro Ogane as the Emperor's Grand Chamberlain. Mr. Mitani, who had been Japanese Ambassador to Switzerland and then to France, I had already known as President of the Joshi Gakushuin, but I met Mr. Tajima for the first time in July.

I found him a man in whom one immediately had confidence: a man in his middle fifties or early sixties, with a rather square face and direct, keen eyes, a straightforward, even occasionally abrupt, manner, and a smile which lights up his whole face. His English had got rusty, but he had begun to polish it up again and during the following months it improved steadily. He brought with him a fresh breeze, and some doors which had been closed blew open.

CHAPTER NINETEEN

On the train, on my way back to Tokyo after a trip, an American on the seat behind me kept up a running conversation with a young sergeant, which I could not help overhearing. He was a businessman in Japan on a three-month assignment with the Economic and Scientific Section to advise Japanese industry, one of many such groups known to the more permanent part of the Occupation as "ninety-day wonders." His job seemed to take him all over Japan and give him many contacts with Japanese businessmen in key positions.

"I didn't much want to come here at first," he said. "I lost two brothers in Japanese prison camps in the war, and I came prepared to hate these people and everything about them. But I haven't found a single thing to hate. It's hard for my father to understand, and every letter I write home I try to explain the country to him."

I have heard many people say this same thing or its equivalent in various forms. Wherever Americans have been received in Japanese homes, as this man was, as I so often was, they have come away with an appreciation and understanding of the art of living, the hospitality, the culture that they found there. But his next words smote me with a realization of the impression of American life that he was conveying to the Japanese. In a house in which he had spent a day or two the wife had asked him, "What is democracy?" He had replied, "Democracy means you have as much right to sleep with a stranger as your husband has."

These words overheard on the train returned often to my mind; they seemed to symbolize the best and the worst of the Occupation. When we went back in July to Karuizawa and various friends visited me there, much of our talk was of the

Occupation. On the whole, I found Americans inclined to be critical of it, the Japanese inclined to defend it.

It was deteriorating, some said. The first G.I.'s who had come in, the combat men, had been older, experienced, serious. They had come at the end of the war; the Japanese had feared all kinds of horrors, and the men had been decent and compassionate, and friendly; they had made friends with the children and often and illegally shared their food with Japanese. They were, many said, the best ambassadors for the United States that we have had. The new men, who came in later, were seventeen- and eighteen-year-olds, inexperienced and irresponsible. They were bored. How often have I seen listless boys trailing up and down the Ginza looking in the shop windows, or sitting in the railway cars gloomy and vacant, and have felt sorry for them. There were "incidents," not many, in view of the numbers of boys who were there, but each one ugly in itself and magnified of course by Communist emphasis.

One incident—the only one that came within my immediate ken—brought me a very pleasant acquaintance. Some drunken enlisted men pushed their way into a Japanese house in my neighborhood when the father of the house was away, demanded "girls" and refused to leave. The women, terrified, sent someone running to my house to ask help. I was entertaining some dinner guests at the time, and my staff told me nothing at all about it, but ran next door, to the house of a major in the military government, who telephoned the military police. They came in short order and removed the drunks, who had actually done nothing but threaten and frighten. I first heard about the affair when my neighbor sent a big bunch of pink and white carnations to thank me for my assistance! I sent a note of regret and apology, and a pleasant relationship resulted. This was an incident with a happy ending; others which I heard about at second or third hand were more serious and sometimes tragic.

On the other hand, there were the many cases where the men were seriously trying to interpret democracy through friendship. Two twenty-year-old lieutenants, Stewart Shoyer and Stanley Falk, called on me one evening and told me with great enthusiasm about the class which they had in a Japanese Sunday School, and how they were trying to teach the boys to discuss controversial questions freely and disagree without heat. They had studied Japanese at the University of Michigan, and they were well fitted for this undertaking.

From one of my visitors I heard this story: She was on a military car, sitting opposite to a very young G.I. A "pom pom girl" came in and sat down beside him, and snuggling up to him, cooed beguilingly, "You like love?" The boy stared straight in front of him and replied distinctly: "Yes, I like love. I love God, I love my mother, I love nature, I love trees—and *I love Lana Turner!*"

When the dependents came and the best of the Japanese houses were requisitioned for them, the contrasts between the victors and the vanquished became sharper. The Japanese rode in the hideously crowded trains, while the cars with the white lines, reserved for Occupation Personnel, went almost empty. Former owners of large and handsome houses lived crowded in the servants' quarters while Americans who "never had it so good"—a phrase one often heard—occupied the main rooms and sometimes redecorated them by slapping white paint over woodwork precious for its carefully selected natural grain. The American houses were full of servants and American larders were full of food, while a Japanese former princess was seen returning from the country with a heavy knapsack of potatoes on her back and countless women who had always had servants were now themselves struggling with the dark and inconvenient Japanese kitchens. The waste and extravagance in many places must have aroused bitterness in many hearts.

What impressed me, however, was the absence of bitterness among the people whom I knew. There was an acceptance of things as they were of which I think we as a people are incapable. People who had been burned out two or three times and who now were engaged in a desperate struggle to keep alive and to maintain standards, were able to put the past behind them and to go forward with patience and courage. *Shikata ga nai*—It can't be helped—is one of the most frequently heard phrases in Japan. I have been told that an American evangelist visited Japan before the war and heard this said so many times that he made it his special mission to counteract it by saying each time that he heard it, *Doka koka dekimasho*—Somehow or other let's manage it! It comes perhaps not so much from a deep philosophic fatalism as from centuries of necessary adjustment to a land where everybody expects three times in a lifetime to be made homeless by earthquake, fire, flood, typhoon, or volcano. But the acceptance of the results of war and defeat was due to something more than an ingrained habit of mind. I have heard many Japanese people say, and especially during the early years of my stay when the war and the years before the war were closer, "Bad as things are now, difficult as defeat is, I am glad that Japan was defeated. It is better for Japan in the long run. If Japan had been victorious, we would be now under the heels of our own military." And some people said, "If a Japanese army were doing the occupying, it would not be so generous as this."

In making any kind of balance sheet in regard to the Occupation, one has to be clear from the beginning as to what one expected of it. Some observers have expected perfection, and it has not been that. Some have been desperately disappointed because Japan has not immediately become a model democracy on the western plan, free of all the faults which we ourselves have in abundance. Others, with equal bitterness, complain that we have been entirely too successful in making Japan over in our image, without understanding or appreciation of her ancient arts and culture. Many have pointed out, with regrettable accuracy, the gaps between our profession of democracy and our practice of it in Japan.

A military occupation is inherently undemocratic, and General MacArthur was one of the first and most vigorous in stressing the harm that too prolonged an occupation does to both occupiers and occupied and in calling for an early peace treaty and termination of the Occupation. But within the framework of a military occupation, I think that we must admit this one has been extraordinary and unprecedented in the world's history. Many wise and magnanimous policies, devoted service on the part of great numbers of members of the Occupation, innumerable kindly and friendly individual acts on both sides, plus the extraordinary coöperation given to the Occupation by the Japanese people, following the example of their Emperor, have produced a result, not wholly good, but far more good than bad. Bitter enemies have become friends, and that is unusual enough in the annals of human society to arouse respect for all who have had any part in this great experiment.

Certain definite improvements have been accomplished. The list is long, but I mention only those I have myself seen. Women vote, women hold responsible offices. A woman may control her own money. Young men and women over twenty-one may marry without the consent of their fathers or elder brothers. Boys and girls are getting three more years of free and compulsory education. There are no Shinto rites in the schools. Young girls are not sold by their parents to factories; they may stop working and go home if they don't like their jobs. The health of the people has been greatly improved through inoculations, new sanitary laws and other public health measures. An active group of Japanese, with guidance from the Legal Section under Dr. Burdett Lewis, is working on prison reform. These are not mere laws in the statute books, they are things that are actually happening.

The Communists, that summer of 1948, were gathering strength. They had cells in many universities and colleges. They were making headway in the labor unions. Their appeal to the college students was one of idealism: communism, they said, is human brotherhood; here is something noble to which you can give yourself; you can sacrifice yourself for humanity. They drew on the submerged spirit of nationalism and capitalized on opposition to the Occupation and its mistakes and inequities. They assured people that the Communists were the only ones who really wanted to help them; they offered to get taxes reduced as immediate and practical proof—and often made good on the promise, through undeclared Communists in the tax assessment offices. They put up posters, "Japan needs independence and peace with Russia." In a tiny station on the little electric line far up in the mountains from Karuizawa, I saw a poster in which a railroad engine with a face and hands was rising off its track to attack a large, fat, gross-looking man in morning-coat and striped trousers, with a cigar in his mouth and dollar signs all over his stomach, and the English word Capitalism, to make all quite clear, while the Japanese caption read, "Strike him down, kill him!"

Other posters—some, I was told, in the schools—announced that the United States was arming Japan and that thousands of Japanese boys were being trained as pilots. Still others called on the Japanese to choose between Americanization and communism; communism, it was declared, meant Asia for the Asiatics.

The storms in the world outside were beginning to be felt in the artificially enclosed and protected pond that was Occupied Japan.

CHAPTER TWENTY

THE CROWN PRINCE and Prince Masahito spent the summer vacation in Numazu.

Two nights the Crown Prince spent at the Gakushuin summer dormitory, when seventeen Middle School boys came for a week of swimming. He slept under the same mosquito netting with six other boys and shared in all the fun of the group.

For six days in July he had three of his classmates visit him. This idea was his own, and the chamberlains were surprised but coöperative. Two of the boys were his own choice and the third was suggested by teachers and chamberlains. The four slept in two rooms, and no difference at all was made between Prince Akihito and his guests.

It is customary in Japanese schools for teachers to assign rather extensive homework for the holidays, and so the four boys had regular periods for study morning and evening. They swam twice a day. Sailing and fishing expeditions provided the high points of the entertainment, and there were, as the Prince wrote me, "pleasant talkings on many things all the while." The task that I assigned my class was to write a composition in English on the thing they enjoyed most in their vacation, and this house party was the Crown Prince's choice as well as that of his visitors.

One of the boys had been doubtful about it beforehand, evidently fearing the strain of visiting in an imperial villa, but afterwards he wrote a boyishly frank letter to Prince Akihito confessing his fears and declaring that he had had a wonderful time and was glad he had gone.

The rest of the time, about five weeks, the Crown Prince and Prince Masahito spent in the same house, to my deep satisfaction.

The chamberlains reported to me afterwards that everything went well, the two were "very good brothers" and happy together, and everyone was pleased.

When I saw Prince Akihito again after the holidays I thought he looked brown and happy. He seemed to have grown an inch during the summer. He walked unattended now from his house to school or from his house to his private lessons in the Kokaden. Sometimes with just one chamberlain and a bodyguard discreetly in the rear he would walk down the road to the village of Koganei and buy a book in the bookshop there, unrecognized in the crowd.

He and Prince Masahito were invited by Sir Alvary and Lady Gascoigne of the British Embassy to a special showing of the film *Henry V,* and according to Lady Gascoigne carried on a competent conversation in English during the intermission. When I asked the Crown Prince about the picture afterwards he told me he liked it, all but the French princess, who did not please him. I couldn't get him to say why. "It's too difficult to say in English," he objected smilingly.

Though he took refuge, when it was convenient, in the formula, "It's too difficult to say in English," actually he had made great progress. He could initiate a subject now, and could express thoughts and feelings. The self-consciousness that at one period had overtaken him when he tried to speak to me in English in front of others was gone, and with the increased ease and freedom came a greater friendliness between us. Whereas for so long I had to feel my way, guessing from a turn of the head, a shade of expression, a gesture of the hand, now he could tell me of his interests, his memories, his opinions.

I knew more, too, about his life before I had come to Japan, from things he told me himself, things the chamberlains told me, and from some moving pictures that I had seen at the Palace. Before the summer vacation began, I had dined with the Imperial Family at the Kaintei, and after dinner, after I had shown at their request the color photographs which the two princes had seen the day they came to tea at my house, some moving-pictures which had been taken of the Crown Prince when he was younger were brought out. At first Prince Akihito ran the projector himself, but later he turned it over to one of the chamberlains and came to sit on the arm of my chair to explain the pictures to me.

They were all fascinating pictures, but plainly those that interested the Prince most were the pictures of the Gakushuin swimming party at Numazu, when he was about nine. He spent only part of the day there, then, and the whole affair had been very formal and ceremonious, quite different from the easy terms on which he stood with his classmates when I knew him.

We saw the small Prince setting off to walk down the beach to the Gakushuin dormitory, followed by his chamberlains. At the entrance Mr. Yamanashi, as President of the school, came out to receive him, bowing very low. Behind were the boys, drawn up in formation. Their bow, lower still, lasted a long time. Setting-up exercises followed, then classes, swimming practice, and supervised games on the sand, at the end of which he went home again down the beach, a lonely little figure, followed by his grown-up attendants.

He talked a good deal about this picture, pointing out the boys whom I would know, recounting the history of the swimming-party custom. I realized as I heard the warmth and vitality in his voice that the formality, the ceremony, the loneliness were not oppressive to him in retrospect but represented instead security, the golden age of childhood before the air raids and the defeat.

During the mild days of the autumn sometimes we had the private lesson walking in the grounds at Koganei, and that too made for more natural and spontaneous conversation. We would start out together from the Kokaden, and one of the policemen on guard would fall in discreetly behind us. Along the boundary of the Gakushuin property was a very pretty strip of woods, mostly tall pines, with paths through it. Solomon's seal bloomed there in spring, and sometimes cuckoos sang, and in autumn a tiny blue gentian appeared among the leaves. Beyond the woods was the stable, where horses were kept for the Prince to ride. Once we paid a visit to Hatsushimo, First Frost, the white horse that he was riding at that time. Once a ball came over into the edge of the woods from the adjoining golf links, and the Prince watched with interest the American soldier hunting for it.

Now, in choosing subject material for the English lessons, I could consult the Prince about his interests. History, travel, adventure, cowboys appealed; school stories, stars, plants, airplanes, machines of any kind, definitely did not. I used *My Weekly Reader*, a "junior newspaper" rather widely used in American schools, whenever there was an article that would interest him, or that I thought would be good for him. The issue on the new Everglades National Park interested the whole Imperial Family, including the Emperor, to whom the Empress carried her copy. As a result, the Crown Prince chose, from several books that I offered him, a book about Florida, one of a series of illustrated books about the different sections of the United States published by Harper and Brothers. A series of articles that I chose because I thought they would be good for him was the series on schools in different parts of the world—Africa, France, India, China, Japan—in the *Ladies' Home Journal*. In the lessons shared by two of the Prince's classmates, we were using the third-grade textbook, *If I Were Going*, which contained characteristic stories about various countries of Europe. In the classes at school peaceful relationships between people of differing races or countries, and ways to ease tensions were the main theme, with a variety of examples: William Penn and the Indians, the Olympic Games with their expressed purpose of "not victory but partnership," the story of St. Francis and the wolf of Gubbio, the story of Ryokan San, the Japanese priest who loved children and shared his rice with the sparrows, and incidents of coöperation taken from the foreign service reports of the American Friends Service Committee.

In October I met for the first time the Crown Prince's grandmother, the Empress Dowager. This was a pleasure and privilege to which I had long been looking forward. Nobody could be in Japan long and not be aware of the Empress Dowager, the force and influence of her character, and the respect and affection in which she was held by all. From a number of people I had heard something of the story of her life. The daughter of a noble family, she had been taken away in her childhood from the pomp and circumstance of her home, and brought up on a farm, so that she might grow up unspoiled, with a knowledge of simple things and true values. This was quite a common practice in great families in Japan. Dr. Nitobe and his wife, who had been Mary Elkinton of Philadelphia, brought up two princes in this way, and there are many other instances. Even the present Emperor, from the time he was two until he was four or five, lived in the house of a particularly fine and upright couple, and to this early training is ascribed in some measure his consideration for the people around him and his conscientiousness. In the case of the Empress Dowager, it gave her a lasting interest in people, an ability to talk naturally with ordinary folk, and a knowledge of and interest in silkworms and sericulture that lasted all her life.

She was chosen as the wife of the Emperor Taisho because of her character and her unusually keen intelligence, she bore him four sons, and made a devoted wife and a beloved Empress. After her husband's death, she retired completely from public life and devoted herself to the causes in which she was most interested, sericulture, and various welfare movements, especially the care of lepers. Hers was a deeply religious nature, and it was widely said that she included the New Testament in her regular spiritual reading, though she was not a Christian. After the Emperor Taisho's death, she did not receive westerners, although she made an exception for Mrs. Joseph Grew.

She lived in Omiya Palace, which was adjacent to the Akasaka Palace grounds. During the war her house was bombed and burned and she barely escaped with her life into the air-raid shelter. A new and very simple house had been quickly built for her at the end of the war, and it was to this house that I was invited one day in October. Mrs. Matsudaira, who had been a lifelong friend of the Empress Dowager's, went with me.

The house, though small and simple, had the entrance typical of all the imperial villas, the tile-roofed portico, the planting of evergreens, the open door and the red-carpeted steps, the table to the right with the book and inkstand and brushes, the waiting-room to the left, with the familiar tablecloth, the tea and round scalloped cookies, the faint but unmistakable fragrance, perhaps of incense, perhaps of perfume, perhaps of camphor wood, that I found in imperial palaces and nowhere else.

After a little while of waiting, we were led down a narrow carpeted hall until we came to the room where Her Majesty was waiting to receive us.

She was a tiny lady, with bright eyes, a rather hawk-like profile, an expression of great sweetness, and an immense dignity. She was wearing a black silk dress with a V-neck filled in with a high-collared black lace guimpe, and little black kid slippers with jet beadwork on them showed under her long full skirt. The only light note in her costume was a diamond and platinum pin at the point of the V in her dress. Inevitably she made one think of Queen Victoria, though there is nothing in the records to suggest that Queen Victoria was slender or that she had a sense of humor, as the Empress Dowager unquestionably had.

The conversation never lagged. The Empress Dowager was in command of it throughout. Charming, vivacious, low-voiced, she asked questions, and introduced topics, her fingers turning and moving in her lap.

She spoke of her grandchildren, especially the Crown Prince, and of his education, and thanked me for what I was doing to help him meet the new world. She said that he had seemed to her lately more alert and more interested in things and that she was happy about him. He told her about his lessons and she had heard about the visit to the American school in detail.

I must find very strange, she commented, the custom of separating the members of the Imperial Family according to rank. It was an old Japanese custom, perhaps an old Asiatic custom, based on tradition but outmoded now. I agreed that it was strange to me, and that I felt that it was a pity to deprive growing children of the benefits of family life.

She asked me about my books, two of which, *Sandy* and *Adam of the Road*, had been translated into Japanese, and I promised to send her copies of both. This I did, with *Jane Hope* and *Penn* when they later appeared, and she read them all and sent me very kind messages about them.

Tea was brought in by two ladies-in-waiting and served on little lacquer tables. The tea was the fine, slightly bitter green tea, without milk or sugar, and the little cakes that went with it had been especially selected. Some were small round cakes filled with chestnut paste and one was made of *yokan*, bean jelly, in two colors, with Mount Fuji in the center.

After tea the Empress Dowager pointed out the treasures in the room, a beautiful old *kakemono* with a picture of Mount Fuji hanging in the *tokonoma*, a gold lacquer fish on one table, and on another a tiny lacquer lute made by some imperial craftsman long ago in Kyoto. The lute had been brought out because Mrs. Matsudaira's father had been a famous lute-player.

In another room children's kimonos had been spread out to show me, exquisite ones that had been worn by Prince Mikasa, the Emperor's youngest brother, when he was small, by a little prince eighty years ago, and by an ancestor of the Emperor Meiji two hundred years ago. They were bright things with gay embroidery. One was scarlet, one was black, one was peach-colored; the oldest were brown and gold. The prettiest of all was embroidered in soft bright colors with flowers of all seasons, from the plum blossoms of January, to the seven grasses of autumn and the chrysanthemums of November. They lay spread out on the tables and I could imagine the red-cheeked, black-haired children who had once worn them running about like bright butterflies with their long sleeves flying, serious, intent, and happy. Some of the ladies-in-waiting told Tané that the Empress Dowager devoted a great deal of thought to the selection of the things to show me, choosing each one herself and rejecting some of the suggestions that were made to her.

When we said good-by, Her Majesty accompanied us into the little hall and watched us go. At the bend in the hallway I turned back in final farewell, and she was still standing there, smiling after us.

Ten days later I was invited by the Empress to a concert at the Palace.

The court musicians, I have been told, are the oldest musical aristocracy in the world. In the seventh century musicians came to Japan from Korea bringing with them their music and their dances, some of which were Chinese, some Indian. They were installed at the Palace of the Emperor, where their descendants have been ever since. Sometimes there were adoptions, but the line was direct. Thus here in the court were preserved the ancient music and dances.

In modern times the musicians must be proficient in three things, in *gagaku*, which is the music alone, in *bugaku*, which is the dancing and the music, and in western music. Twice a year since the end of the war, in cherry blossom time or in chrysanthemum time, they gave a performance of *bugaku*, to which members of the Occupation were invited, and to which they flocked in great enthusiasm with their cameras. I had been to those and had been fascinated by the weird music, the stately dances with their slow stampings and strange rhythms, their

1946. The Crown Prince and his classmates sing their school song with fervor.

1946. Mrs. Vining looks over the Crown Prince's shoulder on her first visit to his school at Koganei.

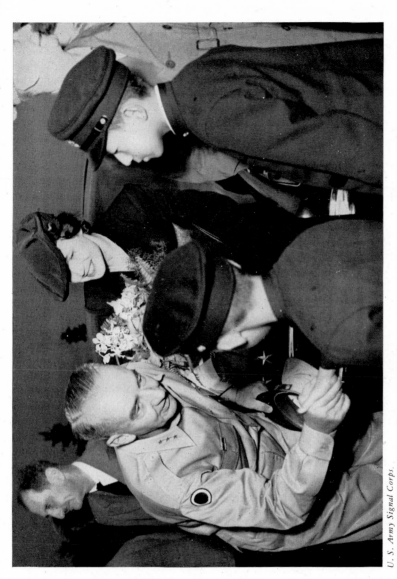

1947. General Eichelberger and the two princes at Haneda Airport. Sir Alvary Gascoigne, the British Ambassador, and Mrs. Vining in the background.

1948. Duck-netting at the Imperial Preserve. The Crown Prince in the foreground, with Mrs. Tsuneo Matsudaira at his left and Prince Masahito across the canal.

The garden of Mrs. Vining's house in Tokyo.

1948. In the sitting-room of the Kokaden.

Tané Takahashi in the garden.

Court Photographer Kumagaye

1949. The Crown Prince at fifteen.

1949. Princess Kazuko.

1949. Princess Atsuko.

1950. Princess Takako.

An inner moat and watch tower within the great outer walls of the Imperial Palace, Tokyo.

Court Photographer Kumagaye

1949. The Emperor's Poetry Party. Their Majesties have taken their places, but the chanters have not yet come forward.

1949. The Crown Prince and Mrs. Vining at Karuizawa.
Mount Asama in the background.

1949. The Crown Prince puts on his shoes before going into the garden of his house at Koganei.

1950. The last private lesson at Tokiwamatsu.

1950.   The Crown Prince, Prince Masahito and Mrs. Vining have tea at Sunset Point.

1950. The people of Karuizawa turn out to see their Crown Prince.

Court Photographer Kumagaye

1950. The Crown Prince and Princess Takako in the drawing-room of Kaintei.

brilliant and exotic costumes. I had been interested that many of my Japanese friends, including some of the imperial children, found the *bugaku* slow and uninteresting, and much preferred western music.

This concert to which I was now invited was a western concert. Several times during each winter the orchestra played western music for Her Majesty and the princesses. Since the war any employee in the Imperial Household who wanted to might attend, and now I was invited.

Tané and I arrived at the appointed hour and stayed in our usual waiting-room in the Imperial Household Building until a smiling young man, Masago San, came to lead us to the auditorium—down a long corridor, up a flight of stairs and down another corridor, to a large rather shabby room, with high windows curtained in brownish brocade.

We went in through a door at the back, and passed the first rows of wooden benches, where the less important office workers sat, then several rows of plain chairs with backs, and then a row of better chairs with seats upholstered in rust-colored plush, with a single chair slightly in front of them and to one side. This chair was for Tané.

In front of these was an oriental rug, and on the rug was a little cluster of chairs. One was an armchair of lacquer with gold decorations. To the left of it and in line with it were three straight chairs; to the right of it and a little behind it was another straight chair. This one was for me.

The orchestra was already in place. It numbered twenty-five musicians, some quite elderly, some very young. Mr. Shiba, the first violin, was a fine-looking old gentleman, gentle, gray-haired, and sensitive. His son and nephew were also in the group; the son played the piano, and I had also seen him take part in one of the *bugaku* dances, in a gorgeous scarlet and gold costume, with a great spreading helmet concealing his modern parted and pomaded hair.

Presently there was a stir at the back of the room and we all stood up. Marquis Yasumasa Matsudaira, the slender, formal head of the Bureau of Ceremonies, came in with the cheerful and helpful Mr. Kuroda also of the Bureau of Ceremonies. They stood along the wall near the rug. After them, walking as *Go Sendo*, Honorable Leader of the Way, was the Emperor's cham-

[161]

berlain Mr. Nagazumi, handsome, distinguished-looking and elegant, gray at the temples, and very erect. Behind him, smiling and acknowledging the bows of the audience who went over in successive waves like grass in the wind as she advanced, came the Empress. Behind her in single file, in the order of age, walked the three princesses, followed by several ladies-in-waiting and Miss Natori and two court officials.

All bowed to the musicians and to me; the Empress smilingly motioned to me to sit down, and they all sat down. Princess Takako's chair was too high for her, but she sat very straight and still, her feet dangling, and never once even leaned back against the chair.

The ladies-in-waiting and court officials filed into the front row of upholstered chairs off the rug.

The orchestra played delightfully for a little over an hour, with a short intermission during which Her Majesty made a brief comment to me, and the princesses turned to smile. The music was light and gentle and nostalgic, and the Strauss waltz made me think of that other ruined city, Vienna, and of the gaiety that had been and was gone.

This was the first of a number of such occasions for me, and they were among my most cherished pleasures. The Emperor never came, nor Prince Masahito, but occasionally the Crown Prince was there and several times the Empress Dowager.

During the autumn I began to know the new Grand Steward, Mr. Tajima. Late in September I had had a long and very satisfactory conference with him about my work with the Crown Prince and the other imperial children. He asked me definitely to consider that my work for the Crown Prince was more than English and to try to think of ways in which my time with him could be increased after the following April.

Mr. Tajima had visited the Crown Prince in Numazu for a few days during the vacation and was a little disturbed because he had seemed more interested in fishing than in his homework. I flew to the Prince's defense, declaring that there would be something wrong with a fourteen-year-old boy who was *not* more interested in fishing than homework. He did do his homework, I assured Mr. Tajima, and furthermore all of the boys in his section of the class had handed in their English work on time, whereas in the other two sections there were a number of late papers. I had noticed that, though the personnel of the three sections was changed from time to time, and though each included a mixture of boys, bright, average and dull, still after a few weeks of shaking down the Prince's section was always the most attentive, most up with their work, and readiest to volunteer in class and I ascribed it to his influence.

This was the origin of the little joke that was much enjoyed by all who were close to the Crown Prince, that whereas the Japanese could be—and sometimes were—quite critical of him, the American who considered herself objective, usually championed him vigorously. The impartial Mrs. Vining, they called me.

The day after the concert Mr. Tajima gave a delightful party for me at the Tokiwamatsu villa, the house which was used as a sort of club for members of the Imperial Family and the court circle. It was an afternoon reception, to which were invited not only those whom I already knew among the court group and outside, but a number of others whom Mr. Tajima thought I ought to know. It would be impossible to name all the distinguished guests, who included several college presidents, two former ambassadors, two former foreign ministers, a former education minister, and the former owner of the office in the Dai-Ichi Building which General MacArthur then occupied.

CHAPTER TWENTY-ONE

EVER SINCE I had been in Tokyo the International Military Tribunal of the Far East, familiarly known as the War Crimes Tribunal, had been sitting. Eleven judges representing the eleven allies in the war against Japan sat on the bench facing twenty-five Japanese defendants, who had been indicted on charges of conspiring to wage aggressive war in violation of international law and treaties, and of abstaining from taking adequate steps to prevent breaches of the laws and customs of war: in other words, of responsibility for the atrocities and horrors of the prisons and internment camps.

The trial opened on May third, 1946. It was expected in the beginning to last for three months, but it dragged on for two and a half years. In all, 419 witnesses were heard on both sides, 773 written affidavits were read, and 4,561 other documents and items of evidence were presented.

When the prosecution was presenting its case, in 1946 and early 1947, the Japanese newspapers carried, by order of the Occupation, full reports of the excesses and outrages committed by the Japanese Army and Navy, and the Japanese people read them, shocked and sickened by the things which they learned for the first time had been done in their name. There is no doubt that these things were done, and all who have come to love and respect the Japanese people must accept the fact which they find difficult to explain: that people so self-controlled, courteous, and kindly in their daily dealings with others could be in warfare so arrogant and so cruel. The explanation lies in the words *in warfare*. War makes beasts of us all. The American people still are in happy ignorance of atrocities committed by our own men in the Pacific. Whether there were many, I do not know. I have heard only whispers, and a single instance, told to me by a captain in the United States Navy, which I wish I could erase from my memory.

During the spring holiday in 1947 I attended one of the sessions of the Tribunal with Diana Kenderdine, who had a pass to the V.I.P. gallery. The trial was held in the Japanese Army War College Building, on a hillside not far from the Yasukuni Shrine. It had been a handsome building to begin with and had been put in beautiful order to give all importance to the proceedings. There was about the entrance, the corridors and the stairs as we went in, a general air of serious and important affairs about to be done, with a definite tinge of theatricality.

We went into the V.I.P. gallery and sat down in the front row. Farther along the row was a smart-looking American woman, who, Diana said, attended every session and took copious notes. Later two American officers came in for a little while and went out again, but for most of the morning the three of us were there in a desert of empty seats. Facing us across the broad room was a similar gallery divided in two sections, one for the Japanese and one for other visitors. Both were well filled, but the Japanese side was crowded.

Below us was the courtroom, paneled in fine wood, with flags of all the countries (except Japan) and all the dignity and panoply of a high court. To our right was the bench; in the center, the witness stand and tables for the attorneys, stenographers, and so on; to our left, facing the Bench, was the dock. A well-setup American captain seemed to be in charge of the production. He had under him two or three very young corporals who had blue bands on their left sleeves marked Page.

To increase the sense of theater, each of the spectators was given a little diagram of the seating in the courtroom: the row of judges and the two rows of defendants. It seemed rather like a program.

The defendants were brought in: twenty-three small and shabby men. Two were absent, Mr. Togo and Mr. Shigemitsu, who were ill.

In marked contrast to that shuffling entrance was the arrival of the judges. The Captain barked, "Rise," and we all stood up, while the eleven justices came in and took their seats. At the command, "Be seated," we sat down again.

Floodlights went on, and there were a few moments of active

[165]

photography. I felt very conspicuous in the almost empty gallery, when the glare was turned full on us. Then the camera men vanished and the business of the day began.

I had met at different times seven of the judges who sat in a line with the flags of their countries behind them: Radha Binod Pal, of India, a tall, fine-looking, dark-skinned man; Bernard Victor A. Roling, of the Netherlands, lean and white-haired with a fine, humorous face; Edward Stuart McDougall, of Canada, small, gentle, urbane; Lord Donald Patrick, of Great Britain, one of the Scottish Lord Justices, who looked as if he might have stepped out of an eighteenth century portrait, handsome in a spare and fine-drawn kind of way, and reputed to be a woman hater; Major General Myron K. Kramer, of the United States Army, stocky, grizzled, shrewd; Sir William Webb, of Australia, the Chief Justice, a large man with keen blue eyes under dark eyebrows, a big nose, and heavy lines beside his mouth, able, keen, unimpassioned; and Major General Ivan Micheyevich Zaryanov, of the USSR, one of the broad-faced, blond, jovial Russians. The other four, Delfin Jaranilla, of the Philippines; Erima Harvey Northcroft, of New Zealand; Mei Ju-ao, of China, and Henri Bernard, of France, I did not know personally. The two generals, the Russian and the American, wore khaki uniforms, the rest were in black robes.

Facing them in two rows were the defendants. The general effect was that of a collection of tired, bored, seedy, discredited men. It seemed almost incredible that they could have had any connection with the might and fury and horror of aggressive war. As I looked at them, individuals gradually began to stand out of the mass, and I consulted my program to see who was who.

Hideki Tojo, war Prime Minister, hated and feared by many Japanese and symbol to the outside world of all that was evil and relentless in Japanese militarism, was in the front row, a little to the left of center; a wispy-looking little figure in a khaki suit, he was thin and gray after his recent illness. Jiro Minami, who was held responsible for the Manchurian Incident in 1931 and who had called the war against China in 1938 a "holy war," was more erect and self-confident. He sat with his head thrown back and his chin lifted; he had an egg-shaped face and a little white chin beard. On the row behind, an aged gray man attracted notice because he appeared to be the most dillusioned, de-

[166]

jected, and bored of them all; he looked as if he were tired out with waiting for an end he neither desired nor feared. This was Kuniaki Koiso, Chief of Staff of the Kwantung Army, Overseas Minister in two wartime Cabinets, director of the war in China and of the occupation of French Indo-China. Next to him, in contrast, Hiroshi Oshima, who was held largely responsible for the pact with Germany and Italy, was younger and better-looking; he sat with out-thrust jaw and a look of sardonic amusement, the only one of them all who seemed to be emitting defiance and hatred. Shigetaro Shimada, who had combined the posts of Navy Minister and Commander of the Navy in the Tojo Cabinet, sat toward the far end of the second row. He bore himself erect, with a look of calm and patience on his broad, high-cheekboned face. The oldest of them all, eighty-one-year-old Kiichiro Hiranuma, who had been a member of the Privy Council and Prime Minister, appeared to sleep.

Mamoru Shigemitsu was ill that day. He had been included on the insistence of the Russians, though his friendship for the western countries and his liberalism were well known and there was a widespread feeling that he was unjustly indicted. Marquis Koichi Kido, who as Lord Privy Seal had been closest of all to the Emperor and who was generally said to have deceived the Emperor by withholding important information from him, was there, but his appearance made no impression at all upon me and I cannot remember what he looked like.

The prosecution had finished presenting its evidence two months before, and the defense was now in full swing. Three witnesses in turn presented their affidavits and were questioned. Ear-phones were in front of each of us, and both Japanese and English versions came over them. When a speech was being interpreted, red lights shone on the desks of the judges, the witness stand and the attorneys' tables.

After the reading of the first affidavit, the witness was cross-questioned, rather ineptly, by the Chinese prosecuting attorney. Sir William Webb from time to time made comments in a quiet voice. At length he said, "We've spent forty-five minutes on this and we have not learned anything that was not in the document," and the next witness was called.

His testimony was attacked by Brigadier H. G. Nolan, Cana-

[167]

dian attorney, as being based on opinion and argument, not fact, and was thrown out by the judges on that ground.

The third and most interesting was the statement of the legal adviser of the Japanese Manchurian Army on the incident at Mukden when the Chinese were alleged to have blown up a Japanese train. The prosecution was trying to establish the fact that the affair was actually arranged by the Japanese as an excuse for the occupation and punishment of Manchuria. Mr. Comyns Carr, the British attorney, cross-questioned this man in his beautifully mellow and controlled voice. Mr. Carr, who was a Bencher at Lincoln's Inn, was tall and thin, with a lock of brown hair that fell over his forehead and a thin, lined face full of kindness, intelligence, and humor. He was billeted at the Canadian Legation, where I sometimes saw him. Once when someone commented on the considerable number of men with brains in the Occupation, he replied, "Oh, yes, my dear, but brains are a penny a dozen. The real question is, what have you got in the way of character?"

Mr. Carr's questions to the witness were on the long-winded side, and twice Sir William Webb broke in with a question that anticipated the point toward which the attorney was heading in a roundabout way, but he was not to be cut short and laboriously pursued his own route to the end. His questions brought out the flimsiness of the Japanese investigation of the Mukden Incident, which took note of the dead bodies of three Chinese soldiers who had been shot by the Japanese guards after they had supposedly blown up the railway, but made no effort to interview anybody who was on the scene at the time.

There had been much delay in the first testimony over terms. Was the landing at Shanghai made on a *hulk* or a *wharf?* The third witness used a phrase, the *remains of explosives,* and it took many questions and many objections by the defense attorneys to determine whether that meant bits of the actual explosives or splintered rails and ties.

The American attorneys defending the Japanese contested every point. It was obvious that they were taking their work seriously and that, having a cause to defend, they had made it theirs emotionally as well as legally.

The trial was being carried out with a thoroughness, a patience, and an absence of recrimination that were impressive.

But as I looked at the eleven judges, able, honorable, distinguished men, some of whom were serving at considerable personal sacrifice, I could not escape the fact that they represented only the victorious nations. There was no Japanese among them. There was not even a neutral, no one from Sweden, Switzerland, Spain, Turkey, or any other nation who had stood outside the conflict. Could a court be impartial and justice be served, when the judges were also the prosecution and the outcome of the trial was known from the beginning? Under ordinary circumstances would we consider a trial fair in which the judge and jury were friends and relatives of the murdered man?

The question troubled some of the judges, and at least one of them made a serious attempt to study and understand the Japanese mind, and its philosophy of right and wrong. Judge Roling had, he told me, gone to Kamakura to talk to Dr. Daisetz T. Suzuki, the venerable Zen Buddhist scholar, and to learn from him. The Tokyo trials, said the Dutchman, were entirely different from the Nuremberg trials, because the Germans on the whole shared our philosophy; they understood the rules in the same way that we did. But the eastern philosophy is different. The same act may be good or bad according to whether a man is "enlightened" or not, and according to whether he is activated by self-interest or an ideal, such as patriotism, or "Asia for the Asiatics." He was impressed by the quality of the defendants; by the fact that Tojo, on trial for his life, spent his time writing poetry, and others studied the great religious literature of the world, Christian as well as Buddhist. As he sat facing the twenty-five defendants day after day for so many months, he came to know them in a curious sort of way. Shimada, he said, was his favorite among them. He called him "a good man."

"I am afraid to go home," he said. "I came here with the Dutch hatred of the Japanese, based on the horrors of war in the Netherlands East Indies and our losses, but after nearly two years I have come to like the Japanese people. They are idealists, and sensitive, and they have something to offer to us westerners, with our emphasis on material things."

The evidence, the counter-evidence of the defense and the prosecution's evidence in refutation, and all the final arguments and summing-ups concluded in April, 1948, and the court recessed while the judges went into their deliberations.

It was a time of tension and strain among the Japanese, as the probability of future executions hung over them like a cloud. Many said that it was not just those twenty-five who were at fault, but all the Japanese people. The Communists, taking their cue from Russia, said that the Emperor should have been among the twenty-five. Elements in the United States and Australia also declared the Emperor responsible, and in some quarters his abdication was called for. There were persistent rumors that if Marquis Kido, who had been the Emperor's closest adviser, was given the death penalty the Emperor would abdicate. There was ample precedent in Japanese history for such an act; many an emperor in the past had withdrawn from the cares of state to devote himself to religion or philosophy or simply the pleasures of retirement. Certainly it would have been the easiest course for the present Emperor, who could then have enjoyed without interruption the scientific pursuits which he loved. I was very much concerned and worried, because I thought it would be a tragedy for the Crown Prince, who would have lost immediately the measure of freedom that he had gained, if he became Emperor at fourteen, no matter who might be the regent.

Among Americans the comment on the trials which I heard most frequently was: "I hope we win the next war!"

Early in August it was announced that the decisions had been made and that a battery of translators shut up like prisoners themselves was translating the verdicts into Japanese; that they would be pronounced in October. It was not until November, 1948, however, after the elections in the United States, that the court reconvened.

On the fourth of November Sir William Webb began reading the verdict. Japan was found guilty of aggressive war. The sentences were read on the twelfth of November.

Tané and I came home from a field day near Koganei, in which eighteen schools had competed, including the Gakushuin, and the Crown Prince had taken part in the Gakushuin's traditional game of *kibasen*, or tournaments. We sat down in the living-room, and as tea was brought in to us, I turned on the radio.

It was the final session of the tribunal. While we sat there, hushed, sipping our tea, we heard the names of the accused

[170]

called, one by one, and Sir William Webb pronouncing sentence in a high monotonous voice.

Seven were condemned to death: Tojo, and six others, of whom only one was a civilian. Sixteen, including Kido, were condemned to life imprisonment. Togo, the Foreign Minister in Tojo's Cabinet, was given a sentence of twenty years, Shigemitsu seven, the time to begin from the day of arraignment. Within the next two years Mr. Shigemitsu was released on parole, and Mr. Togo was freed by death.

The *Nippon Times* on the morning of the thirteenth was filled with the news of the trial, with pictures of the judges and of the defendants, both separately and as they stood together to hear the verdict. The bored, weary, shabby look was gone; they stood erect, with dignity in their impassiveness as they faced the end of the long ordeal.

It had not been easy for the judges to reach their decision. Justice Pal, of India, wrote a long dissenting opinion, in which he declared that the defendants should have been acquitted on all charges, questioned the legality of the trial by the victor nations, and denied that there had been any conspiracy on the part of the Japanese to wage aggressive war. Justice Jaranilla, of the Philippines, on the other hand, criticized the court majority for imposing penalties so "lenient" that "our action may be construed as weakness and failure." Sir William Webb, in a separate opinion, said that since the Emperor, whom he regarded as the leader, had been granted immunity, he considered that no death penalties should have been given.

An editorial in the *Nippon Times* called upon the Japanese people to "strive to hold their emotion in check in order to view objectively and calmly the true significance of the verdict. . . . Its greatest significance," it concluded, "lies in its attempt to contribute to the evolution of the regime of law which must constitute the hope of the world. The execution or imprisonment of a few misguided and exhausted individuals is a relatively minor episode in history. The passing excitement over such an episode must not be allowed to obscure the real significance of the work of the Tribunal as viewed in the light of its long-range historical purpose."

No announcement was made beforehand of the time of the executions. No pictures were shown.

Tojo and the six others were hanged on the twenty-third of December, 1948. The Emperor spent the day in retirement, and the Crown Prince could not go to the Palace to celebrate his fifteenth birthday with his family.

CHAPTER TWENTY-TWO

In November when flocks of brown-eared bulbuls were feasting on the last of the persimmons in the garden, my sister came. Her plane arrived at Haneda Airport a little after three in the morning, and when we drove through Tokyo she saw the moat and walls of the Palace silent and lonely and glimmering faintly in the moonlight. Later in the day, while she was catching up on sleep, flowers of welcome came from the Empress, and from others. Her Majesty omitted one of her lessons that week so that I might take Violet for a drive up into the mountains where she could see Mount Fuji with the sun on her snow shawl and the maples in their full scarlet leaf.

A week later when I went to Koganei for the Prince's lesson, Mr. Nomura told me before the Prince came over to the Kokaden from his house, that he was not feeling well that day, but that he had decided himself that he wanted to have his English lesson just the same. I was concerned when I saw him, for I thought he was pale almost to the point of looking gray, and that his face was drawn. I asked him more than once if he really wanted to finish the lesson, but he declared that he did, and he went through with it in good form, putting his mind fully on his work.

Afterwards as we walked down the hall together, I thought he walked a little bent, and as if he were in pain.

That night he was operated on for appendicitis.

They rushed him in the car at midnight from Koganei to the Palace, and his comment along the way, given with some satisfaction, was that now he would miss his examinations.

The little hospital in the Palace grounds which had been used before the war exclusively for the Imperial Family, and where the Empress's children had all been born, was now the home of Prince Masahito. The large hospital across the Moat for employees of the Imperial Household had been converted during the previous year into a hotel for the traders who were beginning to enter Japan under special limitations and regulations. The Crown Prince, accordingly, was operated on in a temporary infirmary in the Palace enclosure. It was there that I saw him two days later.

He was making a very good recovery, and looked quite bright and cheerful. Mr. Shimizu was reading to him when I arrived and I was interested to see that the book was the Japanese translation of my own *Adam of the Road*. A few days later, the Prince was so much improved that he could be moved to a sunny and pleasant room on the third floor of the Imperial Household Building, where his mother could sit with him every day.

Three boys from his class at school visited him, bringing him notes from all the others. They were thoroughly boyish messages, most of them with humorous intent. One of them commiserated with him because he must be hungry, but urged him to remember the greater hunger of Gandhi in his fasts. Others envied him because he would miss the examinations. The boy who sat behind him lamented that the Crown Prince was no longer there to hide him from the teacher. I don't suppose in all the history of Japan a Crown Prince ever before had such natural, informal, spontaneous letters from his contemporaries— or from anybody, in fact—and all around him were delighted about it. Their Majesties had seen and read them all with great amusement, and the Empress told me about them with obvious pleasure. The Crown Prince himself showed them to me, and though I could not read the Japanese, I could see how they were written, all on one big sheet of paper, at all kinds of angles, and squeezed across corners, so that you had to turn and twist the paper to read them. The chamberlains were pleased, and I noted one more precedent happily broken, one more barrier breached.

Though the Prince was out of school for the rest of the month, he was very soon well enough to be up and about, and on the twenty-first of December he gave his regular birthday party for his English tutors.

After the party, which was a luncheon, I dashed home to

pick up my sister and take her to the Palace, where she was to be presented to the Empress.

The audience, which was very informal, was held in the room where Her Majesty regularly had her English lessons. The Empress, who was wearing a lovely dark purple kimono that day, shook hands with my sister, told her in English that she was glad to see her and glad that she had come to Japan, and invited her to sit down. Mrs. Takaki and I were there too and we all sat in a circle, and talked. Mrs. Takaki interpreted in her easy and skilful way, but some of the time, to my great pleasure, the Empress spoke in English. After about half an hour, a lady-in-waiting brought in a lacquer tray on which was something of silk. Her Majesty took it and handed it to my sister, saying, "This is for you." A similar one was brought for me. They proved to be padded silk kimonos, made to our measurements by the Palace dressmaker, and they were the lightest, warmest, and softest of garments, as well as the loveliest. Violet's had a black background, with multi-colored balls all over it, and was lined with scarlet; mine was a mass of white and pink and lavender peonies, with a shell-pink lining. The Empress had thought the guest from America might be chilly in the cooler Japanese house, and had thoughtfully provided these warm and lovely things.

She urged us to try them on at once, and there were outcries of horror because we folded the right side over the left in the American way, which, in Japan, is the way only a corpse wears her kimono!

Soon the princesses came in with little *furoshiki* which they had made for us with tie-dyed designs, Princess Kazuko's for *Oneisama*—Honorable Elder Sister—was lavender, Princess Atsuko's for me was blue, and Princess Takako's for Tané was pink.

After that we all went off in procession to a concert in the auditorium, the Empress first, bowing to the various chamberlains, ladies-in-waiting, and functionaries along the way, the princesses next, and the rest of us following. Somewhere along the way a gentleman was waiting with our coats, by order of the Empress, who was afraid we might be cold in the concert hall.

The New Year is the great holiday in Japan. Tremendous preparations are made beforehand, houses cleaned, bills paid, all the hanging threads of the previous year carefully gathered in

[175]

and tied. Special food is prepared, so that for the first three days at least of the new year there need be no cooking in the house. The pounded rice, *omochi*, is the particular New Year dish, and it involves much work and ritual. The rice itself is an especially glutinous variety grown just for this purpose. Early one morning toward the end of December it is pounded. The early morning is best, because that provides just the right degree of cold and damp. In the farms they get out the big wooden mortar, hot steamed rice is put into it, and three or four stalwart young people with great wooden mallets walk around it pounding it in turn. Someone with a quick hand and eye crouches beside the mortar turning the hot rice over between thumps. I have been out in the country to see it, and a fascinating scene it is, with the rhythmic pound of mallets, *petán-petán-petánko*, the steam rising in the frosty air, the men and girls going round and round, while the old grandmother sits in the corner by the hearth and watches with a critical eye. When the rice has been sufficiently mashed into a paste, it is taken out and rolled on a board with rice flour into great pillows of dough, and put aside to dry. Squares of this, toasted, appear in the special New Year soup, and in numerous other ways during the festive season.

Houses are decorated with special arrangements of pine, bamboo, straw and white paper cut in a particular way to indicate purification; inside there are arrangements of flowers considered appropriate to the New Year, one of them being a ruffled purple cabbage that looks like a flower, or perhaps it is a flower that looks like a cabbage. Family and friends visit one another, and a game called *caruta* is played by old and young together. The game consists of a hundred cards bearing the first lines of the most famous Japanese poems, and as they are turned up the player who can first supply the rest of the poem gets the card. The point of the game of course is to amass as many of the cards as possible. Out of doors, boys fly kites, and girls play a sort of battledore and shuttlecock, with brilliantly decorated bats.

Young women have their hair done in the classic way, stiffened with camellia oil and piled in high mounds on their heads, decorated with all kinds of elaborate and charming pins and ornaments. Everybody appears in her best kimono and most people at some time or other visit one of the famous shrines.

The scene at the Meiji Shrine was always brilliant beyond description: the beautiful setting of pebbled paths between tall trees, the towering *torii*, and the ever-moving kaleidoscope of people in their brilliant costumes, little family groups, the tiniest scarlet-kimonoed girl in her father's arms, loops of small girls holding hands, their long sleeves almost reaching the ground, their faces painted white and pink, their black hair tied up with bright ribbons, bells tinkling inside their high-soled scarlet clogs, and near the shrine itself the priests in white kimonos with blue or purple or scarlet *hakamas*.

On the third of January I always went to the Palace to "sign in the book," as a gesture of respect and good wishes toward Their Majesties. The second year that I was there I was invited to go in and have some of the New Year food that was peculiar to the imperial court. Mrs. Takaki came to join Tané and me in one of the drawing-rooms, and trays were brought to us, most beautifully arranged, and laden with delicacies that appeared at this time and no other. The *omochi*, instead of being in the soup, (where I always found it very gummy and difficult to swallow) was in two thin cakes, one pink and one white, folded over to make a sort of sandwich, with *gobo*, or slices of burdock root, in between. In the delicious hot soup were quail's eggs, hard-boiled (which were more than difficult to capture with chopsticks), and there was also pheasant cooked in wine, and *tai*, or sea bream, the fish particularly valued for congratulatory occasions.

This year I was invited to see the Empress dressed in her ceremonial costume, which she wore for the special New Year functions. As usual Tané and I waited in one of the sitting-rooms, and Mrs. Takaki joined us. From the window we could see Her Majesty's car arriving from Obunko, a dark red Rolls-Royce with the imperial chrysanthemum in gold on the door. Another window gave on to the corridor, and through it we could see the ex-princesses and their children coming to be presented. There were a number of princes and princesses, descendants of the Emperor Meiji, who had been deprived of lands and titles by the new Constitution and the laws implementing it, but who were of course received at court as before. After a little while I was given a signal.

I crossed the corridor to another room with a screen across the door, skirted around the screen—and there was a picture.

Against the far wall of the room was a gold screen, and standing in front of it, the Empress, looking like a princess in an ancient scroll painting. Her black hair was lacquered into a high wing-like arrangement that made a frame for her classically beautiful face. She wore a bright, soft green outer robe of silk brocade with white medallions of plum trees and blossoms, lined with scarlet. Under this robe, which was long and lay along the floor, was a white brocade kimono, and a scarlet *hakama*, brilliant and stiff. She carried a folded fan in one hand, and used the other to shake hands with me. To complete the picture, beside the Empress there was a stand bearing a classic New Year flower arrangement of a pine branch and a purple cabbage flower.

After a few minutes' talk, I withdrew, and returned to the waiting-room with Mrs. Takaki, where I tried to describe the costume to Tané, who asked questions that I could not answer. Did Her Majesty wear shoes or *geta*? I did not know. What was her hair like in the back? I had not seen her back. Mrs. Takaki asked us to wait and slipped away. Soon Mr. Matsumura, one of the younger prince's chamberlains, came in with Prince Masahito, who had been formally receiving second and third cousins and was unusually stiff, though smiling. After they left, Mrs. Takaki came back to say that the Empress would let me have a second look, and that Tané might come too.

As we hesitated, deciding which side of the screen to go around, I heard Her Majesty's delightful, gleeful little chuckle. We went in, and she turned around so that we could see the back.

Her own hair fell nearly to her waist, tied between the shoulder blades with gold ribbon; and again farther down where a switch was attached that fell beyond the hem of her robe. Her little shoes were red, to match the *hakama*. Prince Masahito hovered in the far doorway, smiling. He was to have lunch with his parents. Prince Akihito was spending the holidays at a seaside resort on the Izu Peninsula, where he had for the first time the ordinary New Year's food which, he told me later, was not so good as that which they had at the Palace.

CHAPTER TWENTY-THREE

BEFORE THE HOLIDAYS were over I gave a party for the Crown Prince. This was to be the second time that he came to my house, and remembering my disappointment over the stiffness of the first affair, I asked permission to include also the six boys who during the year had shared his private lessons on Thursdays.

We worked very hard beforehand, all three of us, my sister, Tané, and I, preparing the Treasure Hunt which was to break the ice in the beginning. I had planned to have the hunt extend to the roof and into the garden, but it began to rain when the day came and at the last minute we had to take out some of the clues and adjust the others to fit the omissions.

A little before two o'clock five plain-clothes policemen arrived, and after bowing to me and promising through their interpreter their full coöperation, began to pace up and down the lane outside. Michiko San was in her dark red kimono for the occasion, Takenaka San was on hand to entertain the Prince's chauffeur and the guards from the Palace. The house was electric with anticipation. At precisely half-past two the long black Imperial Household Packard came slowly around the curves in the winding road and struggled through our narrow gateway.

Prince Akihito had come straight from Omiya Palace, where he had been having lunch with the Empress Dowager. He bore a big sheaf of New Year's flowers, camellias, purple cabbage and plum blossoms, which he presented to me, saying, "My grandmother sent these to you." A man servant behind him carried a big basket wrapped in a blue and white *furoshiki* and containing two *tai*, the congratulatory fish of the New Year, also from the Empress Dowager. (The *furoshiki* was returned, but the basket was considered by my staff too common an affair to send back and it descended to the cellar entrance, where my sister rescued

[179]

it, scrubbed it up, and carried it in triumph to her room. It was woven by hand, of split bamboo, and stood on short chunky bamboo legs, altogether an object of admiration to western eyes.)

Mr. Toda, the tall, boyish chamberlain, accompanied the Prince, with Dr. Yumoto, the newest and youngest of the three doctors, a good-looking man who had a connoisseur's eye for flower arrangements and used to comment on ours after we began to take weekly lessons.

While the Prince was signing in my guest-book the other boys arrived in a body, much concerned about being late. The train had been delayed by the recurrent plague of the period, a stoppage of electricity, or, as the sign in the elevator in one of the American billets expressed it, "Electric currency ceased." Five boys had come; the sixth was in bed with a bad cold.

I explained to them all slowly in English the rules of the Treasure Hunt. The clues, which were written in English on slips of paper, were hidden upstairs and down, in the study, the halls, the parlor and the living-room. They were numbered, and each series was written in crayon of a different color. If they found another boy's clue, they must put it back. If they could not understand any English word they might borrow the dictionary from Miss Takahashi. The Crown Prince's face lighted up at once; the others caught on more slowly.

They drew their first clues out of a pottery jar, and the hunt was on. We had carefully planned the clues so that they would alternate between the upstairs and the downstairs rooms, and great was the rushing back and forth. Some of the clues were simple, some rather difficult. "Find a symbol of courage," led to the arrangement of plum blossoms in the parlor; "You will find your next clue in the key of middle C" puzzled one boy until he thought of opening the piano, where the folded bit of paper was wedged between two of the keys. "Consult Benjamin Franklin" led to a book in the living-room. Other clues were clipped to the month of June in a calendar in the study, pinned behind a sofa cushion with a design of vines, folded under the carved wooden figures of the Old Man and Old Woman on the mantelpiece, or tucked under the carpet on the stairs. Prince Akihito's face was alight as he raced up and down the stairs, the sheaf of paper in his hands fast growing thicker, but the boy who came in first was the one who had been born in the house and had lived there until the end of the war and so felt most at home in it. All the "treasures," which I regret to say were nothing more exciting than notebooks, came to light in the drawer of one of the tables in the parlor, and when the last one had been retrieved, we turned to the next event, which was a quiz game in English.

The game, which I had bought at the PX, was intended entirely for American consumption, and the questions were based on what American children learn in school or from radio programs. Even so, there were few that one or another of the Japanese boys could not answer. The mathematical puzzles, though in a foreign language, were easiest for them, but they could manage those based on sports and geography, and most of the history questions, and one of the boys unexpectedly came up with the correct answer to a question about "The Village Blacksmith."

At four I led them into the dining-room where the table was set for six. Tané had made place cards, and the Crown Prince, instead of being escorted with bows to a particularly splendid chair, had to find his place like everybody else, though I did put him at the head of the table. I told them that from now on they might relax and speak Japanese, and except for going in from time to time to make sure they were getting plenty to eat, I didn't bother them.

The sliding doors were open between the dining-room, where the six boys were, and the living-room where the five grownups had their tea. There was, in the dining-room, the usual "ice-cream silence," and then suddenly came a burst of talk and laughter.

The Prince was scheduled to leave at four-thirty, and the police were alerted for that hour along the twenty-five-mile route between there and Koganei, but he was having such a good time that the understanding Mr. Toda did not interrupt him until there was a lull nearly half an hour later. Then the Crown Prince said good-by and thanked me very gracefully in English, and we all followed him out on the doorstep to see him into his car.

He enjoyed it, he told his chamberlains afterwards and they told me, because it was "such a carefree time." We three were exhausted but elated, when all the boys had left, the police had been fed and departed and Michiko San, back in western dress, for she shed her kimono as quickly as possible, was straightening up the rooms. It had been a success. The only casualty was our little cook's stiff neck, which she had suffered from prolonged peeking at the Crown Prince through the keyhole of the dining-room door!

The September before, when I had seen Mr. Tajima, he had told me of a great innovation that was to be tried out soon. The Crown Prince's advisory council was to meet in the presence of the Emperor and discuss the Crown Prince's education with him. In the past, the Prince's Grand Chamberlain had made a formal report once a year to His Majesty and that had been all. Early in January this meeting actually took place. I never heard how it went or what happened at the meeting.

It must have been considered a successful experiment, how-ever, for shortly after that another innovation was launched. I was invited to confer with the Emperor and Empress about their son. Though I had often been with both of Their Majesties together, the occasion had always been a social one, with some or all of the imperial children present, and there had been no op-portunity for any serious talk about their education. On the two mornings a week when I taught English to the Empress, I spoke rather freely about the children, but there we were necessarily limited to very simple English. So it was that now for the first time in more than two years I was to have the kind of conference with my pupils' parents that is part of normal routine for the teacher of ordinary children.

Their Majesties were in Hayama, as they usually were in January, and I was to give the Empress an English lesson in the morning, have lunch with both Emperor and Empress, and after lunch we would have the serious talk together. I devoted a good deal of careful thought beforehand to what I would say if I got the chance. Mr. Tajima urged me to speak frankly.

Early clouds were blowing away when we stopped for Mrs. Takaki at nine one January morning, and by the time we reached Hayama the sun was sparkling on every pine needle and glint-ing from all the ripples of the deep blue waters of Sagami Bay.

Violet and Tané, who had been invited to come too, were given a picnic lunch and sent off to eat it in the sunshine on the rocks while Mrs. Takaki and I went upstairs for the Empress's lesson to the room with the glorious view of the bay, the islands, the Izu Peninsula, and Mount Fuji.

During the hour the wind rose and whitecaps ruffled the blue of the water. Above the sound of the wind in the pines and the surf on the rocks came the steady beating of drums from the shore, where two Nichiren priests in big bamboo hats kept a self-imposed guard. The Emperor was out in a small boat on the bay, hunting for specimens, and they were beating the drums and praying for his safety.

A little after twelve we went downstairs to lunch in the dining-room, from which there was a view of the garden with white paths through the pines and glimpses of the sun-silvered sea. The Emperor came in and after greeting me said that he had seen my sister when he came up from the beach but as he had not recognized her until he got by he had not spoken to her, and he apologized for the omission. As he had met her only once before and then she had been in dinner dress, I thought it remarkable that he should have recognized her at all.

With Mrs. Takaki there were just the four of us at luncheon, and the conversation was general. After lunch we went upstairs again to the room with the view, where we had coffee. When we had finished, Mrs. Takaki slipped away, and Mr. Mitani, the bland and genial Grand Chamberlain, came in to interpret.

So, as we sat in easy chairs around a small table, the conference began. The hour or more of very frank and direct exchange of ideas that ensued is one of my most cherished memories of Japan. It was neither superficial nor limited, and we discussed most of the problems inherent in the education of a crown prince in a changing world, the tug of tradition, the aftermath of the war, the confusions of the modern world, the personality and needs of this particular Crown Prince, and the sources of religious faith.

The Empress had little to say during the hour, but she followed every word intently and joined in the laughter when, once or twice, we found something that was funny. We closed with the hope that the Crown Prince might grow up in a new world, in which he could make a real contribution to peace.

About a week later Dr. Hozumi and Mr. Nomura called formally at my house. After they had signed in my guest-book and we had had tea, they informed me of the final decision about the Crown Prince's education after he should complete the Middle School course in April.

Months of exploration and discussion, in which every possible person had been consulted except the Crown Prince himself, had resulted in a compromise between those who wished to take the Prince out of school and have him privately tutored and those who wished him to go through the Gakushuin High School with his class. It had been decided that he was to have four days each week in school and two days of private lessons. As the High School had a six-day week instead of the five-day week of the Middle School, he would spend two thirds of his time with his classmates, one third by himself. History, mathematics, English, chemistry, calligraphy, ethics and music, poetry and art, he would study with private tutors. During his four days at school he would have English, biology, calligraphy, social science, Chinese literature, and gym. Altogether, he would be having eight hours a week of English, more than any other one subject.

All of this I already knew from the chamberlains and from the Emperor's Grand Steward, Mr. Tajima, but this was the occasion of the formal announcement.

There was one piece of news. As a concession to my well-known feelings in the matter, one of the Prince's days of private tutoring would be spent at the school, so that he could have the lunch hour and the ten-minute intervals between lessons with the other boys.

The private lessons that winter continued in the Kokaden at Koganei as usual. The two companions that I had for the Prince that term were especially mature and thoughtful boys with interesting ideas. One was the son of a professor of French and himself read and spoke French with ease. His tastes were literary and he was a Roman Catholic. The other was the son of an admiral who had been killed in the war. From his earliest childhood he had expected to go into the Navy. Now his whole life had been cut away from its foundation and he was trying to adjust himself and to find a guiding philosophy. He was a very good baseball player and had a talent also for music.

The book that we used as a basis for discussions was Sophia Fahs's *Tales From Long Ago and Many Lands,* a collection of stories from many countries and periods emphasizing the theme, "Under the sky all men are one family." The stories included

[184]

simple animal legends of Uganda, some of the Jataka tales of India, stories from the Bible, and from Greek and Roman sources. They were simply but not childishly told and the principles involved were fundamental.

The story of Damon and Pythias drew forth an interesting discussion. Pythias, convicted of criticizing the tyrant Dionysius, was condemned to death. He asked for two weeks' leave to go home and provide for his aged parents, and this was granted only when his friend Damon offered to take his place and be executed if Pythias should not return. Pythias settled his affairs and started back in good time, but was delayed by storms, floods and washouts. Just as Damon was being led to the gallows, Pythias staggered in. The tyrant was so moved by the devotion of the two friends that he pardoned both.

I asked the boys what they thought of it. All agreed that such conduct was "ideal." One said that people did not act that way often, but they ought to; another, that perhaps they behaved so in ancient times but not in modern times; that it was a good lesson in human virtues but that love and trust were more rare than betrayal, and he cited Brutus and Judas.

The Crown Prince said that it was a nice story but declared sweepingly that people never acted that way. What interested him was Dionysius. It was not just, he declared, for the king to forgive Pythias. Other people had been executed for the same offense and no doubt they loved their parents too. It was a "breach of the law" for the king to forgive only Pythias. I asked him who had made the law, and he replied, "The king." After a discussion of whether it was a good law or a bad law, I asked, "Do you think that if a king makes a bad law he should not change it?" To which the Prince replied, "If he changes it one day and then another day, the people will not trust him." From which point we went on to laws made by the people themselves and Penn's definition of freedom: "That country is free where the laws rule and the people are a party to the laws."

Another day I had asked the three of them to prepare an oral report in English on their particular interests. The Crown Prince led off with the origin of his interest in biology, his early memories of his father's laboratory and the books that he saw there. He told how when he was small he could not read the difficult books but had enjoyed looking at the illustrations. How his father explained them to him and told him the names of the animals and plants. How his eldest sister, Princess Shigeko, was interested in moths and butterflies and had taught him what she knew. At Hayama he had enjoyed finding and studying little creatures in the pools among the rocks. At Numazu, however, the beach is sandy and so there he turned his attention to fish. This report, he concluded, covered the period of his primary school days. "I love all living things," he said.

The next boy, reporting on his search for a purpose in life, opened up a subject that occupied not only the rest of that hour but all of the succeeding one as well. When he was thirteen, he said, his purpose was to die for the Emperor, but then the war ended and all Japanese thought was changed. He had a long illness when he had nothing to do but think, and he thought about the meaning of life and tried to find a purpose that would satisfy him. His music teacher, "a sweet Christian lady," tried to interest him in Christianity. Now he was not a Christian but was still seeking.

The questions that came out in the course of the discussion were searching and fundamental. They were asked not by me but by the other boys. "Why do you think prayer is the most important thing in religion?" "Why do people say that Catholic is right and all other ways are wrong?" "What is God?" "Why do Christians pray?" "I do not understand about love. I love a person. Where is God?" "Why are you a Quaker?"

For the benefit of the Crown Prince, who considered himself a scientist and an agnostic, I put on the blackboard a list of modern scientists who have turned away from the nineteenth century theory of scientific materialism to a spiritual understanding of the universe: Albert Einstein, physicist, Julian Huxley, biologist, Sir Arthur Eddington, mathematician and astronomer, Sir James Jeans, astronomer, Lecomte du Noüy, bio-chemist, with Alfred North Whitehead, philosopher, and Arthur Toynbee, historian, thrown in for good measure.

They were all listening carefully. The Prince's expression, and I knew his expressions well, was serious, thoughtful, attentive. He leaned forward a little over the table.

I do not know of any more demanding exercise than to have to explain one's basic faith in simple terms, not to children, but to intellectually rather mature young people who are both skeptical and seeking. Fortunately I did not have to answer all the questions; the boys demanded answers of one another too, and the best thing that was said during the two hours was said by one of them: "No, I cannot see God. But I can find him in my heart." When, however, the most philosophic of the three began to spin distinctions with the aid of the dictionary between symbols and abstractions I decided that the moment had come to go on to something else.

The religious education of the Crown Prince was a matter of continuing concern among those around him. The plan which had been adopted was to have a Buddhist, a Shintoist and a Christian lecture to him in turn. Some of us felt that this, while good as far as it went, was formal and inadequate, but we had nothing better to suggest. The experience of attending religious services and being among those who were actually worshiping was denied him in Japan, for the minute he appeared at such a service, whether in temple, shrine, or church, he would himself immediately become the center of attention, and the atmosphere of worship would evaporate. He had had regular instruction for years in the principles of Confucius. He had been given Bibles in both English and Japanese, and perhaps he read them. One of his classmates, in a newspaper interview, said a year later that he "respected" the Bible and sometimes quoted from it. Dr. Saito, President of the Women's Christian College, an outstanding scholar in the field of English literature as well as a noted Christian, was asked to lecture to the Prince, and he devoted an hour to David Livingstone and Albert Schweitzer. I was encouraged to include among my stories accounts of of people whose lives were influenced by religion, and this I did, though to what effect I cannot say. Once I was asked to lecture to the Crown Prince and a group of classmates on Quakerism and Christianity, and this also I did.

But religion is not alone a matter of ritual or of intellectual understanding; it is emotional and spiritual, and the best way to get it is to absorb it in childhood from the atmosphere of one's own family. A child who grows up surrounded by people whose lives are rooted and grounded in faith has the best chance of understanding and living by the reality of the unseen God. Later in life it comes generally in answer to great need or because the heart is opened to it by great experiences of sorrow or joy,

[187]

and he who would give help must wait until he is asked for it, or at least until there is some evidence of receptiveness. Repetition of dogmas before one is ready for them often repels fatally. I felt that perhaps the most effective religious education which the Crown Prince got was the occasional discussions with his friends.

In the lessons alone with me that winter, the Crown Prince read Genevieve Foster's fine *George Washington's World,* in which events and developments that were taking place all over the world while Washington grew from boy to soldier to statesman are described. It included Voltaire and the Japanese artist Hokusai, the Chinese Emperor Chien Lung, Catherine the Great of Russia and a score of others and skilfully wound the threads of their lives and Washington's into the fabric of the period.

There were changes that winter in the little circle around the Prince. First Mr. Sumikura came one day to tell me that he had resigned in order to head up the legislative reference division in the new Diet Library. He had been chamberlain for three and a half years and though his devotion to the Crown Prince was undiminished—and his eyes filled with tears as he spoke— he felt cut off from the world and believed that the time had come for him to establish himself in his profession. In his position as vice-grand chamberlain he would be succeeded by Mr. Tadatsune Sakaki, who had been in the chamberlains' group ever since I had been there. I was sorry to see Mr. Sumikura go for I had enjoyed working with him, but I knew Mr. Sakaki and liked him well, though as his English was limited we could not talk so freely.

Mr. Sakaki was a lawyer, had been at one time secretary of the Gakushuin. His eldest son was in the Crown Prince's class and had shared the Prince's Thursday English lessons during one term. He was a rather short man with a thick crop of hair, keen eyes behind round spectacles, a very bright quick smile, and a decisive, open-hearted manner. He was particularly good on public relations.

Later in the winter Dr. Hozumi also resigned, to become a justice in the Supreme Court. Mr. Nomura took his place as Grand Chamberlain to the Crown Prince, and Dr. Shinzo Koizumi was with difficulty persuaded to assume Mr. Nomura's duties as director of the Crown Prince's education. Mr. Tajima told me that it took fourteen visits on his part to Dr. Koizumi before he yielded to persuasion. His health, which was, however, steadily improving, his desire to devote himself to writing, his sense of the responsibility involved, and his feeling that anyone so publicly an opponent of communism as he had been should perhaps not be so close to the Crown Prince, were the factors that held him back, but once the decision was made, he threw himself into his work with all his heart and soul.

On January twenty-sixth the Emperor and Empress celebrated their silver wedding anniversary. Because of the war and the Occupation, it was done with a minimum of fanfare, but it was a happy family occasion, with a dinner party at the Kaintei and an entertainment by ladies-in-waiting and the chamberlains, of which I got rapturous descriptions from all the imperial children in turn. The performance of the serene and elegant Mrs. Takaki as a gentleman in a drama was especially popular. "It was a kind of dance," the Crown Prince told me, "if you want to know what kind, you must ask her."

CHAPTER TWENTY-FOUR

In Japan almost everybody writes poetry, to express emotion, to celebrate a day, or sometimes to say through its veiled symbols what cannot be uttered in bald prose. Our little maid Michiko San responded to my birthday gift of a resplendent casket of cosmetics in delicate and graceful verse. At the other end of the scale was the historic occasion, already described, when the Emperor made clear his opposition to the war through the medium of poetry.

In the court, poems are written by the members of the Imperial Family and the court officials for all imperial birthdays and other anniversaries and occasions, and of course for the New Year, when a subject is assigned by the Emperor, such as New Grass, Spring in the Mountains, Morning Sky and so on. The poems are all *waka,* the classic thirty-one-syllable verse.

Since the tenth century there had been an annual party when the New Year poems were read in the presence of the Emperor and Empress. Ten years after the Meiji Restoration commoners too for the first time were permitted to send in poems, and a board of judges selected the best to be read. Three of the four years that I was in Japan I was invited to attend the Emperor's Poetry Party, and it was one of the privileges that I most valued.

I was not the first westerner to be invited, but there have been few of us. The first was the British wife of Baron Sannomiya. The second, also some years before the war, was Mrs. C. B. Burnett, wife of an attaché in the American Embassy, who used to send in every year a poem in Japanese, written with a brush; her poems are still kept in the Palace archives and one of them was shown to me. In 1950 Edmund Blunden, the poet whom Great Britain sent to Japan after the war as cultural adviser, and his lovely young wife were also present.

Before I went the first time, Mr. Sukemasa Irie, head of Outa-dokoro, or the Bureau of Poetry in the court, came to see me and to explain the whole procedure, which is precise and complicated and follows a thousand-year-old ritual. It was arranged that Mrs. Takaki was to accompany me, so that I should be quite comfortable. The sensitive thought and care for the western guest never failed to impress me in Japanese hospitality, not only that of the court but in the simplest of country villages.

The party in 1949 was held at ten o'clock on the morning of January twenty-fourth in the Imperial Household Building. It was in a large room, paneled in dark wood, and decorated for the occasion with beautiful screens and hangings. At one end of the room were the three gold-encrusted lacquer chairs for the Emperor, the Empress and the Empress Dowager, with three tables in front of them, each covered with brocade in scarlet, gold, blue and the brilliant light green of Japanese paintings. Behind the three chairs were gold screens painted with scenes from *The Tale of Genji*, and high on the wall behind the screen an embroidered hanging, depicting a peacock with tail outspread. In the center of the room was a table, covered with violet brocade patterned with chrysanthemums, with seven chairs of lacquer with the imperial chrysanthemum in gold, for the chanters. Down the right side of the room were chairs for the judges and the Grand Steward and the Grand Master of Ceremonies; down the left side were chairs for the guests, who numbered twelve or fifteen; at the far end the chanters sat, and behind them, where sliding doors stood open into a smaller adjoining room, were places for the poets, who for the first time were actually there to hear their poems read, and a very few other guests.

The order of entrance into the room was prescribed. First the poets and members of the Bureau of Poetry, then the chanters, with their own master of ceremonies, a former prince, then the judges, then the guests, who included Mr. Shigeru Yoshida, whom the recent elections had made Prime Minister for the second time, several Cabinet ministers and vice-ministers, some assistants to the judges, Miss Yamakawa, lady-in-waiting to the princesses, whose poem was to be read, Mrs. Takaki and myself.

In a few minutes Princess Takamatsu and Princess Kazuko came in and we all stood up for them. Princess Takamatsu wore a little hat with feathers and a dark blue chiffon velvet dress with a long full skirt. Princess Kazuko wore the stiff silk leaf-brown *hakama* of the imperial princesses and a kimono of deep, soft, wine color, embroidered with snow-covered branches of red plum, with birds flying from branch to branch. It was the first time that she had been considered old enough to attend the party.

Now the doors were flung open again and the Emperor and Empress entered, preceded by the Grand Master of Ceremonies, Marquis Matsudaira, and followed by Mr. Mitani and two ladies-in-waiting in blue and violet court kimonos. Everyone rose and bowed.

The Emperor was very well turned out in morning clothes, and the Empress wore court kimono of an exquisite shade of lavender brocade, with paulownia leaves in gold. She had at her belt a diamond and sapphire pin in the shape of a crown and a small diamond ornament in her hair.

After they had sat down behind their tables and the rest of us settled back again, the seven chanters moved forward and took their places at their table, on three sides of it, the side nearest to the Emperor and Empress being left empty. Their own poems were now brought to Their Majesties with great ceremony. Mr. Mitani, the smooth, slightly plump Grand Chamberlain who gave the impression of smiling even when, as now, he was dead serious, carried the Emperor's poems in a long lacquer box, of the gold-spattered type known as *kinmakié,* took it out of the box, and placed it in a square *kinmakié* tray that was waiting on the table. The poem was written on white paper, rolled, and bent in the middle. Mrs. Hoshina, small, bright-eyed, rather quick in her movements, brought the Empress's poem and placed it before her in the same way. This poem was written on fawn-colored paper with a sheet of deep plum color behind it. There is a book of color schemes from which the paper is chosen. Each combination has a name, such as red plum or azalea, and there are fifteen or twenty choices for each season.

As the Empress Dowager did not attend the Poetry Party, her chair was empty, but on the table before it was her poem, written on a lighter shade of plum than the Empress's and placed there by her secretary.

Mr. Irie, tall and very thin, in striped trousers and cutaway, formal and intellectual-looking, with a lean face and high nose, brought the commoners' poems on a square lacquer tray and set it on the chanters' table. The master of ceremonies for the chanters took the poems off the tray and placed them face down before him; turning the tray over, so that it made a little platform about an inch high, he put it in the center of the table. Very deliberately he took the bottom poem from the pile and spread it on the tray, so that it faced the Emperor, but was upside down to those who were to read it. It was written on a large sheet of white paper, and he secured it with two narrow silver paper weights.

The man in the center seat read the poem to himself first, gave a satisfied little nod, and then read in a loud, monotonous voice first the name of the place where the poet lived, then the poet's name, and finally the poem itself. When his voice died away, another man sang the first line, and the four other chanters came in on the second line and finished the poem. The pattern of the *waka* is set for five lines of a definite number of syllables each, 5-7-5-7-7. The chanting itself was strangely lovely, the men's voices rising and falling in a weird, sad, yet tuneful rhythm, drawing out certain syllables, shortening others.

The chanters all belonged to noble families and were descended from a long line of hereditary chanters. Some of them came up from Kyoto for the occasion, others were in business in Tokyo. Most of them were middle-aged or old, but there was one young man, tall, with long eyelashes, full cheeks, a turned-up nose and short upper lip, who looked more European than Japanese. I learned later that his grandmother was a Belgian, and his mother had been lady-in-waiting to a princess.

The poem written by the princesses' lady-in-waiting was read third. When her name was read she rose and bowed to the Emperor and Empress and remained standing till it was finished, a slender pretty figure in the court dress of the 1890's, with a fan furled in her white-silk-gloved fingers. At the end she bowed again and sat down.

Sixteen commoners' poems altogether were read, though not all sixteen poets were there. Some were from distant prefectures, one poem came from California and began nostalgically, "In my native village . . ." Among the poets who were there I was interested to see a schoolgirl in uniform; it must have been a proud day for her family.

The subject of the poem that year was "Morning Snow," and the words *asano yuki,* which appeared in each poem were among the few that I could understand. Each year I sent in a verse myself to register my interest and because I loved this ancient and unique poetic ritual and took delight in having a small share in it. I wrote in English, of course, not trying to approximate the form of the *waka,* which is not practical in English, but to approach its spirit. Someone in the Bureau of Poetry translated my efforts into Japanese and they were circulated among the members of the court and sometimes got into the Japanese newspapers, somewhat to my embarrassment, for they were only tokens, not poems. That year I had written:

> The morning snow
>   Lies deep and white
> And gleaming in
>   The early light.
> I wonder what
>   Footsteps will mark
> Its innocence
>   Before the dark.

After the sixteen winning poems came the poems of the five judges. They were all specialists in one or another school of *waka* and poets of note themselves. Again this year, as the year before, I was struck by the countenance of Dr. Mokichi Saito, a fine, white-bearded face with a noble brow and a look of serenity and wisdom. He is a Christian and the director of a mental hospital.

The judges' poems were on larger pieces of white paper than the sixteen poems first read. The next poem in vivid contrast was written on a sheet of scarlet. This was Princess Takamatsu's poem. She rose and bowed deeply and gracefully, stood while it was read, and bowed again before she sat down.

Twice or more in the long reading period of nearly an hour and a half the pitch and tune were changed. The Emperor and Empress sat as motionless as their counterparts in the Doll Festival, and there was no sound in the big room but the monotonous swelling and ebbing voices of the chanters.

The room became more silent, if possible, and the atmosphere more tense, when the tall, slender, elegant Grand Master of Ceremonies rose and went to get the Empress Dowager's poem, which he reverently carried back to the chanters' table. All the men at the chanters' table stood up and bent over it to read it silently. When they had finished, they sat down again. The reader began his preliminary reading; all in the room except the Emperor and the chanters rose. This poem they chanted three times, the man who sang the first line beginning while the other four were still on the fifth line, rather like a round.

The Empress Dowager's poem, translated, was "The scent of early plum blossoms floats over my garden covered with morning snow."

Everyone sat down while the Empress's poem was brought, and then once again we all rose, the Empress too, and stood while her poem was read three times. Her poem was written in Japanese simple enough for me to understand, and the picture it painted was one that I too had seen:

"In the morning sun I see snow glistening on the pine trees that line the Palace Moat."

The Emperor's poem was the only one not placed upside down before the chanters. The others were placed so that from where he sat he could read them if he wanted to; the inference was that he knew his own by heart. His poem, "At the sight of snow deep in my garden of a morning my thoughts go to people who are shivering in the cold," was read five times, everybody standing except the five chanters and the Emperor himself. Most people stood with their heads bowed, as if in prayer.

At the end of the reading His Majesty's poem was returned to the tray in front of him by the Grand Master of Ceremonies. The commoners' poems were put back in their tray and taken away by Mr. Irie. The chanters left the table and returned to their seats at the far end of the room. One of the chamberlains of the Emperor came and put His Majesty's poem into the long lacquer box and took it away, and Mrs. Hoshino, moving slowly and sliding her feet on the floor like a Noh dancer or a tea-ceremony mistress, came for the Empress's poem.

Their Majesties rose to withdraw and all in the room stood up and bowed low. My bow being western and rather quickly over, my glance met the Empress's as I came up and she gave me a charming and friendly smile. The procession passed through the double doors, Princess Takamatsu and Princess Kazuko following the Emperor and Empress, and all the chamberlains and ladies-in-waiting following them. The doors were closed quietly behind them, and a faint sigh went up in the big room.

CHAPTER TWENTY-FIVE

EVEN AFTER THE compromise about the Crown Prince's studies had been reached, another major problem remained. Where was he to live?

The Koganei school grounds would be deserted, for the High School department of Gakushuin was located in Mejiro, the section of Tokyo in which I lived, and the Middle School, after the Crown Prince's graduation in March of 1949, would be moved to the Girls' School campus at Toyama. As it was a forty-minute drive from Koganei to Mejiro, and it was well known that the Crown Prince himself did not like his house at Koganei, it seemed to me that the obvious solution was for the Crown Prince and his brother to live together in the Palace enclosure, which was only twenty minutes from the Gakushuin High School. Prince Masahito's house was large enough for the two of them, I thought, but if not some other building could no doubt be found.

But it was not to be. The chamberlains to a man opposed this arrangement. Many conferences ensued. As early as January I heard the first rumors about the dormitory.

From the spring of 1946 there had been on the grounds at Koganei a dormitory for boys who lived too far away to commute easily. About twenty boys stayed there during the spring and autumn terms; in the winter it had been closed because of the difficulty of heating. The Crown Prince from time to time took meals with the boys and joined in some of their activities. It was situated in a group of buildings behind a hedge of fir trees at some distance from the Kokaden. I had never been invited there and when I went walking with the Crown Prince he obviously wanted to avoid going near it, so that I knew it only from distant view as a shabby and rather dreary building.

Now it was proposed that this dormitory should be renovated and that the Crown Prince should spend three days a week there, three days at his own house at Koganei, and one day at the Palace.

This plan filled me with misgivings. A well-established dormitory, properly equipped, situated on the school campus, where the Prince might spend the whole week, would have been splendid, but this divided week seemed to me disjointed and lacking in continuity and the dormitory itself too primitive, too far from the school, and too casual. The Prince would have to spend forty minutes twice a day on the road, the other boys two hours each way—four hours a day altogether—commuting on the train. They would start before daylight in the winter and get back after dark. There would be little time for recreation together, just time for bath, dinner, homework, and bed. The boys, seven from each of the two upper classes and five from the Crown Prince's, would be chosen from those who applied, and as there was not much enthusiasm for the idea among the student body, there would probably not be enough applicants for a real choice. Two of the Gakushuin teachers, who were married and had their own homes, would take turns spending part of each week at the dormitory as housemaster.

On the afternoon of March sixteenth, I was invited to meet with Mr. Tajima, Mr. Nomura, and Dr. Koizumi at the Toki-wamatsu club, and we talked it all over from three-thirty until almost six. Mr. Tajima sat a little apart from the rest of us on a sofa with his feet up, his arms folded, his side to us, silent but attentive. "I am here only to listen," he said, and not till the end did he join in.

Mr. Nomura, still looking a little frail after a serious illness in the autumn, seemed radiantly happy over his new appointment. Dr. Koizumi, big, honest, warm-hearted and open-minded, began by expressing the hope that this would be the first of many conferences and that we "would be all good comrades together."

I was asked to express my views and I did. They listened to me with extraordinary patience and fairness as I urged again the advantages of the two brothers' living together, the Crown Prince's dislike of Koganei, and my feeling about the difficulties and dangers inherent in a makeshift and part-time dormitory.

They not only allowed but encouraged me to express all my fears. Some of them they admitted as valid, but felt that they would be compensated for by the advantages. I was torn as I talked, for ever since I had been in Japan I had urged that the Crown Prince be more with his classmates, and I had done everything I knew to encourage such occasions and opportunities; now here I was questioning seriously a venture that would be a tremendous step in the very direction that I wanted to take.

They reassured me about the points that troubled me most: the character of the teacher who would be chiefly in charge, the care with which the other boys would be selected. As to the physical disadvantages, the cold, the damp, the dreariness and discomfort of the building, they said that many boys all over Japan were having to accept uncomfortable and inadequate living conditions and that it would be good for the Crown Prince to share their difficulties.

To this I could only agree, with respect for the point of view behind it, as women in all ages and countries, longing to shelter boys from unnecessary hardships, have bowed to men's stern dictum: "This will make a man of him."

We finished the session with a dinner, after which the subject of foreign study for the Crown Prince was also discussed. The desirability of his studying in both England and the United States as well as some general travel was agreed upon. The questions centered around the time, whether before or after his Japanese education was completed, and the order, America first or England first. Nothing of course would be possible until after the peace treaty was signed, but they were looking ahead, thinking about different schools and universities, their educational principles and practices, the hazards and benefits to a Japanese crown prince.

The next day I visited the dormitory, which was in the process of repair. Dirty and broken *tatami* were being replaced, and carpenters were at work. The building was H-shaped. On the front bar were the bleak study-room, the dining-room, the dark kitchen with its great cauldrons for boiling rice and its small wooden sink with a single, cold-water spigot, and the bath. On the back bar was the row of bedrooms, which faced south so that there would be sunshine on good days. They were all the same size, ten mats, which meant about twelve by fifteen feet, with a

[199]

cupboard in which the bed-quilts were kept during the day. Each room had two low wooden desks without legs before which the boys would sit cross-legged on the *tatami*, and the lighting consisted of a bulb with a white shade hanging from the ceiling. The Crown Prince's room was just like all the rest, except that his perhaps had more new mats than some of the others. A chamberlain would sleep next door, but the Prince would have one of the boys for a roommate.

Outside there was a sea of mud, beyond which were the brown frame dormitory for the police guards, the barn-like school auditorium with several broken windows, the laboratory, and a "music building" which contained a tinkly practice piano or two.

As I looked at it all, I tried to forget the school dormitories that I knew at home. Equipment, I reminded myself, was the least important thing, provided the essentials for health were there. This was Spartan, but there would be safeguards. And here for the first time in history a crown prince of Japan would live among boys of his own age in the democracy of youth, which is age old and eternally of the future, natural, unconscious, yielding yet persistent, like flowing water.

The Gakushuin Commencement was a great affair that year, for two of the imperial children were graduating: Princess Atsuko from the Girls' High School, Prince Akihito from Middle School. The Emperor and Empress would both attend the ceremony.

Saturday, the twenty-sixth of March, was cloudy and cold, as most Commencement days in Japan are, a surprise and relief to one who had grown up in the tradition of graduation days so hot that the suffering guests stick to their chairs. The Gakushuin boys and girls and all the guests, who were mostly mothers in lovely Japanese costume, lined the long driveway of the campus to welcome the Emperor and Empress. At the door of the main building were the imperial children, the top-ranking teachers, and distinguished guests, who included a sprinkling of former ambassadors and several American women.

There was a good deal of chatter and running about on the part of the students until a shouted command froze everybody to stillness. The mothers, obedient to the rule of etiquette which forbade wearing coats before royalty, shed their *haori* (outer garments) and stood in their blue or violet or green kimonos like chilled flowers in the raw wind.

First came an open touring car, rather battered, filled with policemen, followed by a noisy motorcycle and side-car with more policemen, and a mammoth touring-car with the top down containing very high-ranking policemen fortified with much gold braid and buttons. A jeep with two white-helmeted M.P.'s directly preceded the imperial car, which rolled along slowly and majestically with the Emperor and Empress together on the back seat and the Grand Chamberlain on a jump seat, facing them. Cars filled with attendants and a final jeep-load of M.P.'s completed the procession. The welcoming lines bowed low.

The Empress looked beautiful in a violet and gold court kimono with sables around her shoulders, and the Emperor wore formal morning clothes. They returned their children's bows as they passed on their way to the waiting-room which had been prepared for them, where they stayed until all the crowd had been shepherded into the auditorium.

It was the same auditorium in which I had met the students of the Joshi Gakushuin for the first time two and a half years earlier, but great changes had been made. Not only had the leaking roof been repaired, but the whole building seemed brighter and more substantial. The platform end had been provided with a back curtain of cotton brocade of a rich currant color woven with a design of anchors and cherry blossoms. This material must have been made originally for Navy clubs and houses, and large supplies of it apparently became available to the Imperial Household after the war. Most of the curtains in my own house were made of it, and I saw it later at the dormitory at Koganei, and even in the upstairs room at the Hayama villa. It was a beautiful color and glowed softly wherever it appeared.

The imperial children came in first and the audience rose to its feet. The teacher at the piano began to play the *Kimigayo*, the slow, solemn, stately national anthem, and the Emperor and Empress came in. To the command *"Saikeirei,"* everybody bowed very low indeed. *"Rei"* demands the ordinary bow, which is almost unattainable to stiff western backs; *"saikeirei"* calls for something even beyond that.

On the low platform provided for the Emperor and Empress

were two tables covered with gold brocade and two very elegant lacquer folding chairs patterned with the imperial chrysanthemum. Their Majesties sat down, and the audience followed suit.

Dr. Abe, white-haired and forthright, bowed before the Emperor and Empress to indicate that the ceremony was beginning and took his stand on the right, beside the table of diplomas and prizes. The Crown Prince came forward to receive his diploma first, bowed twice before his parents, walked to Dr. Abe, bowed again and returned to his place. Princess Atsuko followed.

Representatives of the four classes, Boys' High School, Girls' High School, Boys' Middle School, Girls' Middle School, received the diplomas for their groups. Dr. Abe made a speech, and the Minister of Education made a speech, both admirably brief. A boy and a girl recited valedictory addresses. Awards were given for the highest scholastic honors and for perfect attendance.

The Emperor sat motionless and impassive through the whole exercise; the Empress's eyes followed her children. The Crown Prince was growing up, I thought; his face had fined down and with his shy poise was coming a quiet unconscious air of command and authority.

The brief ceremony closed with the singing of the school song by all and by the Girls' School a song especially composed for it by the Empress Shoken, consort of the Emperor Meiji, who had been the school's first patroness. For that song the Emperor and Empress also rose, and when it was finished they withdrew, to the strains of the *Kimigayo*.

Curiously enough, Japan owes her national anthem, as she does her national flag, to western influence. She had neither until after her emergence from the Tokugawa seclusion, when she found that other nations set great store by these symbols. She then reached back into her past and provided herself with flag and song. The rising sun flag, which had been used by some of the clan chiefs in long ago days, first appeared as the national flag in 1860 when the first embassy ever sent abroad by the Japanese government set sail for the United States in the Navy ship, *Powhattan*. It was not used in Japan itself until twelve years later, when the Emperor Meiji attended the opening of the first railway in Japan. The words of the *Kimagayo* are a poem from the *Kokinshu*, the tenth century anthology, and the music is an old Japanese melody, harmonized and arranged for western instruments by a German bandmaster named Franz Eckert, who was asked to compose a national anthem for Japan. It was played for the first time at court on the Emperor Meiji's birthday in 1880. Roughly the meaning of the words is, "May you reign thousands of years until what are now pebbles grow to mighty rocks," and the music is beautiful and impressive. It is an interesting example of the fusion of western patterns with Japanese substance, and more successful than many. What is more difficult is the combining of western substance, or ideas, with Japanese forms.

I had thought that when the Crown Prince graduated from Middle School my work would be finished, insofar as a teacher's work is ever finished, and that at the completion of my contract the following October I would return to the United States. Three years had been rather vaguely mentioned in the early days as the probable period of my service. When the invitation came to renew the contract for a fourth year, I declined with sincere expressions of gratitude and regret.

Smoothly as everything had gone, it was nevertheless a heavy responsibility and a strain, and I was beginning to feel physically tired and mentally separated from my life at home. I was losing, I felt, my freshness, which had been one of my greatest assets in the work that I was doing and necessary to it. There comes a point when anyone who has spent any considerable time in the Orient must decide which he is going to do: yield to its charms and become faintly yet indelibly imbued with its point of view and subtly yet unmistakably cut off from the currents of thought and feeling in occidental countries, or break away and go home before it is too late. I thought that that moment would have come by October, 1949.

I found, however, that the Imperial Household was not prepared to say *"Gokuro sama deshita"* (Well done, thou good and faithful servant) and let me go. The Crown Prince's councilors, Mr. Tajima told me, had unanimously decided to urge me to stay. The Emperor himself had asked Mr. Tajima to put it to me as strongly as possible without forcing me to stay against my will. Prime Minister Yoshida either had gone or was going to General MacArthur about it. Dr. Koizumi was hoping to have my coöperation in his new work with the Crown Prince. The Emperor had especially asked him to work closely with me, and he had counted on more than six months of such association. The Crown Prince needed a woman's influence, Mr. Tajima said persuasively, and now that his English had reached the point where he could understand the expression of ideas, he was ripe for the kind of things I could teach him.

They would heartily welcome, Mr. Tajima continued, any suggestions I had to make in regard to the Crown Prince's education. And then, he voiced—as Dr. Koizumi was to do more than once subsequently—the only criticism of my work which they were ever to put to me, and it was a criticism that surprised me. They wished, he said, that I had not so much *enryo*. *Enryo* is a word frequently used by the Japanese and almost untranslatable. It means delicacy, reserve, hesitation to push oneself, one's idea, or one's interests. I made efforts to overcome this fault, but I was always held back by the realization that it was an old and very complex civilization on which we westerners were laying reformative hands and that there were many pitfalls and infinite possibilities of making serious mistakes through well-meaning ignorance. Where I knew that something could help to prepare the Crown Prince for the meetings with westerners that he would have in the future, I spoke out freely; where it was a question of purely Japanese relations I usually kept silent. Yet I rejoiced again and again when some bit of freedom won for the Prince through his western contacts was extended to his Japanese life.

My decision to stay involved also my sister and Tané, and I took a day or two to talk it over with them before I gave my final assent.

It would have been well-nigh impossible for me to continue without the daily help of Tané. She went everywhere with me, so that at any time when a word of clarification was needed, she was there to interpret so unobtrusively, so sensitively, that she was almost an extension of my own mind. Her understanding of my motives and of the Quaker ideals which we both shared, eliminated the difficulties that often arise even with highly skilful interpreters. During the hours at the Palace and other imperial houses when she was not actually with me, she was usually in a waiting-room talking to chamberlains, ladies-in-waiting, or officials, and I knew very well that many times she must have made explanations that would clear away misunderstandings before they had a chance to arise. When I reflected sometimes on the harm that an interpreter who was malicious or simply dull could have done, I was flooded with gratitude for this wise, sensitive, and loving spirit, who was as eager as I was to promote international peace and understanding.

She had heavy duties in the house, too, keeping the complicated accounts, acting as liaison with the household staff, typing my correspondence, taking my Japanese telephone calls, translating my articles and speeches, of which there were a good many, and steering me through the intricacies of Japanese social relations. She even taught me to speak a little Japanese and to recognize a hundred of the characters. She was as pretty as ever, with her wide cheekbones and the shadows of beauty under them which gave her a slightly Mona Lisa smile, her graceful little figure and delicate, long-fingered hands, but she had lost twenty pounds, and I was troubled about her health. Her own life she had put aside, her teaching, her leadership in the Friends Meeting, the possibility of marriage, to follow day in and day out at my heels, and this I thought was a sacrifice that ought not to go on too long.

Violet had joined me with the idea of staying just a year. Though she was enjoying her experience and finding much to interest and please her, the damp climate did not agree with her, so that she suffered frequent onslaughts of a virus type of grippe, and never, even at best, felt quite well.

These two, who were so vital to my happiness and effectiveness, agreed to cast in their lot with mine for another year, and we all settled down after the flurry. Once the decision was made, it became the only tenable one, right and inevitable.

CHAPTER TWENTY-SIX

WITH THE OPENING of the new school year in April, I began to
meet my classes on the main school campus at Mejiro instead
of at Koganei. The big brick building had once been a handsome one but soldiers had been billeted there and there was
little money for repairs after the war. Doors lacked handles;
the white plaster walls were dirty and scarred; in the mornings
the janitor sprinkled the corridors with water in order to lay the
dust.

The Crown Prince's class were now first-year High School
boys. Most of them were letting their hair grow out. Before and
during the war all students, both school and university, had
shaven heads, like soldiers in the Army. During the war even
civilians were enjoined to follow the Army custom and a civilian
with hair long enough to part was liable to have his face slapped
by a soldier on the street. After the war the rule was dropped
and the boys might suit themselves. In the Gakushuin they decided to shave their heads through Middle School and to let their
hair grow in High School. Now I suddenly faced a forest of
stiffly sprouting hair and some of the boys were so changed in
appearance that I had to learn their names all over again. It was
two or three months before their hair was long enough to be
parted and plastered down with a hair oil so richly perfumed
that the atmosphere of the classroom was almost overwhelming.

I had also a good many new boys to learn to know. Between
twenty and thirty boys from other schools passed the examinations and entered. There were now 110 in the three sections, six
of whom were repeaters in English from the class above.

As a means of getting acquainted with the new boys, as well
as of testing their knowledge of English, on the first day of the
new term I had the whole class take down from dictation a

series of questions about themselves and answer them. The questions included one about their interests and one about what they wanted to be when they grew up.

The interests were varied, and usually a sport was listed first with some intellectual pursuit second. Baseball and reading was the most frequent combination. Football, tennis, and swimming came next, with *judo* (wrestling), mountain-climbing, riding, fishing, skiing following along. After reading, music and drawing or painting were the most popular; model trains and airplanes, archaeology, photography, stamp-collecting, radio and movies had a few adherents each. One lad, obviously with an eye on teacher, avowed a passion for "demokrace." The Crown Prince had switched his favorite sport from swimming to riding.

Their ambitions varied even more widely. Six wanted to be doctors, six to be scientists in different fields, five simply and grandly to be "great men." Banking, teaching, journalism, and engineering were chosen by three boys each, and there was a sprinkling of businessmen, "officials," hotel managers, scholars, statesmen, philosophers, writers, sportsmen, and travelers. One boy wanted to be a chamberlain. Two wanted to do something to help people. One said, "I want to be litterature," another, "I want to be grow-up violinist or pianist and I want to be *good.*" One announced, "I want to be a gentleman," but did not explain what he meant by the term.

I was interested to see what the Crown Prince's answer would be. He wrote, "I shall be Emperor." There was no question of what he wanted to be; he was aware of his destiny and he accepted it.

This term, I told them, we were going to study Great Men and Women of the Twentieth Century. I took a little time to discuss the meaning of the word century, and to explain that while our subjects might have been born before 1900, the major part of their lives must have been spent in the twentieth century. A great man I defined somewhat arbitrarily as one who was not merely a figure of power or fame but one who had done something to help the world. We would study ten, of whom they were to chose five and I would choose five.

They made up their lists, and I wrote the names of their candidates on the blackboard and the five most often mentioned were chosen. Gandhi, Einstein, Noguchi, and Madame Curie came out ahead in all three sections. Edison was fifth in two sections, Winston Churchill surprisingly in the third. Lenin, Stalin, Hitler, and Tojo were mentioned, probably to get a rise out of me. I wrote their names on the board without comment and they got one vote each.

To the five whom the boys chose I added Roald Amundsen, Eleanor Roosevelt, Helen Keller, Albert Schweitzer, and Pierre Ceresole, the last one not because he is universally known but because I wanted to include one whose life had been given wholly to peace and whose *Service Civile Internationale* offered the moral equivalent of war that William James advocated.

I varied the classroom procedure as we studied these great figures. Sometimes I told the story and they asked questions. Sometimes they told the story and I asked questions. Sometimes they carried on prepared conversations in pairs about them. In the examination at the end of the term they were required to say which one of the ten was their favorite and why. Some of the answers were interesting.

"My favorite is H. Noguchi because he is a great man produced by my own country."

"My favorite is the woman whose name is Marie Curie because she gave her life to scientific truth."

"One of my favorites is Miss Helen Keller because she is deaf and dumb and blind and yet she worked hard to learn to speak and to read books by touching the pages with her hand. And she got money for the deaf and dumb and blind and other poor people."

"My favorite is Albert Schweitzer because he found his true happiness by offering all his earthly happiness to helping poor Negroes."

"Gandhi has helped the world in two ways, one he unified India and made it free from English rule, second he showed throughout the world that non-violent resistance is very strong and peace is very important."

Their English had advanced far since the first days, but the class was now badly split between those who could speak and understand a good deal and those who had given up the struggle and hoped for nothing more than to get by. The latter would rise to recite in class and would stand speechless for so long that sometimes I forgot the question waiting for the answer. I tried always to frame easy questions for the poor students so that they would get some sense of achievement and a measure of confidence in English, but some of them were so panic-stricken at being called upon that all their shreds of knowledge vanished and they could not have told their own names. At the other end of the scale, the good ones were capable of fairly long and thoughtful observations in English, and I used to regret that I could not carry them ahead as fast as they were capable of going.

Sometimes they came to see me during holidays or wrote me letters, and I got to know them very much better than I did their less articulate but also interesting and likable fellows. One of them wrote: "The cold war is booming violent more and more as if it will become the hot war. I wish it return to the peace and atomic energy will be used to the engine peacefully. I hate war very much because I met the air raid during wartime."

Another who, like many of them, was a devotee of Tolstoy, wrote of his pleasure in reading "The War and the Piece."

Still another wrote to explain his absence from school with the dramatic declaration: "Suddenly I became appendicitis on the Yokosuka Line."

The two boys whom I chose for the Crown Prince's companions that spring were to have a particularly happy and unusual series of experiences, partly owing to luck and partly because their own personalities were such that they could make the most of opportunity when it came. Masayoshi Shiba was a quiet, alert boy, actively friendly. He was a good rider, and though his natural bent was toward mathematics and science he did well with his English and sought friendships with Americans. Akira Hashimoto, cheerful and eager, with an unusually sweet expression on his round face, had been one of the Crown Prince's especial friends since primary schooldays. He had been one of the house party at Numazu the previous summer.

With the Crown Prince these two now came once a week to my house for a lesson and a tea-party. Every Wednesday afternoon a few minutes after three there would be a great sputtering in the lane outside as the motorcycle and side-car with two policemen preceded the Prince's car around the narrow curves. At the gate the Prince and the two boys would get out of the car and walk up the driveway, followed by a doctor and one or two chamberlains.

I always took the boys upstairs to the study for the lesson. Meanwhile Tané entertained the doctor and chamberlains in the parlor, and the chauffeur and bodyguard, after the car had been backed into the driveway so that it would be ready at the door for the Prince's departure, would come into the little waiting-room where they would amuse themselves with tea and cigarettes and American publications, the Sears Roebuck catalogue being one of the most popular.

That spring we read together, with difficulty, Kipling's story of the White Seal, and I taught the boys to play Monopoly. I did not seriously entertain the idea that the Crown Prince would have any need of the English vocabulary for buying and selling lots or buildings and mortgaging houses, but Monopoly was a game popular in the American school and I thought it might be a good ice-breaker in the meeting of the Crown Prince and American boys toward which I was slowly working.

After the lesson we went downstairs to the living-room, called in Tané and the chamberlains, and had tea with sandwiches and cake or cookies. And more English conversation. Hashimoto San shone particularly in the conversation, and used to provide himself beforehand with conversational gambits such as, "Mrs. Vining, what is your opinion of Japanese culture?" Most of our talk, however, was of a much simpler nature and I learned a good deal about what was going on at school.

It was through these talks and through Tané's conversations with the chamberlains that I heard about the dormitory, though the Crown Prince also told me a little about it in the lessons which he had alone with me.

The experiment seemed to be working out well. The Prince had a very nice boy, a Third Year boy, for a roommate and they got along well together. He did his share of the work of the dormitory, sweeping his room, helping to clear the table after dinner, waking early one morning at stated intervals to rouse the other boys and get out the cleaning implements and materials. The cook made up all the lunch-boxes of rice and cold fish or vegetables and the Crown Prince took his from the shelf at random, just like all the rest. One evening a week the boys all gathered in the living-room of the dormitory and two of them, by turns, made oral reports on any subject that interested them, while the rest listened and later made comments on delivery and content. Some of the subjects which they took up were sleep, vitamins, the Musashino region, Lafcadio Hearn, the type of satirical poetry called *senryu,* and school uniforms. The Crown Prince when his turn came chose "Animal Worship." He looked up the subject in the Encyclopaedia and other reference books, and his account included the sacred crocodile of the Nile, the cows of India, the deer of Nara, and the fox. The other boys approved the content but felt that his delivery left something to be desired and told him quite frankly that he dropped his voice too much at the ends of sentences. He took the criticism in good part and made efforts thereafter to improve his enunciation. The whole program was managed by the boys themselves; they drew lots for their turns, and the subjects were kept a secret until the day itself.

Adjustment to the dormitory life was not easy for the Prince, but he met it manfully. When I asked him point-blank how he liked it he said, smiling, "A little," but would not specify what it was that he did not like. The benefits began to show up almost at once in the form of an increasing ability to pitch in and help naturally, whenever it was necessary, and an increasing capacity for leadership among the boys. When they decided to form an alumni association of the boys who had been in Elementary School together, the Crown Prince was on the committee to arrange the first meeting, which was to be a party in the Yotsuya school building. The affair was a great success, and when it was over the chamberlains looked around for the Prince to take him home. For some time they could not find him, but at length discovered him upstairs in the room where they had met, all by himself putting the room to rights again.

Now I decided that the time was ripe to introduce some western boys to him, and I asked for permission to invite two to join the Crown Prince and the other boys at my house one Wednesday afternoon. The proposal was accepted with alacrity and I made full reports about the boys whom I had tentatively decided upon.

One was Tony Austin, the son of my friends Oliver and Elizabeth Austin. Dr. Oliver Austin was an ornithologist of note, and headed up the wildlife program of the Natural Resources Section of General Headquarters. His wife was a very warm-hearted, outgoing person, who had hosts of friends both in the Occupation and among the Japanese. Tony, yellow-haired, gray-eyed, roly-poly, irrepressible and friendly as a puppy, was fourteen, nearly a year younger than the Crown Prince but in the corresponding class in school. He had several Japanese friends of his own age and had learned to speak a little Japanese, to which his mother referred disparagingly as "kitchen Japanese." Tony was my first choice. I then went to his mother for advice about a boy who would make a good team with Tony, and she suggested his boon companion, John O'Brien.

John seemed to me ideal for several reasons. In the first place he was an Australian, and I was very glad to introduce a British boy as well as an American. Then I knew his parents pleasantly through meeting them at dinner parties. His father was Brigadier General John W. O'Brien, who was Chief of the Scientific and Technical Division of the Economic and Scientific Section of General Headquarters, one of the very few Allied nationals who worked alongside of Americans in the Occupation. I had met John himself in Karuizawa and liked him. Like Tony he was fourteen, but there the resemblance stopped. John was very tall, already over six feet, very thin, curly-haired, quiet, and gentle. They complemented each other well.

Tony and John arrived first, in John's jeep, on the afternoon of June eighth, 1949, and I had a chance to brief them a bit before the Prince came. Dr. Koizumi was the next to appear, and he made friends at once with the two western boys. "Where will the Crown Prince sit?" he whispered to Tané, seeing John and Tony on the sofa, and I realized, not for the first time, how much Americans tend to let things take their natural course, and how carefully the Japanese plan each detail ahead.

The Prince brought Hashimoto San and Shiba San in his car with him when he came, and he was accompanied by Dr. Yumoto, the youngest of the three doctors, and Mr. Kuroki. There were introductions and handshakings all around, and then I took all the boys upstairs for the game.

John and Tony were adept at Monopoly, the Japanese boys knew the rudiments of the game. I acted as banker, the boys threw for first turn, and the game was on. The Prince was a little quiet and reserved at first, feeling his way in the new situation, but relaxed after a while. Tony the irrepressible played with zest and loud outcries, the others enjoying themselves more quietly. Presently Dr. Koizumi came in to watch, standing up and looking over their shoulders, laughing at Tony, helping with the translation of a Japanese or an English word when necessary. His natural gift for people and his long association with boys in especial made him always a positive asset in any such group.

They played for about an hour and a half and then I called a halt for scoring and we went downstairs. Monopoly is an all-day affair, and the game was nowhere near its end. At the half-way point the Crown Prince's score was low, as might be expected. He was not in the least bothered by the fact nor were the Japanese boys; the western boys were a little uneasy, wondering if they had been rude to defeat him, and they commented afterwards admiringly on his being a good loser.

As I had done at the party in January, I put the boys by themselves in the dining-room for refreshments, the Crown Prince at the head of the table, with John on one side and Tony at the other, and the two Japanese boys one on each side beyond. Violet came in to speak to the Prince and the others, and they all rose politely to greet her. She then retired to the living-room where Dr. Koizumi, Dr. Yumoto and Mr. Kuroki were gathered.

The double sliding doors between the dining-room and living-room were open. The boys ate and laughed and talked, the Prince taking the lead now. They talked about school and the people they knew, the sports they liked, the school subjects they didn't like, and so on, the usual schoolboy talk in any country. They managed with gestures supplementing the words to understand one another.

We in the adjoining room talked too, but desultorily, listening for scraps from the boys. Now and then Dr. Koizumi or I slipped in for a minute or two.

"That place your father has at Zushi—"

"You mean Hayama?"

"The only thing I don't like about Japan is the way people get in front of the jeep when I'm driving—"

"I went to visit the American school and what I admired about American boys was—"

"Do you know what a bow and arrow are?"

"Yes, I do, but I don't like it."

Five o'clock passed. Mr. Kuroki looked into the dining-room but the Prince avoided his eye. He came back and said that

[213]

they were having too good a time to break it up. At twenty minutes of six he went in again and stood behind the Crown Prince's chair, and then the Prince rose to leave.

There were thanks all around and the Prince's car left, filled with chamberlains and boys. Dr. Koizumi left next in his own car, and John and Tony, after a few enthusiastic comments on the afternoon, departed last in the jeep.

They were impressed by the Prince's entirely natural manner with the other Japanese boys, and they gave him the accolade of schoolboy praise. "He's a regular feller," they said.

The affair might have ended there but it did not. It was a very happy combination of boys, and the acquaintance flowered into friendship. After the Crown Prince invited them all to his house in Koganei and they had a thrilling afternoon there, the mothers of the western boys sounded me out and I sounded the chamberlains out, and as a result both families entertained for the Prince and the others of the group. At the O'Briens' the Prince was introduced to the new toy that was a feature of many Occupation parties that year, the wire recorder, and had the fun of hearing his own voice come back to him. I did not go to any of these parties but the farewell to the Austins, which came later, but I was told in some detail about them. There was, it seemed, the usual difficulty of thinking of anything to say to the wire recorder, and so they decided to read to it passages from *Julius Caesar*, which the western boys were studying in school. That was difficult going for the Japanese boys, but I was proud to hear from several sources that the Prince did himself great credit.

The party at the Austins' was an early Christmas party. Elizabeth Austin, who was of Viennese background, had that especial flair for Christmas that Austrians and Germans have, and their Christmas tree turned slowly around showing all its balls and angels while a music box in the base tinkled out "Silent Night."

John O'Brien had a younger sister Jill, and Tony a younger brother Timmy, so that the Prince's circle was further enlarged. In January, 1950, before the Austins returned to the United States, the Prince gave a farewell party for them at the Palace, to which he invited both families, and of course Hashimoto San and Shiba San. Dr. Koizumi asked me to be there as "hostess," and Tané was of course with me.

[214]

It was a beautiful day with moments of cloud and snow flurries. The western guests had the coveted passes to the Palace, and the party began in one of the drawing-rooms in the Imperial Household Building. Because Dr. Austin was an ornithologist, the hangings and screens brought out that day all featured birds and offered an immediate subject for conversation, for Oliver Austin recognized them all and knew their names in Japanese as well as English. Some were to be found in Japan, some only in China and the islands of the South Seas and must have been drawn by the artist from caged specimens. It was interesting to me that the woven, embroidered, and painted birds were accurate scientifically as well as artistically beautiful.

The second stage of entertainment was a tour of the Palace grounds. The Prince and the boys went ahead in one car, the rest of us followed in other cars. Jill, who in spite of being unusually tall and slender, was still a little girl with pigtails doubled up behind her ears, had a little girl's shy delight in everything. She stuck close to her beautiful mother, but responded very sweetly and naturally when spoken to. Timmy, who was yellow haired, blue eyed, and engaging, was two or three years younger than Tony and determined to keep up with him in everything. He was about the right age for Prince Masahito, who was unfortunately at home with a cold.

The tour of the Palace grounds included the famous Nijubashi, the double bridge used by the Emperor and overlooked by the Fushimi watch tower brought long years ago from Kyoto. At this historic spot Timmy was caught by his mother scooping up a handful of gravel to stuff in his pockets as a memento and forced to relinquish it. Past the Kashikodokoro, the Imperial Shrine, past the Emperor's laboratory, we went to the greenhouses where the dwarf trees were kept, including one which was a thousand years old and other younger ones merely six or seven hundred years old, and on past the entrance to Kuretakeryo, the princesses' house, to the Music Hall, where we saw the red lacquer stage and the cases of ancient costumes, and then on to the stable and carriage house.

Four white horses were brought out and lined up, a groom at each head, for the guests to see. They were beautiful Arabs, with the Arab's small and gentle face, but full of spirit, as we saw later when the grooms started to lead them away and they reared up on their hind legs and pranced about. The Crown Prince was in the habit of riding any of the four, but Mineyuki was his favorite. Sakurakage, Prince Masahito's bay, was brought out saddled and another white horse, and John and Tony both mounted and rode about for a few minutes while their mothers held their breath.

The carriage house was a large building, filled with carriages in rows, carriages of all kinds and degrees of grandeur. The chief among them was the glass coach built for the Emperor's enthronement and intended to be drawn by eight white horses. Next to it were two slightly less grand carriages for four horses which the Emperor formerly used when going to open the Diet, and those used in pre-war days for bringing foreign ambassadors to call upon the Emperor. Across a passageway were rows of other fine carriages under cloth covers.

The immediate reaction of the western boys was to climb upon the coaches; they did not want to get inside but simply to sit upon the highest seat, which was the footman's perch at the back. No objection was made, but I noticed that the Japanese boys did not follow suit.

Tea, which was really an elegant and lavish buffet, was served in the Imperial Household Building. It was the Crown Prince's first big party for foreign guests and the imperial chef, Akiyama San, outdid himself. Food by that time, 1950, was much more available for all Japanese and there was no particular reason to hold back. The table was decorated with orchids, and there were beautiful platters of lobster, duck, ham, salads, and cakes, with punch and orange juice to drink. The Imperial Family when alone had very simple and even frugal meals, and the chefs loved to have a chance to display their skill when there were guests.

The six boys sat together at one table. The Prince looked particularly handsome that day and very happy. I saw him passing the plate of mandarin oranges and apples to the other boys, and he was talking and laughing very naturally. When the time came to say good-by, he presented Mrs. O'Brien and Mrs. Austin and me with sheafs of flowers which later proved to be mostly orchids.

There was one final note of informality. As we were putting on our wraps in the hall, I heard laughter and turned to see everyone clustered around the Crown Prince and Timmy. They were wrestling, hands clasped and foot to foot, each one trying to make the other move his right foot.

"Did you ever expect to see that?" I asked Elizabeth Austin.

"No," she said emphatically. "Did you?"

"No," I replied.

At that moment the Prince pulled Timmy over and there was a general exclamation of satisfaction. We all went downstairs through the now dim and cold halls to the side door, where one after another the cars were loaded and departed. The Crown Prince shook hands again with everybody on the steps. Tané and I were the last to go and we exchanged congratulations with the people directly responsible.

After the Austins had gone home, the Prince continued to see John at intervals. I invited two more American boys to my house, with John and the two Japanese boys who were sharing his current lessons, in the spring of 1950. Harry and Bruce Brenn were the sons of Mr. Harry Brenn of the Civil Property Custodian Section, who had come up from the Philippines with General MacArthur, and whom with Mrs. Brenn I had met at various times. Their home was a sound, wholesome one with high standards of behavior and the boys stood well in the American school. They were both thoroughly likable and fine boys and fitted in well. Both were riders, having grown up in Idaho practically in the saddle, and the Prince had plans for inviting them to Sanrizuka, the imperial stockfarm in Chiba, for a riding party in the fall, but by then that family too had gone home to the United States.

The O'Briens in their turn left early in 1951, two months or so after I had gone, and so I heard about the Crown Prince's farewell party for John only through letters. It was a dinner party, and Princess Takako, who had met Jill at my house one afternoon, was included, with Jill and Shiba San and Hashimoto San. The boys and girls had dinner together and afterwards the grownups joined them for some travel pictures.

But that was a long way from my first tentative Monopoly party that rainy June afternoon!

CHAPTER TWENTY-SEVEN

ONCE OR TWICE a year I paid a courtesy call on General Mac-Arthur, to report on the Prince's progress. In April of this year I took him some recent photographs to show how the chubby little boy whom I had first known had grown into a slender and handsome youth. He said that when the Prince could speak enough colloquial English for a conversation, he would like to see him. "I don't want anybody else here—except you, to make him feel comfortable—so I'll wait till you think he's ready. When that time comes, you bring him over."

When I broached the matter to the Imperial Household, there was no objection; rather a general feeling that it would be a valuable experience for the Crown Prince. It was left to me to decide when he was ready and there the matter rested.

Two months later, after the successful meeting with the western boys, I decided that the time had come. The Prince's English was by no means fluent, but he did well enough, if the General did not expect too much. I mentioned the possibility to the Prince, who made no comment but looked interested and thoughtful.

Though it had been approved in principle earlier, now that there was a definite proposal it had to go through various stages. First I spoke to Dr. Koizumi and Mr. Nomura, who told me to go to Mr. Tajima. Mr. Tajima then went to see the Emperor about it.

After Mr. Tajima had seen His Majesty, he came to my house to talk to me. On ordinary occasions if Mr. Tajima had anything to say to me, he would ask me to stop in at his office in the Imperial Household Building after one of the Empress's lessons. When, however, there was some direct word from the Emperor to be given to me, Mr. Tajima always came all the way to my house to deliver it, sometimes at the end of a long and busy day. He was very punctilious about this.

Late on the afternoon of June twenty-first, Mr. Tajima came to report that the Emperor was pleased with the idea of the Crown Prince's calling on the General but stipulated that there should be no publicity until afterwards.

The next stage was that I called Colonel Bunker on the telephone and told him that I thought "a certain young person" was ready to see the General. He called me back a little later, with a choice of three days for the appointment, and proposed either six or seven as an appropriate time. The General suggested that the Prince come in my car; he said an officer would meet us at the entrance and take us in. As to publicity, no one would know beforehand but the General, Colonel Bunker and myself; afterwards I could refer any questions to the Imperial Household or to SCAP.

The next morning I went again to Mr. Tajima, who had meanwhile had a conference with Dr. Koizumi about it. The hour of seven was considered better than six because fewer people were about; the first of the three dates given was chosen, since that gave less chance of leakage. There was one remaining problem; could the Crown Prince go alone with me in my car, or should Dr. Koizumi or Mr. Nomura accompany us and sit in the waiting-room during the meeting?

The next day Dr. Koizumi came to tell me that it had been decided that the Prince was to go alone in my car with me, with a bodyguard on the front seat beside Takenaka San. The time was set for seven p.m. on Monday, June twenty-seventh. Dr. Koizumi said, "It will be recorded in our history: the first time that a crown prince of Japan has ridden alone with a western lady, going to visit a westerner," and then he added, "It shows not only the Imperial Household's trust in you, but the whole nation's trust," which left me a little breathless.

June is the rainy season in Japan; day after day the rain comes down, or hangs in heavy clouds waiting to fall. The twenty-seventh, however, was a beautiful day, mild and sunny and fresh. All day I went about my regular business with my mind suspended, feeling as one does when something important is going to happen later, like graduating from school or going abroad for the first time.

[219]

The Crown Prince had his regular English lesson in the morning at Koganei, and I tried to prepare him a little, describing the General and his office and the usual procedure there, suggesting the kind of questions I thought the General might ask him, but leaving the answers, of course, entirely to him. He seemed to me to be looking forward to the meeting with interest and I saw no sign of nervousness.

He was to go to the Palace in the afternoon and have an early dinner with Prince Masahito, and I was to call for him at six forty-five. The tires of my car had picked up several nails recently and I was haunted by the fear that we might have a puncture halfway between the Palace and the Dai Ichi Building. Takenaka San could change a tire faster than anyone else I have ever known, but in even a short delay the Crown Prince would be discovered by passers-by.

Prince Masahito's house was near the Imperial Household Building on the edge of the cleared-away ruins of the former Palace. In the drawing-room when I arrived that evening I found Dr. Koizumi and Mr. Nomura, as well as three of the chamberlains. Prince Masahito had been put to bed with a slight cold, and I went in to see him for a few minutes. When I returned to the drawing-room, the Crown Prince joined us. He wore his summer school uniform of dark trousers and immaculate white jacket, and his hair, so recently in the awkward stage of growing out, was parted and lay flat. He showed me the snake which Prince Masahito had found in the grounds and brought in as a pet, and then it was time to go.

The secret had been well kept; even the guards at the great gate did not know. My car of course was familiar to them. The policeman gave me his usual polite salute—and swiftly made it into something very much more formal when he saw who was sitting beside me. Out of the corner of my eye after we had passed, I saw him dive for the telephone, no doubt to find out if it really was all right.

It was only a five-minute ride from the Palace to the Dai Ichi Building. The outer Palace grounds with the late shadows over the grass and the late sunshine on the tops of the twisted pines were serene and lovely. A few people strolled along the paths, and no one gave my car a second glance.

As we drew up in front of the Dai Ichi Building Colonel

Bunker came out and opened the door for us. I presented him to the Prince, and we went in, the honor guard smartly saluting as we passed. The big bank-like building was cool and empty. We went first to Colonel Bunker's office on the sixth floor, where the Colonel put the Prince's hat on the table, the dark-visored white cap which is part of the summer uniform, and asked him to sign in the guest-book, which he did without any ado, writing "Akihito, June 27th" in his firm and rather distinguished hand. There was just a moment to look at the view of the outer moat and the Palace rising on its hill beyond, before Colonel Bunker said the General was ready and would I show the Prince the way in.

"How do you do, sir," said General MacArthur. "I am glad to meet you."

The Crown Prince replied, "How do you do, General. I am glad to meet *you*."

The General led the Prince to the sofa, drew up a chair for me and another for himself. There was a small round table in the middle. The General lit his pipe and the conversation began.

General MacArthur, having a beloved son of his own, knew how to talk to a boy. He suited his topics to fifteen-year-old interests and simplified his vocabulary, though he occasionally used some idioms which the Prince had not yet encountered and which I then translated into phrases that I knew he would understand. Otherwise I took little part in the colloquy, and so was free to savor the occasion.

I saw a conquering general putting the son of his former enemy at ease, speaking to him with an older man's kindly interest in a promising boy and at the same time with the courteous deference due to a crown prince. I saw the son of the Emperor of the defeated country facing the former arch-enemy without a trace of fear or shrinking, frank and responsive, with boyish dignity. And I rejoiced that in this day and world, such a thing could happen.

When the Crown Prince spoke of the Gakushuin, General MacArthur turned to me, "Is that the old Peers' School?" and the Prince said quickly, "There are not many peers there now."

When universities in various lands were mentioned the Prince asked the General what university he had gone to, and when

[221]

the perennial topic of sports came up the boy surprised the man by saying suddenly, "Do you have any sports?"

"I used to when I was young," the General answered, "but they're all gone now. I used to swim and play tennis, but baseball was my best game."

He reminisced about the Davis Cup matches at Forest Hills when the Japanese team played against Tilden and Johnson, and the Olympic Games in Amsterdam in 1928 when the Japanese won the Hop-Step-and-Jump. The Prince followed with interest. One of his classmates, Masao Oda, was the son of the Olympic champion. The difference between *amateur* and *professional* arose and was explained.

Throughout the call the Prince was natural and at ease. He smiled and looked interested, met the General's eyes squarely, or turned to me squarely, never letting his eyes stray around the room. He managed his limited English well, frankly saying so when there was some word or phrase that he did not understand. It was one of those heartening times when you see a young thing suddenly fulfill a promise, and it bode well for the future. He was evidently to be one of those few people who can produce their best at need, not one of the unfortunates who blow up in a crisis.

After they had talked for about twenty minutes the General asked me if the Prince would accept a box of candy. The Prince thanked him and tucked the box under his arm, and the historic meeting came to an end.

General Marquat was in Colonel Bunker's room when we came out, and he was introduced. Colonel Bunker escorted us down to the car. At the last moment an American in a gray suit carrying a briefcase rushed to get into the elevator. As I had told the Prince a gentleman removes his hat if there is a lady in the elevator, he kept his cap carefully in his hand, but the newcomer's remained on his head, as he joined most informally in our conversation.

Five minutes later we were back at the Palace, without having had any punctures. Two men, employees in the lower ranks of the Imperial Household, were playing catchball near the entrance, inside the gate. One looked up, saw nothing unusual about my car, and threw the ball. The other man's jaw dropped and he let the ball go by, as he bowed low.

Mr. Tajima was at Prince Masahito's house waiting for us. After saying good-by to me, the Crown Prince went off whistling to see his father and tell him about the meeting with the General. Mr. Tajima, Mr. Nomura and Dr. Koizumi gathered around me eager to hear all about it. Tané translated from time to time.

Shortly after I reached home, Colonel Bunker telephoned to say: "I thought you'd like to hear that your charge passed his examination with flying colors. The General said immediately when he came out that he was very favorably impressed—the Prince had poise and was charming and attractive."

It had been, I felt as time went on, a milestone in the Prince's path to maturity. He had successfully met a challenge, and with the knowledge came confidence and a new initiative.

CHAPTER TWENTY-EIGHT

WHILE THE CROWN PRINCE was making brief excursions into the western world, I in my turn was having experiences that gave me some insight into the enduring life and thought of Japan, not the post-war Japan, which lay all about me, but the Japan which existed before the war and apart from all wars, and which would continue into the future untouched by political storms.

Flower arrangement in Japan is an ancient and honorable art, dating from long centuries ago when a Buddhist priest first brought a pine branch into the temple and after bending and shaping it set it up before the altar. Lessons in flower arrangement are part of almost every young girl's education, and married women often continue them for years. Many men too are experts.

You see flower arrangements everywhere. Every room in a private house has an arrangement in the *tokonoma*, not a four-sided affair to be viewed from every angle as ours are, but a picture to be seen from the front only. Almost every shop has one. Even in the simplest and roughest kind of place, a blacksmith shop or a garage, you would frequently see a handful of flowers artistically arranged on the tool bench. The flower arrangement for a tea ceremony was always particularly simple and exquisite, perhaps a single pale camellia with one perfect leaf and one that was brown and insect-touched in an old celadon vase.

At almost any time of the year you might find an exhibition of flower arrangements in a department store, a museum, or in a temple or shrine in connection with some festival. The amazing thing about it was the number of people who turned out to see the exhibits, the great interest they took in them, and the serious and critical understanding that they brought to bear on them. I have always thought that the program notes for the Philadelphia Orchestra provided about as intricate an interpretation of musical patterns as was humanly possible to make, but the comments of the connoisseurs on flower arrangements could equal if not surpass them.

The rudimentary principle of Japanese flower arrangement is easy enough to grasp, the three points of heaven, man, and earth, with man as the reconciling element between heaven and earth. But beyond that there are symbolisms and subtleties that only years of study and experience can enable one to understand, not to mention the practical difficulties of making the flowers conform.

There are, moreover, a number of different "schools," each with its organization and literature, its "headmaster supreme" and devoted followers. The three that I learned to recognize were the classical school, Ikenobu, the most artificial and difficult, and the two modern schools, Sogetsu and Ohara. The Sogetsu school had a good many students among the Occupationaires and showed considerable western influence. Some of its productions were really beautiful, original, strong, and daring; others verged on surrealism, with bits of mirror applied, or dead branches painted blue or silver. One Sogetsu arrangement which I saw, of calendula and brussels sprouts, was uncomfortably bizarre. The Ohara school, also modern in its freedom, went in much more for arrangements that showed the flower in its natural growth and habitat.

When my sister and I started taking lessons, soon after her arrival, we knew nothing about the different schools, nor did we know to which one our teacher belonged. I had seen some of Miss Koha Taira's lovely arrangements at the house of a friend, had heard that she often went to Kuretakeryo, the princesses' house, to arrange flowers there, and knew that she had taught at Keisen School, where Tané had been first a student and then a teacher. The wish was expressed, and Tané did the rest. For nearly two years Miss Taira came late one afternoon each week to our house, and we had the lessons in flower arrangement and the friendship with our enchanting little teacher that were among the joys of our stay in Japan. Sometimes I was too busy to be present, though I never missed a lesson if I could help it, but

my sister worked consistently and rose in time to entering arrangements in exhibits and the final dignity of a "Certificate"
and a professional name—*Kofu*, or Shining Maple.

Early on the day of the lesson a man would come from the
flower shop with the flowers ordered by Miss Taira, and very
unpromising they seemed to us at first: a few stalks of shrubs
with tight buds, a handful of narcissus, three rather small
chrysanthemums. They cost about seventy cents in our money
and they were enough for a least three arrangements, sometimes
with the addition of something from our own garden.

Late in the afternoon, after dark on winter days, we would
hear the click-clack of Miss Taira's *geta* in the driveway. She
always wore Japanese dress, and had a great variety of beautiful
dark kimonos, in gray or violet or blue or brown, and brocade
obis to harmonize. She was a tiny person; her black hair with
a few threads of gray was done up in a little knot on the top of
her head, she had big eyes behind spectacles, a little turned-up
nose, and a shining look of joy that never faded, no matter how
tired she might be. And tired she must often have been, for
she made long journeys "to North" to give lessons to teachers
there, while her Tokyo schedule alone was horrifying, with
trips by crowded trains to all parts of that vast sprawling city.

She knew a very little English and was learning more as
quickly as possible. She would write new words down in her
notebook and con them over on the trains. Even with Tané
there to interpret, she used her English with us as far as it
would go.

The method of her teaching was something like this. Each
of us in turn would make an arrangement. "This is Heaven,"
she would say, handing us a long spray. "Take off dirty leaves,"
and we would clip and shape at her direction. Next came the
crucial matter of putting it into the vase. Sometimes it was
necessary to split the end and insert a crosspiece to hold it in
place, sometimes to lengthen the stem by tying on an extra piece
with raffia. Sometimes when a branch continued to be stiff and
refractory she would say, "Bend him," and would show us how
to place our fingers so that he would bend and not break. Man
and Earth followed, and the extra sprays called "fill-in" pieces.
"More one," Miss Taira would say from time to time.

When it was all finished, she would bow very low and say,

"Veree nice, *Oneisama*,"—or Vining *Sensei*, or Taneko *Sensei*— "Veree nice." She would stand looking at it for a moment with her head tipped on one side. "But I think much better this way," she would pronounce, and with a few deft movements of her magical little hands she would draw a beauty and a meaning out of the flowers that had certainly not been there before.

Gradually we learned a little. Between the lessons we would make arrangements for her to criticize and repair when she came. She knew the style—if it could be dignified by such a word—of each of us and could tell at a glance who had done the arrangement. Or if some friend came in and made an arrangement for us, she knew that too, recognized at once that a stranger's hand had been at work, and to what school the stranger belonged.

Her hours were generous in length, and when she left, she would slide out of her house slippers, turn and step quickly into the wooden clogs waiting for her in the entrance, bow deeply, chirp, *"Gomen asobase"* (a particularly polite form), and then she was off in a swift cheerful walk which reminded me of a flower swaying in the wind or a bird running over a lawn, I never could decide which.

One spring there was a big flower arrangement exhibit at the Ueno Museum, which the Empress was to visit. Miss Taira was to have an entry in it, and we heard about it for some weeks beforehand. Her preparations were the kind that a *samurai* might have made before his great test. First she purified herself outwardly by paying up all debts and obligations. Inwardly she cleared up all mental confusions and got herself into a frame of mind in which more than usual she felt love toward everyone. On her last trip back from Sendai before the exhibition she watched the countryside from the train windows so as to get an inspiration from nature for her arrangement. She did not want to use expensive, rare flowers that most people could not afford to get but the plants that were available to everyone. On the morning of the day itself she would try not to see or speak to people on the way, so that she could concentrate with undisturbed mind upon her arrangement.

We went to the exhibit, of course, and among the scores of striking and lovely arrangements (with some that were odd to the western eye and a few that were odd to any eye), among the

[227]

orchids and bird-of-paradise blossoms, the branches of camellias, we recognized Miss Taira's arrangement at once: a woodland scene, with the suggestion of a brook, and the ferns and flowers that would be growing beside it.

Silk before the war accounted for forty per cent of Japan's exports. During the war the production of silk almost came to an end, and since the war the demand for it has been very much smaller, with the competition of nylon and rayon and the loss of markets during the war years. Silk within Japan, however, is still an important part of the national life. The kimono is made of silk, and the sleeping quilts for people who can afford it are covered with soft and lustrous silk. The raising of the silkworms gives gainful occupation to farmers' wives and children to supplement the small profits from their two-and-a-half-acre farms, and the spinning and weaving of the silk gives work to countless girls in large and small factories.

From egg to cocoon is a matter of approximately six weeks, and one way or another I saw all the stages: the minute eggs, so small that it takes about thirty thousand of them to weigh an ounce, the worm, not more than an eighth of an inch long to begin with and growing to about three inches, the cocoon, which it takes less than three days to spin, and finally the unwinding of the long, fine filament from the cocoon and the twisting of it with other strands into a thread. About 1830 there was a silkworm craze in the United States, which took the form chiefly of speculation in mulberry trees. When it came to the actual raising of silkworms, the American farmers' wives and daughters found that the amount of time, space, and effort that must be given to it brought in too small financial returns to make it worth while for them. The more patient and hardworking Japanese, however, work day and night feeding the silkworms, keeping them warm and clean, and manage to labor as farmhands in the fields in the cracks of time that are left.

Just as the Emperor had his rice field within the Moat and each year symbolically planted some rice and worked in the mud of the paddy so that he too might experience and share in the life of Japan, so the Empress had her silkworms. Special houses had been built for them on the little hill called Momijiyama, and two or three times a week the Empress went to inspect them.

One day after her English lesson she asked me if I would like to accompany her.

We crossed the courtyard on one side of the Imperial Household Building, and walked along a wooded path, a guard in front, and three ladies with us, Mrs. Takaki, Mrs. Hoshina, and Miss Daté. As so often, I thought of the old English ballads that begin, "The Queen and her ladies sat in her bower . . ."

An old man, a specialist in silkworm culture, came from Yamanashi Prefecture to supervise the care of Her Majesty's silkworms. He had a straight, narrow body, slightly bent, a round gray head with wide-apart eyes, and a mild but intent expression. With his four or five assistants he was out in front of the buildings, bowing when the Empress arrived. The houses, two or three, were of the usual type of Japanese dwelling, with black tile roofs, sliding doors, and little *engawa* (a sort of very narrow porch) but the rooms were floored with polished wood instead of *tatami*.

As silkworms must be kept at a temperature of seventy-two degrees Fahrenheit, the rooms were warmed by charcoal fires under the floors. In each room were tall bamboo racks, in which the big trays rested in ranks.

At the beginning of the season, I was told, the Empress performed a little ceremony in which she brushed the first eggs out onto a tray with a little feather brush. The minute worms begin to eat and to grow as soon as they are hatched. At first the mulberry leaves are chopped very fine and the worms are fed every four or five hours day and night. There must be no moisture on the leaves, and if necessary they are individually wiped dry. As the worms grow they are moved to other trays, and larger leaves may be fed to them. They eat for several days and then they rest for a day or two, their heads raised. In all, the eating period occupies about forty days.

The old man set up a sort of luggage rack in the center of one room and took down one tray after another for the Empress to inspect. Those that we saw were about three weeks old, an inch and a half long, a thousand of them on a tray. The sound of their eating was audible in the room.

I was interested to see Her Majesty's real knowledge of the worms. She quickly spotted one small one that had gone off by himself and was not eating, and she wanted to know if he was

[229]

sick. The expert told her that he had got separated from the especial group of worms with which he had started out, and that when they do that they will not adjust themselves to the other worms but sulk alone, refusing to eat. Very like people, I thought, insisting on being with their own kind, scorning all others.

Her Majesty picked up one casually with her fingers, and so, after a moment's revulsion, did I. It was cold to the touch, but not unpleasant.

One tray of worms, from China, I think, had yellow legs, and their cocoons would be yellow. In the entryway of the building were some cases and jars of specimens, including some of the yellow cocoons and a skein of the most beautiful yellow silk, the natural color without a trace of dye.

Also in the Palace enclosure within the Moat was the Ka-shikodokoro, the Imperial Shrine. I have never been inside any of its simple, white-walled, steep-roofed buildings, but I have often walked about outside it, under its great trees, and felt the serenity and the solemnity of its atmosphere. Magnificent trees planted for a religious purpose seem to be a part of nature worship in all parts of the world, and I imagine that the groves of the Druids must have had some of the feeling of the shaded, sun-splashed corridors of trees in Japan.

In the Kashikodokoro were kept the Jewels and the Sword of the imperial regalia, the Mirror being at Ise Shrine. No regular services were held here, it was not in any sense a royal chapel, but here at different times in the year came the Emperor as head of the Shinto religion to perform certain ceremonies. One of them, I know, was the annual thanksgiving for the harvests, and one was the New Year ceremony, but there were others also. The Crown Prince, being not yet of age, took no part in these celebrations.

I was always interested to see which of the Japanese customs belonged to the Palace and which to the world outside the Palace. O Bon, or the Festival of the Dead in midsummer, was a festival of the people, as also was Otsukimi, or Moon-Viewing. I have delightful memories of a party in the country near Tokyo to which we went when the September moon was full. We sat in the twilight before an arrangement of autumn grasses and an offering of foods which the moon liked, and watched the great golden sphere rise above the dark fields.

Incense-hearing parties, on the other hand, originated in the court a thousand years ago, and for years were confined to the court, but have now got out into the world. The word *hearing* is used, not only because hearing sounds more refined than smelling, but also because one does actually seem to listen intently as one tries to distinguish minute differences in odors.

I was privileged to attend one of these parties presided over by the head of the cult, an ex-prince who had come up from Kyoto. The atmosphere of concentration, of detachment from the world, of alert leisure; the beauty of the appointments, tiny cabinets for holding varieties of incense, fabulous incense burners, exquisite counters for scoring in the games that are played; the sensuous wealth of subtle, evocative, oriental fragrances; the delicate, playful, yet serious formality of the participants: all made the occasion memorable. Yet perhaps most memorable was the exquisite Japanese care for the clumsy western guests. We could not maintain the proper sitting position (knees bent, legs tucked under, our weight resting on our heels, backs straight, and hands folded in our laps) for more than half an hour at best, and our long western legs seemed to be everywhere. Our untutored noses could not detect even the most obvious differences between the incenses with the poetic names, and the only success we had was due to lucky guessing. We took hold of things all wrong, grasping at them with our fingers spread, or using one hand casually when it was proper to use two. But our hostesses never betrayed by the flicker of an eyelid that they noticed any lack in our behavior; they praised our skill in guessing and quietly manipulated the scores in the game to our advantage; they explained every detail with thoughtful care; they brought out their treasures to show us, and shared their best and rarest incense with us as if we had been connoisseurs.

CHAPTER TWENTY-NINE

ON A HOT, breathless Sunday morning in mid-July we left Tokyo for Karuizawa, five of us and the newly acquired puppy packed tight into the car, with suitcases, lunch basket, coats, books, cameras, coffee percolator and other last-minute necessities.

After we passed through the long, dusty, sterile edges of the city, we entered beautiful country. Picturesque figures in the big straw hats and cotton *mompes* of the old prints bent over weeding the rice fields where occasional white herons stood one-legged or rose on slowly flapping wings.

After we had left Takasaki the road began to climb, and the last twenty miles of the way took us through a series of hairpin turns with dramatic views behind and ahead of us. About half-way up the air suddenly grew fresh and cool. The fantastically jagged peaks of the Miyogi range showed distinct but pale, as if cut out of gray crepe paper. Along the roadside we saw fox-gloves, wild roses, wild hydrangea, and a tall drooping white flower whose name I did not know.

At the top of the pass was the line between Gumma and Nagano prefectures. The road widened and there was a stone monument and a magnificent view back over the country through which we had struggled. In the other direction was the flat plateau of Karuizawa, the gray roofs of the town itself, and the wooded knobs of Hanareyama and Atagoyama, with the volcano, Asama, its head veiled in mist, brooding over all. I looked at this place with especial interest this year, for here, it was planned, the Crown Prince would pause on his way to visit me, and would be formally welcomed to Nagano Prefecture by the Governor and the Chief of Police.

Our house was ready, and both Sakata San, the caretaker, and

Sato San, the keen and efficient factotum of Kaurizawa, were there to greet us. The men with the truck from the Imperial Household had been there the day before with furniture and other equipment, Masako San had come by train earlier that day and already had started the fire in the water heater, so that we could have the luxury of warm showers.

The air under the trees was deliciously fragrant with balsam, pure, fresh, and cool. We heard the bush warbler calling across the valley and saw the orange flash of the little narcissus fly-catcher in the trees. It was good to be back. We had two whole months to look forward to this year, and a little over three weeks in which to prepare for the Prince's visit.

The idea had originated with the Crown Prince and the chamberlains early in July, and the decision had been reached and the plans made with unusual dispatch, for the ordinarily slow-moving Imperial Household. As it was not to be an official visit to Nagano but a private and informal visit to me, it was to be kept as quiet as possible. They would bring two cars with chauffeurs and bodyguards, two chamberlains and a doctor. The retinue would stay at the inn, while the Crown Prince spent three nights in the house with us.

Though I would never in the world have ventured to suggest such a thing myself, I was delighted that it was going to happen. Delighted—and very much aware of the responsibility. I left nothing to chance. My sister and Tané and I went over and over the arrangements, the plans for entertainment, the menus, with alternatives for every contingency. I was determined that the Prince should have a really good time, not an interesting time, or an instructive time, or a "good experience," but a lot of fun. The two most important elements, I thought, were the weather and other boys. The weather I could do nothing about; Karuizawa was one of the wettest places I had ever been. I concentrated on the other boys.

Many people gave me wonderful help throughout the Prince's visit, but to no one am I more grateful than to Mrs. Shibusawa. Her son was in the Crown Prince's class at school. The Shibusawas had a summer house in Karuizawa, and each year that I had been there I had seen something of them. Mrs. Shibusawa was one of the most exquisite-looking Japanese women I have seen; she was as lovely in a simple American sports dress as in kimono. She herself had come of a well-known Japanese Christian family, and her husband's family had long stood for friendly relations with the western countries. Now I went to see Mrs. Shibusawa and told her my problem. Two or three days before the Crown Prince arrived she went down to Tokyo and returned with three boys from his class, friends of his and of her son, Hiroshi.

The Prince was to arrive on the eleventh of August. All through the week before there was a great bustle in our house. Representatives of the local newspapers came. The local police set up an office in an empty house near the foot of our hill, and prepared their routines. Mrs. Takaki, who was visiting an American friend, came with a message from Their Majesties. Two gentlemen from the Liaison Office of Nagano Prefecture offered their assistance. Mr. Ishitani from the Imperial Household came to go over the final arrangements with us, including the way the Prince was to be met on his arrival, who was to be his *Go-Sendo* and at what point on the path I was to greet him.

With the car we went over all the roads that might be used for picnics and sightseeing, to determine for ourselves which were merely poor and which were impassible. Beyond the little town of Komoro, about ten miles away, there was a very old Buddhist temple called Nunobiki set high on a wooded cliff looking over the valley of the Chikuma River to Mount Asama and, on clear days, to the Japan Alps in the far distance. Above the temple was a rocky ledge, shaded by pine trees, that was a perfect place for a picnic. The difficulty was that between Komoro and Nunobiki the Chikuma River must be crossed, and the bridge was in very bad repair. I had driven over it myself, weaving in and out to avoid the wide holes in the planking, but I was afraid to risk it with the Prince. Takenaka San had driven us up to Karuizawa, and then, as usual, returned to Tokyo, for I liked to drive myself during the summer. He came back, however, to make himself useful during the Prince's visit, and he in turn tried the bridge near Nunobiki and confirmed my fear of it. Reluctantly we gave that plan up.

Wednesday had been chosen as the day for the Prince to arrive, because on Tuesday evening the commissary train made its weekly stop. I did my final marketing, and checked everything in the kitchen. Michiko San and Masako San were more experienced now, and they were very good little cooks, but they had to work under difficulties. The icebox was tiny, and they had to cook on two small flower-pot charcoal stoves and a single electric plate, with a portable tin oven.

The morning of the eleventh dawned clear and sparkling, with a deep blue sky. Later in the day it grew warmer and the distant mountains paled a little, but the sun continued to shine. We got the Prince's room ready in the morning, the master bedroom of the cottage, which had its own large tile bath. The little *tatami* room next to the kitchen, with the brick terrace on which it opened, was prepared for the three bodyguards, who were to sleep in the house but take turns going to the inn for meals. Takenaka San, on the other hand, was to sleep at the inn and get his meals in the kitchen. Besides driving the car when it was needed, he ran errands, helped with the dishes and proved himself invaluable.

At quarter past four the Prince arrived. Tané was at the foot of the hill waiting for him, and she said there were only a few people standing about to watch him get out of his car. She greeted him and led him up the hill; I met him at the turn of the path. Mr. Shimizu, Mr. Sakaki, and Dr. Saburi were with him, and we walked together up to the terrace, where my sister was waiting to greet him. The bodyguards followed and the chauffeurs with suitcases and baskets. It was all as simple and natural as any long looked-for arrival, with the usual spatter of conversation about the trip, the dust, and the inquiries and messages.

We had cool fruit juices in the big living-room while we caught up on the summer's news. The Crown Prince had been at Numazu for the swimming and then had stopped at Hayama to spend a few days with his parents before he started for Karuizawa. He brought a box of fruit and a wonderful smoked ham from Numazu, and a big basket of fresh vegetables from the Empress. He was as brown as a berry and looked very fit. His face lit up when he heard about his classmates' being in Karuizawa, and I felt that the visit had got off to a good start.

He had a bath before dinner, Mr. Shimizu stayed to help him get settled in his room, and then all the chamberlains went off to the inn, which was about half a mile away, leaving the Crown Prince of Japan unattended in a western house. I wondered what qualms they felt. They showed none.

[235]

The Prince reappeared looking very nice in a lightweight gray suit and we had dinner at seven. He ate everything as if he enjoyed it and chattered freely in English, about Hayama and the things he had done there, yachting and fishing, the new boat, and collecting specimens.

Just as we finished dinner, the four boys appeared, as arranged: Hiroshi Shibusawa, Kenochi Yamaza, Hiroshi Kusakari, and Masao Oda. After they had made a little polite conversation in English with my sister and me, I turned them loose in Japanese, and they were all very effervescent. There were several games on hand, but what they really wanted to do was to play bridge, which they did. At ten we had fruit punch and cake, and discussed the plans for the next day, and a little after that the boys went home. Mr. Shimizu came back to see if the Prince wanted anything, but departed after a few minutes. The Crown Prince for the first time in his life slept without a chamberlain in the adjoining room. He told us next morning that he slept well.

The next day, too, was warm and sunny. We had breakfast at eight, and after breakfast as usual, Masako San and Michiko San joined us at the table, and we had our Bible reading in English and Japanese. I chose the Sermon on the Mount, which was spread over three mornings.

The four boys joined us for the excursion to Onioshidashi which had been planned for the morning. Onioshidashi was the lava beds on the slope of Mount Asama, and the name, which meant the Rocks the Devil Threw Out, was very appropriate for those jagged, sombre piles of barren rocks. The police car, and the chamberlains, with Tané, went ahead, to lead the way over the steep, narrow, twisting mountain roads, the Prince and I followed in his dark maroon Lincoln, and the four boys in my car brought up the rear. The Prince talked as we rode along about rowing and swimming and about the Gakushuin riding club, which now had only one horse, a good one from the imperial stables. "Before the war there were many horses in the Gakushuin stable. Now there are pigs in it!" He laughed.

We stopped at the Imperial University Research Laboratory on the way for a few minutes, and then went on. The road was rough, and the Prince commented on that, but on the beauty of the mountain vistas not at all. He was eager for life and had no time for scenery.

At Onioshidashi the photographers were waiting and the clicking of the cameras made a sound like rain. As soon as that was over the Prince and the other boys tore off to climb over the jagged lava rocks. Tané and I followed for a bit, and then stopped to pick the tiny flowers growing in the crevices and take photographs and wave to the boys on the distant heights which they scaled with great rapidity, while the chamberlains toiled behind.

When we got back to the house at twelve, we found Princess Kitashirakawa waiting to call upon the Prince. A daughter of the Emperor Meiji and therefore the Prince's great-aunt, she was a charming and gentle elderly lady and a very royal one. With her were her daughter, Princess Tokugawa, and the Swedish friend, Mrs. Gertz, at whose house in Karuizawa they were staying. The Prince was obviously very much pleased to see his aunt, and pleased when he and I were invited to have tea with her at Mrs. Gertz's the next afternoon.

Tennis occupied that afternoon, which was Thursday. Mr. Uchiyama of the Liaison Office had arranged with the Captain of the First Cavalry detachment billeted at the Mikasa hotel, for the Crown Prince to have the use of the courts. There were two of them, in excellent condition, away from the road and surrounded by trees. New balls were provided and two little Japanese boys to chase the balls. Hiroshi Shibusawa's younger brother joined the group, so that there were six boys altogether and they could keep doubles and singles going all afternoon. Mr. Shimizu, Tané, and I watched them get started and then came away. About quarter of six the Crown Prince, with his bodyguard in discreet attendance, drifted up the hill.

The chamberlains came for dinner and after dinner the Prince went off to spend the evening with his friends. With a flashlight in his hands and accompanied only by the bodyguard, he walked along the narrow lanes of the little mountain village to the Shibusawas' house. The chamberlains stayed with us until the Prince's return.

During the afternoon the Prince's chauffeurs had gone to see for themselves the condition of the bridge near Nunobiki, and they reported that they were not afraid to take the cars over, if all the passengers got out and crossed the bridge on foot. So it was decided that we would go ahead with the picnic, and the local police were informed of our plans for the next day.

There was a brief, sharp thundershower during the evening, but by the time we saw the Prince's flashlight like a firefly in and out among the trees as he came back up the winding path, it had cleared off. The stars were out and the air smelled freshly of wet balsam. We talked a little while on the terrace before bedtime and for the first time the Prince began to ask questions spontaneously about America. I remember that Indians and boats especially engaged his interest.

After breakfast on Friday morning our guest tactfully buried himself in the book which he had brought with him—*Gone with the Wind* in Japanese—while we all pitched into the job of preparing a picnic lunch for ten people. At eleven the boys came and the chamberlains, and we loaded up the three cars. I suggested that one boy ride with the Crown Prince and me and that they *jan-ken-pon* for the privilege. (All such matters are settled by *jan-ken-pon*, which to us is the stone-paper-scissors game.) Masao Oda won, and was put in the maroon Lincoln between the Prince and me. The cars started off, my Chevrolet with Tané and the boys first, then the Prince's car, then the black Packard with the chamberlains.

Though it had rained in Karuizawa the evening before, and everything was dewy-fresh, outside the village the sixteen-day drought still prevailed, and the dust rose in clouds. But the sky and sunshine and puffs of cumulus clouds were lovely and Asama loomed very high and only slightly veiled at the top.

In most of the villages that we passed, people, especially the children, were waiting to see the Crown Prince go by, and he was kept busy bowing. Mothers held their babies high to see him, and one very small girl ran out naked in her haste and got spanked and chased back by her scandalized parent.

At Komoro we dropped down a steep winding hill and took the narrow road through the rice fields of the river valley. When we came to the bridge, we found all the holes mended with new clean yellow wood and we sailed across without anybody's having to get out of the cars.

The full story I learned later. It seemed that in the little village responsible for it, the repair of the bridge had long been held up because of lack of funds and a dispute in the village council about the raising of them. At nine o'clock that morning word reached the village that the Crown Prince would be there at a quarter of twelve that day. The bridge! The dispute was forgotten. One of those outbursts of energy and good will took place. The young men of the village volunteered their labor. A lumber company gave the wood. In an hour they mended the bridge. It cost the village nothing.

We found several cars already parked at the foot of the path up to Nunobiki and a number of officials were there waiting. The village head of Kabemura, an old gentleman with a straw hat, handlebar moustaches, and formal morning clothes, preceded the party up the long climb. It was hot on the lower reaches, but as we climbed higher, following the path in and out among the towering rocks and across the bed of a stream now dry, the shade was refreshing and a cool breeze reached us. At the temple, where the big ancient thatch-roofed buildings occupied a level shelf in the side of the cliff, the priest and his family were lined up to bow. Above the temple we wriggled through a narrow opening in the rocks and came out on the tree-shaded ledge overlooking the long valley of the Chikuma River and the vast waves of mountains beyond.

At this spot, which I remembered as a wild and remote mountain hideaway, I was staggered to find a red carpet, three tables with white silk covers, and four wicker armchairs complete with cushions. The thirty young men of the village, after repairing the bridge, had carried all these things up the difficult path so that the Prince might have his picnic in the proper manner!

The village head man, having received our thanks, retired, and we spread out the steamer rug I had brought over the carpet, pushed back the chairs, used the tables for our supplies, and had our picnic sitting on the ground in American style!

We had the usual sandwiches, hard-boiled eggs, thermos bottles of cold drinks, cake, oranges, and peaches. The peaches of Japan are completely beautiful and delicious, huge white globes with pink cheeks, juicy and full of flavor. Indeed, all of the Japanese fruit was a surprise and delight to me; somehow I had not been prepared for it. At every season of the year there is something to enjoy: the persimmons of the autumn, mandarin oranges and wonderful apples during the winter, sweet and delicate loquats in the spring, peaches and nectarines all summer, and superb grapes, and then the figs of September.

After lunch there was the usual picnic restless resting. Mr. Shimizu, who had a real gift for painting and never went anywhere without his sketchbook, perched on the edge of the cliff and drew a picture of the valley. The Prince and the boys climbed over the rocks and explored the surroundings, with Dr. Saburi keeping a careful eye on them and saying a quiet word when they got too near the edges.

When we started back by a different trail over the top of the bluff, the village head appeared from nowhere to lead the way again. At the temple the priest gave the Crown Prince three lotus blossoms from the temple pond, which he later presented to my sister for her to arrange.

We were home again in time to bathe and dress for Mrs. Gertz's tea-party, to which Mr. Shimizu and I accompanied the Prince. He had been twice before to western houses, to the O'Briens' and the Austins', but both of those were boys' parties. This was his first excursion into the western adult world.

Mrs. Gertz had lived for many years in Japan, and after the end of the war and her husband's death, her summer cottage in Karuizawa had become her year-round home. The little parlor was filled with Buddhas and brocades, with photographs of her four attractive children, now married to people of four different nationalities, and with oil paintings.

Besides Princess Kitashirakawa and Princess Tokugawa, several friends of Mrs. Gertz's were present, and the Prince had not only to change back and forth from Japanese to English but he had to cope with Swedish English and Swiss English as well. He was moreover the focal point of the party and everyone hung on his words. It was something of a test for a shy boy of fifteen, but he met it beautifully. His innate dignity and his boyish diffidence made a charming combination, and when he took a second piece of the cream cake, all strain went out of the atmosphere and everybody visibly rejoiced.

At six, when a pause came, the Prince rose and very composedly broke up the party. We were all lined up on the front steps for a photograph, and the final farewells and thanks took place at the gate.

We had wonderful trout for dinner, which had been sent by the Governor of Nagano, but the Prince and I, after Mrs. Gertz's feast, were not hungry. He gave me the most mischievous smile when I put down my fork.

The boys came again after dinner, and another card game was in progress when the Governor himself arrived with Mr. Sakaki. He had had to go to Tokyo for a governors' meeting on the day that the Crown Prince first came to Nagano and the vice-governor had taken his place at the ceremony at the top of the pass. This, then, was his official visit to the Crown Prince. The Prince left the card table and came to the other side of the room, in front of the fireplace, to speak to the Governor.

He was a young man for a governor, and quite fine-looking. He bowed to me, and then bowed very formally and very low to the Crown Prince, who bowed low in response. The Prince thanked the Governor for his gifts of trout and peaches. The Governor told the Prince about his friendship with a former doctor of the Prince's, and about the Empress Dowager's inspection of the silkworm industry in Nagano in June, and he invited the Prince to visit Nagano again and to see more of it next time. The Prince made a smiling and cordial answer, and they both bowed low. The Governor withdrew.

Most of the time the Prince was to me a pupil, a very special and royal pupil, to be sure, but primarily a growing boy of whom I was very fond, whom I wanted to help, and to whose development I devoted a great deal of thought. Today I had twice seen him in his role of Prince, once in an international group and once with a high Japanese official, and I was impressed by his demeanor on both occasions. He will do well, I thought, and prayed that nothing would happen, either in his personal life or in the life of his country, to change or warp him.

We had decided on six-forty-five for breakfast, but at six-forty the Prince had not stirred. I woke him up, and he was ready, in school summer uniform, by seven. He talked quite a bit at the table, speaking of Nikko and Yumoto, where he was during the latter part of the war. "Nikko was a weary place for me," he said, "but Yumoto is good."

Mr. Shimizu arrived while we were still at breakfast, had a cup of coffee with us, and then went to work with the guards on the Prince's packing. We had our reading, the Crown Prince

[241]

attentive and serious, not commenting but not bored, and after breakfast he and I talked alone together for a little while.

Presently Dr. Saburi and Mr. Sakaki came. Things had been carried down to the car. It was time for the Prince to go. He and I walked down the path together, the rest followed. In the fresh morning air the shadows and sunlight through the trees were beautiful. At the turn in the path Mrs. Shibusawa and the four boys were waiting to say good-by.

At the foot of the hill the Crown Prince thanked me and I thanked him, and he got into the car, followed by Mr. Sakaki. Mr. Shimizu and Dr. Saburi took the other car. Our neighbors, the girls and teachers at the Japan Women's University summer camp next door and people from the houses near by, were all out to watch the departure. The Russian gentleman across the road still in his blue pajamas was standing in the bushes like a deer in the underbrush.

The cars moved off. The visit was over.

We watched them out of sight, and then we turned to go up the hill again, babbling our satisfaction, saying out loud those things which we had been whispering in snatches during the visit. Really a perfect guest, thoughtful and considerate, responsive, eats everything with apparent enjoyment, amuses himself with his book in odd moments, seems happy and interested always. So clear and honest a nature, coöperative, anxious to do his part and meet his obligations. An ideal guest, and a very lovable boy. Nothing had gone wrong. The Prince had been safe and happy here.

I have had many happy times in Japan, but for pure bliss this moment was the peak.

CHAPTER THIRTY

THREE FIRE FESTIVALS of ancient tradition still linger in Japan: one on Mount Fuji, one in Kyoto, and one in a little village in Nagano Prefecture, called Mochizuki. To the festival at Mochizuki, through the good offices of the friendly news photographer of Komoro, Mr. Kitago Kodama, we were invited.

We had no idea at all what we might be getting into, as we set off late in the afternoon from Karuizawa. Takenaka San had returned to Tokyo and I was driving. We took Masako San and Michiko San with us because we thought they deserved some fun after the splendid way they had worked during the Crown Prince's visit, and we had asked our friends the Botts if they cared to take a chance and trail us in their car. Mr. Ernest Bott was the representative of Church World Service on LARA. He and his charming and lovable wife had been in Japan many years before the war; both spoke Japanese and they knew the life well, but neither had ever heard of the festival at Mochizuki.

We drove about thirty miles into the mountains in the late afternoon light. The shadows were long and mysterious, and the sun-warmed rice, nearly ripe, had a subtle, characteristic fragrance. There were winding rivers, temples deep among tall trees, farmhouses with lilies growing out of the thatch roofs, and villages where swift streams flowed between the road and the solid line of houses, with a footbridge to each front door. As we drew near Mochizuki we saw that the roads were full of people on their way to the festival, a steady stream of old people in dark kimonos, boys in western clothes and girls in brilliant kimonos, young women with babies nodding on their backs, small children in every kind of costume, but all clean, all well mended and patched.

[243]

It was nearly dark when we reached Mochizuki. The streets were so crowded that we could make our way only slowly, our horns screeching monotonously. Special buses were discharging their loads of country sightseers, and a bevy of girls in brilliant blue kimonos scattered before us as we drove up a steep hill to the village hall.

Out of the plain two-storey building swarmed a flock of officials to greet us, and when a young girl thrust into my arms a sheaf of chrysanthemums as heavy as a baby and considerably larger, I got my first inkling that I was to do more than stand anonymous in a crowd and peer over their shoulders at the celebrations. The news of the Crown Prince's recent visit had spread all over the countryside, and since there was no chance to see him, the people were eager at least to have a look at his American teacher, and to honor her in some degree as they would have liked to honor him.

Officials led me upstairs, clutching my sister firmly but separated from the rest of the party, to a big room at the far end of which was a long brocade-covered table. The Soncho San, the village head, a big-eyed man with waxed moustaches turned up at the ends like the Kaiser's, welcomed us and thrust me firmly into an impressive armchair at the center of the table. There I sat in state holding my flowers, with my sister beside me, wondering what was going to happen next.

What came next unhorsed us both and almost fatally upset our gravity. The Botts and Tané, appearing at the far end of the room and beholding us enthroned, doubled over in profound and mocking bows.

Now the Soncho San brought up other village officials and visitors and there were many introductions: the head of the Women's Association, the English teacher in the village school, a visiting professor of architecture from Tokyo University, and a number of newsmen and others. The Botts were escorted to the table and seated with honor, Michiko San and Masako San had their turn, and the other places soon filled up, and the girls in blue kimonos whom we had scattered before us on the road, brought plates of sweet omelette and vegetables, with *saké* for the men and cider for the women. "It may not suit to your mouth," said the Soncho San earnestly, "but please to eat anyhow." This was difficult, because we had had an early dinner before we left.

Various people were eager to tell us about the festival, and before Tané could finish interpreting for one, another would tap her shoulder and pour forth a spate of words. She turned her head from side to side like a mechanical doll and talked steadily, while the village English teacher with considerably less fluency held forth on his own account and on behalf of those who could not reach Tané.

The purpose of the festival was the worship of the sakaki tree, a kind of broad-leaved evergreen considered sacred. Sprays of sakaki figure in Shinto funerals and are part of the symbolic decorations at the shrines. On the top of the mountain above the village there was no shrine, but a great sakaki tree which was the object of worship.

A shout suddenly went up that the festival had begun, and we all jumped up and rushed to the windows.

After the heat and the lights and the crowd in the room, the night air at the window was fresh and cool and the darkness was welcome. On the top of the hill that loomed black against the sky, a great bonfire flamed high. A hundred and fifty young men of the village, from seventeen to thirty years old, were up there lighting their torches from the bonfire. We could see the small flames breaking away from the big ones—and then in a moment the line of light starting down the hill, as they brought the fire to the village, where they would douse their torches in the river.

This was the most beautiful moment of the evening: the flames mounting into the night sky, the line of flaring torches winding down the black hill in loops and curves of golden light.

In a very short time—too short a time—the side of the hill was dark again and the lingering flames on the top sank to a glow. The first part of the festival was over; there would be more later. Please return to the table.

An exhibition of a folk dance peculiar to the village was next on the program. A four-piece orchestra, drum, flute, *samisen* and one other instrument, provided music for about twenty dancers, young men in white kimonos and dark gray *hakamas*, and girls in blue kimonos and bright *obis* (their hair permanently waved). The men danced in a row behind, the girls in front, and the dance was grave and charming.

[245]

When that was finished we were led away to see the procession, which was the main feature of the festival and which had been forming while we watched the dance. A place had been prepared for us in another part of the village, and as we made our way thither through the crooked, crowded streets, we were ourselves a procession, gazed upon by the thousands of people who had come on foot and by motor bus from all the surrounding villages.

First went men carrying lanterns, paper lanterns with black lacquer frames and handles, and after them the Soncho San, now very happy because of the *saké* he had drunk, weaving back and forth, twirling his moustaches and shooing the children before him. Then came Violet and I, stumbling a little on the rough street in the dark, each of us with a Japanese lady to guide and reassure her—another example of the care and thoughtfulness of the Japanese for their western visitors. Behind us were Tané and the Botts, similarly attended, and behind them the first lanterns and *omikoshi* (portable shrine) of the festival procession.

At a fork in the road the Soncho San led us to the left, while the procession behind us veered off to the right. Most of the throng of children and villagers that followed preferred to stay with us. Soon we came to a house built close to the street with its front opened up to make a sort of platform, on which there was a double row of chairs, with a plush armchair for the Crown Prince's teacher directly in the middle. Here we were established while the crowd packed itself solidly in the street before us.

As the procession was to go up to the top of the village and then come down again in front of us, we had some time to sit there under a barrage of naked electric bulbs and the fascinated gaze of hundreds and perhaps thousands of black eyes. We were the only foreigners, we were told, who had ever been to the festival, and the first westerners that many people in the throng had ever seen. People were on the balconies and even the roofs of houses on both sides of us and across the street. They were massed in front of us so tightly that the warmth of their bodies was oppressive and we seemed to lack air to breathe. Yet there was no odor, as there would have been from such a solid pack of humanity in the western world.

[246]

Someone whispered that there were plain-clothes men in the crowd to ensure our safety, but it had not occurred to me to be uneasy. The wonder of that swept over me as I realized that here we were, four Americans miles from the nearest American soldier, in the midst of thousands of Japanese, and the date was August fifteenth, the fourth anniversary of the surrender.

While we sat there, some bits of information about the festival came our way. It was known to be about eight hundred years old; the first mention of it in recorded history occurred in 1464 when a hostile army approaching the village saw the lines of torches and thought that a big and powerful army was ready for them before which it would be wiser to withdraw. The record said that the festival was then three or four hundred years old.

The sakaki tree, we were told, was thought to have the power of keeping off pestilence and everyone tried to get a bit of it to hang over their doors—not just any sakaki tree, but those carried in the procession which were purified by the priests. Pregnant women also kept pieces of it in the family shrine until they were safely delivered.

Two of the young men who were to take part came to our platform and were introduced as officers of the Village Youth Association. Stuck in the towels tied around their heads, like feathers in an American Indian's headband, were short leafy branches of sakaki.

Suddenly these young men began to clear an opening through the crowd, and, as a breath of sweet cool air swept down from the mountain, the procession came.

First were lighted paper lanterns on long poles, carried by quite small boys. Then the first *omikoshi*, a children's one, carried by little boys. Most *omikoshi* are elaborate structures painted, carved, and decorated usually with a gilt phoenix on top; all the *omikoshi* in this festival were simply the sakaki tree. An upright tree, with all its branches, was mounted in the center of a sort of rimless wheel made of heavy beams, which rested on the shoulders of several boys. The *omikoshi* proceeded by revolving round and round and lurching from side to side of the street, the boys chanting in unison to keep the rhythm and encourage one another, *"Washoi! Washoi! Washoi!"* From time to time they stopped and bounced the tree up and down violently, and then rocked it from side to side, so that the top of it dipped within reach of eager hands on both sides of the street. Now and then the older boy directing these younger ones led them in a sort of shouted song with a pronounced rhythm.

After the first *omikoshi* had passed, there came a dragon boat (*tatsubune*) on wheels: a very old heavy boat with a prow in the shape of a dragon. There was a big lantern in the middle and four men lolled at ease around a large kettle of *saké*. No one seemed to know the significance of this boat; it was very old and heavy, they said, and was kept in a shrine storehouse in the village and brought out just once each year.

Three more *omikoshi* followed, two carried by boys and the third and largest by young men. Between the *omikoshi* came the lion dancers. There were five lions in each group, and each lion was made up of two young men; one carried the big head, from which the body, a long piece of cloth, stretched out and covered the second man. The "lion" weaved about making dashes at the crowd, which scattered shrieking.

Lion dancing is featured a great deal in Japanese entertainment. Mr. Joseph C. Grew in his book *Ten Years in Japan* tells of seeing the great Kabuki actor, Kikugoro, do the lion dance at a Kabuki performance, and of the almost hysterical excitement of the audience. Street entertainers, especially at New Year's time, often perform it, and almost any variety show is likely to feature a lion dance. The most recent one I had seen in Tokyo was very gaudy and sophisticated, and the lion spent what I felt to be an unreasonable amount of time biting fleas. I took that to be a modern perversion for comic effect but evidently the fleas were a traditional part of the act, for these Mochizuki lions had in attendance a swarm of young men armed with decorated paper bats with which they danced about driving away flies and fleas from the lions.

These dancers performed a free but definite step in and out among the lions in a never-ending pattern, which had an almost hypnotic effect. Their shirts were plastered to their backs with perspiration and now and then they would reach into a big basket containing cracked ice, which was carried by a helper. We were told that these men danced for four hours without stopping. They must have been in a semi-conscious frenzy at the last.

A week or so later we returned to Mochizuki in the daytime to call upon the people who had been so kind to us and to thank them: the Soncho San, the head of the district, the president of the Women's Association and the English teacher.

CHAPTER THIRTY-ONE

ONE DAY AFTER the Crown Prince's visit to us in Karuizawa two policemen came marching up our hill through the trees, one of them bearing a large wooden box, which the other, his superior, formally presented. The box contained large and beautiful peaches from Okayama, the gift of the Prime Minister. This was followed a few days later by a very cordial letter from Mr. Yoshida and an invitation to visit him at Gotemba where he had taken Count Kabayama's house and was spending August and September.

Mr. Shigeru Yoshida had been the Prime Minister when I first went to Japan, and during my first year had invited me one night to a very pleasant small dinner-party at his house, just a day or so, as it happened, before his government fell and was succeeded by a coalition headed by the Social Democrats. Mr. Katayama, a Christian, and an honest and conscientious man, was the next Premier, and held the position through several difficult and disturbed months, until, because of a shift in his coalition, he was ousted by Mr. Hitoshi Ashida. Mr. Ashida in his turn lost out, and Mr. Yoshida came back to take the helm in 1949. His party, which called itself the Liberal Party, was actually the conservative party, and it had the support of the majority of Japanese people at the polls, though labor was opposed to it. Its platform was coöperation with the Occupation, opposition to communism, and the promotion of Japan's interests.

Mr. Shigeru Yoshida himself is a colorful and strong figure, a liberal of long standing and identified with the group of liberals who stood before the war for international friendship in opposition to the policies of the military party. He was the son-in-law of Count Makino, the liberal statesman who had barely escaped

[250]

with his life in the assassinations of 1936, and it was Mr. Yoshida's daughter Kazuko, now Mrs. Takakichi Aso, of whom Mr. Grew tells a touching story in his book, of her defense of her grandfather in the face of the assassins. Mr. Yoshida was Ambassador to Great Britain at the time of the Coronation and during the war he was under suspicion by the military and indeed imprisoned for six months because of his western interests and sympathies. He speaks English with ease, and Mrs. Aso's English is just about perfect. Since the death of Mrs. Yoshida, Mrs. Aso has been her father's hostess, and her beauty and charm and political acumen are well known and respected. Her relationship with her father seems more western than Japanese, and when one hears her say, "I'm sorry for the Japanese people. Daddy doesn't know anything about economy. He can't even balance his own budget," or "Daddy loves to say things to shock people," it is difficult to believe that one is hearing a kimonoed daughter speaking of her kimonoed father!

Mr. Yoshida wears kimono and *hakama* when he is at home, a most becoming costume for men, with the same cachet that judges' robes and ministerial gowns have. Whenever I saw him he was bland and smiling with an air of enjoying some private joke, perhaps at your expense, and a detachment which suggested that he thought in terms of thousands of years instead of decades or even centuries.

I thoroughly enjoyed the week-end which I spent with Mr. Yoshida and Mrs. Aso in Gotemba in September. Mount Fuji, as usual, did not deign to disclose herself to me, but aside from the mistiness, the weather was beautiful, and the surroundings peaceful and lovely. The house was a very old and spacious farmhouse with a great thatched roof, which had been modernized and made comfortable without destroying its atmosphere of antiquity. Count Kabayama was there too, a fine, spare, elderly aristocrat of the old school, a loyal follower of his "feudal lord" Prince Shimadzu, with the breadth of vision and the warm interest in human personality that frequently belonged to that dying breed of men. He had been a lifelong friend of the United States, having been educated at Wesleyan College and Amherst. He was one of the committee that worked on the new Japanese Constitution, but because of some purely nominal connections with one of the ultra-nationalistic societies of the war years, he was "purged," an extreme example of a number of ironic injustices that resulted from purging by categories rather than on the merits of the individual case.

Princess Chichibu came to dinner on Saturday night and Dr. Koizumi for Sunday lunch. In a week-end of very good talk, the words that have stayed most vividly in my memory are those said by Count Kabayama:

"You know, the most interesting and *tasty* thing in the world is one human being. His Majesty never had a chance to know people as they are, in the old days. Now he meets hundreds and hundreds of people; he sees them as they naturally are. As for the people, he goes about and meets them and they see him as he is. They see something they didn't know existed in the world, a man without ambition or greed, and it's a wonderful thing to them."

As the autumn wore on it was complicated for us by a series of illnesses. Flu swept through the house from one end to the other and back again, we all had it and some of us more than once. Most of the autumn the weather was cold and rainy, and there were only a few of the brilliantly sunny, warm days that usually make the Japanese autumn a time of delight.

It happened that the days that I went to Koganei for the Crown Prince's private lesson were generally fair, and we would have the lesson sitting in the sunshine on the steps of the Kokaden. The sun was silver on the tassels of pampas grass at the edge of the woods, and golden on the yellow leaves that drifted out of the trees. We were reading parts of Carl Sandburg's *Abe Lincoln Grows Up* in those lessons and talking about the ideas that it raised, with excursions into the subject of the sounds that one hears when one lies awake at night, early memories, difference in dialects both in America and Japan, and the quality of the conversation of the people about the boy Lincoln as revealed by the words that puzzled him as a small child: "independent," and "predestination."

Some of the new words that I asked the Crown Prince to use in sentences of his own making were *form, conscience,* and *appreciate.* His sentences, always interesting, showed that he was growing up. "She bothered about her form because her form was not so good to look at." "The man whose conscience is paralyzed is dangerous." "It is unwary to appreciate a person when you first meet him."

In the lessons at my house, with the Crown Prince and two of his classmates, I went on with *Tales From Long Ago and Many Lands* because the stories offered such good starting points for discussion. One of the tales was the Italian legend also retold by Longfellow in "The Bell of Atri." Briefly it is the story of the Duke of Atri who was determined to see that all his people were justly treated. Anyone who felt that he had suffered injustice might ring the bell in the center square and his case would be reviewed. So well did this system work that in time the bell fell into disuse and vines grew over the bell rope. Then one day the village was startled by the sound of the bell. When the people rushed to the spot they found that a work-worn old horse, thin as a bag of bones, had set the bell to ringing. Even the animals should have justice, said the Duke, and ordered the owner to feed and care for his faithful horse.

The boys were to make questions about the story. One question was: Did the poor dumb horse ring the bell for justice on purpose? To which the boy's own answer was, no, he was only hungry. But the Prince maintained that he had, and his argument was a nice piece of reasoning, expressed in competent English.

He first established the fact that it was only a legend anyhow and therefore we could assume that the horse could think. Atri at that time, the Prince pointed out, was not a city, it was only a small country town. The horse could have found fresh grass or low-growing trees anywhere, whereas the vines and tendrils on the bell rope must have been withered. Therefore he rang the bell for justice, not for food.

During that autumn I saw the Prince rather more often than usual outside of the regular hours for classes. One September evening, for instance, my sister, Tané, and I were invited to dine with him at his house in Koganei. Dr. Koizumi was also there and Mr. Shimizu made the sixth. The Prince sat at the head of the table and took on the responsibilities of host in a very charming way. That Tané was included was something new that had come within the past six months. She had been invited also to the princesses' Doll Festival party in April, and instead of having tea in another room with a lady-in-waiting had sat down at the tea-table with the Empress and the princesses, and Her Majesty herself had performed the tea ceremony, in a very happy and informal way, and served us all. Tané was now teaching English to Princess Takako on alternate Tuesday afternoons, while her elder sisters were with me, which perhaps partly accounted for the change, as well as the Imperial Family's appreciation of Tané's own character, but it was a great change nevertheless. It always seemed to me that the innovations made for Japanese persons were more significant than those made for me. Barriers lowered for a foreigner in a unique position could easily be raised again, but barriers lowered for Japanese were more likely to be lasting.

Several times I had lunch alone with the Prince, for practice in western ways, and afterwards Dr. Koizumi and Tané and Mr. Nomura or other chamberlains would join us in the sitting-room and there would be talk of books and poetry, of riding and other sports, of what was going on in the dormitory. The Prince's second contribution to the weekly discussions in the dormitory had been on the subject "The Origin of the Japanese People." He discoursed ably about racial strains, migrations, and so forth without any mention of the Sun Goddess. The boys said that his delivery was definitely improved over the first time, and they commended his subject matter also.

One evening I took Dr. Floyd Schmoe to the dormitory to show his color photographs of underwater life to the boys. Dr. Schmoe was a Quaker from Seattle who had been in Japan during the summer heading up a small international work-camp at Hiroshima. He had done a good deal of work at the Oceanographic Laboratory of the University of Washington and had some fine color movies of fish and other creatures at the bottom of Puget Sound. He showed those pictures primarily for the benefit of the Prince; some others of skiing on Mount Rainier for those who had a less burning interest in marine biology. Between pictures he talked a little about the work-camp at Hiroshima. "Peace cannot be made with words," he said, "it must be worked for, by people of different races, nations, and religions working together." Some of the men around the place, cooks, bodyguards, chauffeurs, had come in and stood at the back of the room to see the pictures, and I saw one of them nod his head in emphatic agreement.

The dormitory that rainy night, with the currant-colored curtains drawn at the windows, the lights and warmth inside, the bright, alert faces of the boys, was a much more cheerful place than I had dared to hope it would be.

Before the showing of the pictures we had looked in at the study-room, where there were tables in groups of two or three, with good lights, and boys' heads bent over them. An air of profound concentration brooded over the room; no one stirred except the Crown Prince who looked up and grinned. Floyd Schmoe said, "They seem to be studying very hard." Mr. Shimizu laughed. "Too hard," he observed shrewdly.

Later that month we were all shocked by the sudden death from heart attack of Mr. Tsuneo Matsudaira, President of the House of Councilors, husband of my friend Mrs. Matsudaira, and father of Princess Cichibu. Before the war his life had been spent in the foreign embassies of the world; as Ambassador to the United States he had been responsible for the gift of the Japanese cherry trees along the Schuylkill River that are the spring glory of Fairmount Park in Philadelphia; during the war he had been Minister of the Imperial Household until the Palace burned, when, taking responsibility for the disaster in the Japanese way, he had resigned. Politics was an unfamiliar and rather uncongenial field to him, but he yielded to the urging that he could do a service for Japan, and as a patriotic duty ran for election to the newly created House of Councilors in 1947. He had the respect of both Socialists and conservatives, and his election to the presidency of the House followed. It is probable that the emotional and physical strain of leadership in those difficult times brought about the heart condition that caused his death. He was a large man, with an almost Buddha-like yet worldly expression of calm, and he had a baby grandson, whom he adored, who was a comical reproduction of him. The baby called him "Jiji," and took the liberties with him which the Japanese baby may take with the most distinguished of grandfathers.

The Shinto funeral, which was held at the official residence of the President of the House of Councilors, was a very simple and impressive one. Shinto priests in white kimonos and *hakamas* with tall black hats performed the brief ritual and chanted the prayers. Afterwards to the weird and mournful music of bamboo flute and pipes, the congregation filed in line before the

[255]

portrait and ashes, which were hidden by a great mass of sakaki, and each one presented a spray of sakaki tree, tied with the cut papers which are a symbol of purification.

Two other things marked the autumn of 1949 in my mind, one large and one small. The former was a rather indefinite yet perceptible change in the atmosphere about the Communist menace. In the January elections of 1949 the Communist representation in the Diet had jumped from four to thirty-five, and the Communists had correspondingly taken heart. The fall of Nanking to Communist armies in April had provided further encouragement, and one heard more talk, and more uneasy talk, about them all the time. Though the Communist magazines continued to print scandalous articles about the Imperial Family, the party had ceased to call for abolition of the Emperor system, a policy which had been very unpopular with the Japanese people, and concentrated on nationalism and opposition to the Occupation. There were also persistent rumors about a "revolution" which was supposed to take place in August. A woman member of the Diet whom I knew had spoken of these rumors with considerable perturbation, and some teachers confessed to a fear of future recriminations if they were known to be friends of Americans.

During the summer of 1949 two acts of violence occurred. Mr. Shimoyama, the head of a government railway, disappeared, and his decapitated body was later found on the railroad tracks. The railways had recently announced the dismissal of a large number of workers in an attempt at "rationalizing" the industry. This "rationalization" was done at the instigation of Occupation officials, who contended that no business was healthy in which there were great numbers of employees on the payroll who did little or no work. The spreading of the work over many poorly paid workers, however, had been the traditional form of social security in Japan, where people are seldom dismissed suddenly and without warning. It was not a bad form of social security, either, and less deteriorating to the character than unemployment and the acceptance of government handouts.

A few weeks later a switch was opened by saboteurs and a railway train ran down an embankment and overturned, killing a number of passengers.

These acts of violence, which were laid to the Communists, roused great revulsion among the people at large and caused a sharp reaction against the Communists, especially among those who had been inclined to support them because of their expressed idealism. Japan had had enough of assassinations and violence in her past history and wanted no more of it. For the moment, anyhow, the tide of communism was ebbing, and some unspoken fears went out of the atmosphere.

The other matter which lingers in my mind is a trivial one and yet, too, a sign of the times. The old street cries of Tokyo were coming back, and with them a little of the normal life and color of the past. When I first came to Japan, the only street cry was that of the man who went about at night clapping two sticks together and calling out his long-drawn warning, "*Hi-no-yo-jin!* Be careful of fires.*" Spring had brought the goldfish man, summer the wind-bell man, who needed no cry, for all the fairy bells on his cart tinkled and delicately clashed as he moved along the uneven road. With the autumn came the bamboo-seller's nasal whine, as he pulled a two-wheeled cart piled with long green bamboo poles, the wail of the mender of bat-umbrellas— "*Ko-mo-ri-ga-sa!*"—the shriller cry of the tinman who would repair pots and pans. In the crisp early mornings came the call of the little boy who sold fermented beans wrapped in straw, a breakfast delicacy; "*Natto-natto, natto,*" sounded his loud childish voice up one street and down another, while we still lay snugly in bed. And at dusk there was the melancholy whistle of the blind masseur who tapped his way along in search of tired bodies to soothe into relaxation.

Shortly after our return to Tokyo, the Tajimas took us to a performance of Kabuki, a sort of congratulation party because of the Crown Prince's visit to us in Karuizawa. Kabuki was one of the things I enjoyed most in Japan, and this was an especially exciting performance because an outstanding actor was to be invested with one of the great Kabuki names in a formal ceremony.

The Kabuki is one of the traditional types of drama. It developed about three centuries ago as a popular form strongly influenced by the aristocratic Noh play and the popular puppet play of Osaka. For the foreigner it is easier to understand and enjoy than the slow and stately Noh.

We had beautiful seats in the center, near the stage, with a good view of the *hanamichi,* the passageway extending through the audience to the stage, along which the most dramatic entrances and exits were made.

In Kabuki there is an orchestra consisting of eight or ten men, some of whom play the *samisen* and some keep up a sort of recitative about the action of the play in the harsh nasal tones and prolonged vowels which characterize the traditional Japanese singing, whether in Kabuki, Noh, story-telling, or praying. These men wore kimonos and *hakamas,* with the *kamishimo,* a sort of pinafore with wide, stiff shoulder bretelles, very striking and handsome.

The action of the plays is much stylized, probably owing to the influence of the puppet dramas. Moments of crisis are marked by the actor's holding an exaggerated position, sometimes with crossed eyes and hideous grimaces, while a man at the edge of the stage claps two sticks together to emphasize the moment. The audience often applauds at this point and the enthusiasts in the top gallery shout the name of the actor or a phrase meaning, "I've been waiting for this!" In the scenes where someone is killed, an inferior dies by turning a somersault backwards, his feet in the air, comic and undignified as befits an inferior; a man of importance, however, like a *samurai,* is permitted to die with more pomp. The property men, lithe young figures in black tights and jerkins, with a black cloth over their faces to show that they are invisible, dart about with whatever is necessary. They thrust a stool under a man about to sit down; take away a bowl or bring a scroll. They help an actor to change his costume, which he does without leaving the stage, simply making himself invisible to the audience by turning his back. The new costume is conveniently underneath the old one. Costumes and settings are incomparably beautiful.

There are certain families of Kabuki actors who have a long history of eminence, and their names are handed down to sons or grandsons (adopted if necessary) who are worthy of succeeding them. On this day, Somegoro, a son-in-law of Kichiemon, was succeeding to the name of Matsumoto Koshiro the Eighth. Kichiemon acted as master of ceremonies, and the whole family was on the stage for the brief but impressive ceremony, including two very small sons of the new Koshiro's; all were dressed in kimonos and *hakamas* with the broad-shouldered *kamishimo,*

[258]

and they wore wigs to simulate the classical hair-do with shaven pate and topknot.

The acting was superb—brilliant and strong and subtle. There was a drinking scene that was really funny, and at the end of the play when Benkei, played by the newly named Koshiro the Eighth, left the stage in a series of extraordinary leaps along the *hanamichi*, the audience went wild.

During one of the intermissions we went backstage and met the famous Kichiemon in his dressing-room. He was an elderly man, with a wise, kindly face. It was hard to realize that he was capable of the vivid ferocities of acting that we had seen.

CHAPTER THIRTY-TWO

THE CHRISTMAS AND New Year season brought the events that had, by my fourth year in Japan, become customary.

On the twentieth of December I was invited to dinner at the Palace with the entire Imperial Family, the usual happy, informal evening with the Empress so gracious and charming, the Emperor smiling benevolently on his children and making occasional comments, the lively, attractive young people, and the Crown Prince the unconscious center of the group. Because Christmas was so near the children decided to sing "Silent Night" in English. They got off to a false start and after a bar or two the voices dwindled away to nothing. The Crown Prince laughed. "Truly a silent night," he said. They began again, and this time, with the aid of the Empress's lovely voice, sang the whole stanza, while I sat there and wondered if it was really I, hearing the Japanese imperial children, deep within the Moat, singing the favorite Christmas carol of the western world.

The next day my sister and I went to a concert at the Palace, where we sat as before, a little apart from the imperial chairs, but on the rug. This time the Empress Dowager was there too, and after the concert she spoke cordially to my sister and then to me. Her force of character, her warm and genuine interest in people, and her sense of majesty were as evident as her quaint black dress, little black toque, and black silk gloves.

The Crown Prince's birthday party this year took the form of a dinner party at his house in Koganei on the twenty-first, to which Mrs. Matsudaira, Mr. Yamanashi, Dr. Koizumi, Mr. Blyth, Mr. Nomura, Mr. Shimizu and I were invited. Mrs. Matsudaira had just been made a member of the Crown Prince's Advisory Council, at which I rejoiced, for I felt that her feminine wisdom and wide experience would be of real benefit to the de-

[260]

liberations of that body. The talk during dinner and after was varied and interesting, good adult talk for a boy just turned sixteen to be hearing.

Mr. Yamanashi, reminiscing about the days when he was a ranking admiral and vice-minister of the Navy, spoke about Admiral Yamamoto, who had once been a protégé of his. He had taught the younger man history and other things, and Yamamoto was with him at the Washington Conference of 1922 and the London Conference of 1931. His experience in Washington had given Yamamoto an affection for America, and in London he had learned to admire and respect Ramsay MacDonald for his integrity and sympathetic understanding. When the war clouds gathered, he lifted up his voice many times in favor of friendship with England and America. It was therefore "sad and ironical," said Mr. Yamanashi, that as Admiral of the Fleet, Yamamoto was ordered to plan the attack on Pearl Harbor.

He had told Admiral Yamanashi in private conversation of his agony of spirit at the task, and the older man had answered that it was his destiny.

"The question arises why he did not resign," said Mr. Yamanashi. But the Army was in the saddle, he went on, it was determined on the war, and Admiral Yamamoto felt that with Japan committed he must do what he could to save her from ruin.

It has been well established that the widely publicized remark about dictating peace from the White House which made Admiral Yamamoto a chief object of hate and fury in wartime United States, was distorted by the Japanese propagandists who first released it. What he actually said and what he meant was that the Japanese Army would have to fight its way into the very heart of Washington before it could bring the United States to sue for peace.

Admiral Yamamoto was killed during the war. His younger son Tadao was in the Crown Prince's class and was one of the finest and most thoughtful of my students.

On the way home in the car after the party, Mr. Blyth told me that he had asked the Crown Prince one day, "Which would you rather be, the Crown Prince or an ordinary boy?" To which the Prince had replied with simple truth, "I don't know. I've never been an ordinary boy."

The actual day of Prince Akihito's birthday this year was full, and sounded happy as I heard about it. He went to the Palace in the morning and had lunch with all his family. After lunch he returned to Koganei to receive the congratulatory visits of his former attendants and servants. In years past this had been a purely formal affair with silent bows on both sides, after which the callers withdrew and were given some small token to take home, such as a box of cigarettes with the sixteen-petaled chrysanthemum stamped on the lid. This year, however, on the Prince's initiative, there was an innovation. They were all asked to sit down and were given tea. The Prince sat down with them. As he did not remember all of their names, he had them introduce themselves, tell what they had done and what they were now doing, and he made comments and little jokes. One man, a former chauffeur, humbly aware that he would be remembered only for an unfavorable incident, said, "I am that X who had a little accident"—and was applauded by all for his honesty and modesty.

The great innovation of the day, however, was having ten of the Prince's classmates to dinner with him. The mother of one of them, who had lived for some years in the United States, had made a birthday cake, complete with sixteen candles. At the proper moment Mr. Shimizu carried it in, lighted, and they all sang "Happy birthday to you." The Prince blew out the candles in three tries. After dinner they talked and played games till late, and those boys who were farthest from home were kept overnight. Such a contrast to the Prince's birthday three years before!

The day after Christmas we had our party for the Crown Prince and the six boys who had shared his private lessons during the year. This time Prince Masahito was included in the party with the older boys.

The day began with an earthquake before dawn, followed by others of increasing intensity. Doors and windows rattled, trees swayed in the garden, and some new cracks appeared in our walls.

The treasure hunt had gone so well the year before that we had another, more difficult one, followed by games. After refreshments in the dining-room, they all gathered around the piano to sing. Hashimoto San, who had a fine tenor, sang "White Christmas" very effectively, and the rest sang "Silent

Night." Prince Akihito stood with his hands behind his back, and I saw the adoring Prince Masahito, who had stuck close to him all afternoon, sidle up and twine his fingers through his big brother's.

When the motorcycle and side-car had rattled noisily away and the Prince's big Packard ponderously rounded the corner, the other boys and the policemen all gone, we returned to the living-room and sank into the nearest chairs. "Four earthquakes in the morning," said my sister, "and two princes in the afternoon are a little exhausting!"

After the party the Crown Prince went to Hayama for a few days. Two or three evenings later, his house at Koganei burned to the ground in half an hour.

We heard the news over the radio and telephoned the Palace at once for confirmation. I wrote a note of sympathy immediately to the Prince and the next afternoon Tané and I drove out to Koganei.

It was a cold winter day with the remains of a recent snow frozen on the ground. The villages along the way were full of people doing their final shopping for the New Year, and branches of pine and bamboo were tied to every telegraph pole and lamp post. At the school a table had been set up for people who wished to "sign in the book" to express their sympathy and a little crowd was milling around it.

The fence around the house was apparently undamaged, but when we reached the entrance we saw the complete destruction that had been wrought. The low concrete foundations looked like a child's blocks marking the rooms of a playhouse, and all between them was ashes and blackened debris, over which two men and a woman were working with hoes. The charred timbers that remained had already been gathered into piles and some burned quilts had been dumped into a corner of the yard. Otherwise nothing was left but a half-burned book whose pages fluttered in the breeze.

The fire had started from the electric wiring and had got such a start before it was discovered that the fire engines on the place and the fifteen more that rushed from neighboring villages were powerless to stop it. Possibly the wires had been dislodged by the recent earthquakes, for the regular inspection had revealed nothing amiss. Tama the dog and the fawn which had been a recent gift from an American general were safe, but all the Prince's books, his beautiful leather albums with his childhood photographs, his records and record-player were gone. The men attached to his household lost most of their clothes, a serious loss for them, for it was still difficult to get men's suits and shoes and prices were out of all proportion to salaries.

The Crown Prince, we heard, took the news very calmly. Prince Rikyu, the son of the heir to the Korean throne, was with him at Hayama, and the two boys were playing cards when Mr. Kuroki called Prince Akihito aside and told him what had happened. He asked at once if anyone had been hurt, and when relieved about that made no other comment. Returning to Prince Rikyu, he said briefly, "My house has burned down," and went on with the game. Later when people commiserated with him about the loss of his cherished possessions, he said only, "They can be gradually replaced." Prince Masahito, however, when he heard of his brother's loss, wept.

It was generally agreed that the Crown Prince had taken the news in a thoroughly royal manner, and admiring references were made to Confucius who, when his stable full of horses burned, asked only if anybody had been injured. The fact that the Crown Prince had never really liked that house at Koganei was also admitted with a smile. For my part, I hoped that now he and his brother could live together.

Fortunately his skis had been sent ahead to Kumanoyu, where he was going with three classmates for his first lessons in skiing, and were there waiting for him when he arrived the next week. Kumanoyu is a small hot-spring resort high in the Japan Alps, not far from the Shiga Heights Hotel which was popular with the skiers of the Occupation.

There was great interest in the Crown Prince's first venture in skiing, and the news photographers were all there in hopes of getting the first picture of his falling down. In one of the dailies the story was told of the present Emperor's abortive effort to learn to ski when he was Crown Prince. He went to a place at the foot of Mount Fuji, and the first day, like anybody else, he fell down. Reporters wrote that he took his fall good-naturedly, got up and went on again. There was an immediate outcry of *lese majesté* from the ultra-nationalists and so much heat was generated about the "disrespect" shown the then Crown

Prince that the Imperial Household officials advised him to give up all further attempts to learn to ski.

Today's Crown Prince, happily, is free to ski and to fall down in front of the cameras, and his rapid progress under the tutelage of Japan's foremost ski-master was a source of interest and satisfaction to his people. He returned to Tokyo well-tanned by the winter sun and full of enthusiasm for the new sport.

Shortly after the first of January Dr. Philip Jessup came to Tokyo as ambassador-at-large, visiting the Orient in preparation for the long-awaited peace treaty. His wife, Lois Kellog Jessup, who accompanied him, was a Bryn Mawrtyr and had been working with the American Friends Service Committee at the same time that I was there. It was a delight to me to see her several times during the week that the Jessups were in Tokyo and to gather together the small Bryn Mawr group to meet her.

One evening Mr. and Mrs. William J. Seebald, of the Diplomatic Section of GHQ, gave a buffet supper for the Jessups, to which the heads of all the diplomatic missions, except the Russian, went and in which I was included on Lois Jessup's account. It was an interesting and significant group of people who gathered that night, and the atmosphere was heightened by awareness of the increasing tensions in the world. Earlier that week the Russians had dramatically walked—or rather, to speak literally, run, pelting down the stairs and jumping into their waiting cars—out of the Allied Council Meeting when the repatriation of the 376,000 Japanese prisoners of war still in Russia had been pressed.

One small incident, like a tiny searchlight, pointed to the seriousness that underlay the surface gaiety that evening. Sir Alvary Gascoigne, the British Ambassador, came late—so late that the Chinese Nationalist representative had just left when he arrived. Great Britain had that day recognized Communist China and severed relations with the Nationalists.

A Japanese friend of mine, who before the war had spent a number of years in various embassies of the world, said to me one day with a heavy sigh, "Japan is in heaven now, but sometimes a cold wind blows in from Russia."

CHAPTER THIRTY-THREE

A GOOD DEAL has been written about Japan's new Constitution and how it was produced. Though I knew some of the Japanese, as well as some of the Americans, who were reported to have worked on it, I have no inside information as to what parts of it were the product of Japanese thought and what parts were shaped by American pressure. It was promulgated with a ceremony on the third of November, 1946, and went into operation with the new Diet the following spring. To me the most interesting features of it were the fact that sovereignty was explicitly placed in the Japanese people, that war was renounced as an instrument of national policy, and that the Bill of Rights provided liberties and safeguards which the Japanese people had never had before.

The criticism of the Constitution of the Weimar Republic was that it was too perfect a constitution, too advanced for the German people, who were not yet ready for the freedom and responsibility that it offered. It may be that the same criticism will be applied to the new Japanese Constitution. I have no doubt that in future times it will be amended and many of the laws implementing it will be repealed or allowed to fall into disuse, but I think that there will be some residue which will be irreducible and out of which new and more solid and characteristic structures will rise.

The Bill of Rights was the occasion for my bringing the Constitution before the Crown Prince. In the winter term of 1950 the two boys who shared the Prince's lessons at my house were mature and capable, and I took for the center of our study the United Nations Universal Declaration of Human Rights. The boys read it in both English and Japanese and we discussed it in English.

We talked about the different rights and what they meant to individuals. The discussions were necessarily very simple. In the course of them I thought it would be interesting for them to compare the provisions in their own Constitution with those of the Universal Declaration, and so we had copies of the Japanese Constitution in English and Japanese. Though they had had some instruction on it in their social studies course at school, only one of them and that one not the Prince had encountered the text itself.

The Crown Prince commented that it was written in "queer Japanese." I was interested, because I had often heard it said by critics of the Occupation that the Constitution sounded "translated" and that the Japanese would therefore never really accept it as their own. I asked the Prince whether he thought it sounded translated and he replied that he did not. Why then did he think the language "queer"? He answered readily that it was a mixture of written and spoken Japanese. He and the two other boys had a short discussion of the question in Japanese and then they confirmed his point to me in English.

One reason why Japanese is such a difficult language to learn is that there are so many varieties of it. Formal written Japanese is so different from ordinary spoken Japanese that it is well-nigh unintelligible to many who have stopped with the six years of elementary education which were formerly all that was required.

I asked the Prince if he thought it would be a good thing to have the Constitution all written in spoken Japanese, so that everybody could understand it. He answered decidedly, "No, written is better." Why? Because, he said, the written language is more beautiful and the Constitution should be in beautiful language. The Meiji Constitution, he said, was all in written Japanese; it had beauty and people respected it.

He spoke, I felt, not for himself alone but for the majority of the Japanese people, who are an aesthetic race and to whom beauty has a value and dignity of its own. This universal love of beauty is one of the purest qualities of the Japanese character and represents a gift which the Japanese people have to make to that other part of the world which is so taken up with utility and equality that it tends to overlook the claims of beauty. We tend also to misunderstand the part that is played by this love of beauty in Japanese thinking and to underestimate its power. One reason for our misunderstanding must be laid at the door of the Japanese themselves. Their taste is faultless in Japanese matters but errs when they enter the western world. Most Japanese western rooms are stuffy, stiff, and clumsy; much of the china, silk and bric-a-brac manufactured in Japan for export, to suit what they believe to be western taste, is cheap and ugly.

At tea-time downstairs in the living-room after the lessons the conversation would be general and sometimes very interesting. I always liked to hear the Crown Prince on the subject of the Japanese language, for his ideas were definite and his own. He had what seemed to me a remarkable knowledge of the history and meaning of the Japanese ideographs, as well as an appreciation of them, and would go to considerable trouble to explain to me in English differences in history and significance of the varieties of *kana*, the simplified syllabary.

One of the burning questions among the Occupation was the simplification of the Japanese writing, which is almost incredibly complicated. It is even more complicated than Chinese, from which it is derived, partly because of the addition of two different sets of simplified characters representing some fifty-three basic syllables, called *kana*, which they sprinkle in among the Chinese ideographs, called *kanji*. The system served well enough during the leisured years when only a small part of the population needed to read and write, and everything was done by hand slowly and carefully, but in a modern industrial civilization it adds immeasurably to life's difficulties. Typewriters are few and almost as complicated to use as it would be to set type by hand. Most business letters are still written by hand and most documents copied by hand. Writers send handwritten manuscripts to their publishers and usually there is but one precious copy.

Extremists among the Occupation wanted to sweep away *kanji* and *kana* alike by directive and require the Japanese from then on to use *romaji*, the Roman alphabet, for everything. They had very good reasons, but there were still better ones for not doing it. Instead, a simplification of *kanji* was urged on the Japanese, a limitation of the number to be used in newspapers and taught in the schools, and changes in the *kana* toward a more consistent and logical use of the symbols.

The subject of *romaji* versus ideographs was always good for a discussion, frequently a heated one. Most people had very decided views which they defended with spirit. Tané, whose education in the United States had given her a western viewpoint about many things, was dead against the general use of *romaji*. She contended that it would change the character of the language, that Roman letters did not correctly represent Japanese sounds, and that the Japanese ideographs with their history, associations, and the overtones of meaning clustering about them were essential to the understanding of anything that was written.

I expected the Crown Prince, with his usually conservative outlook and his regard for the beauty of his language, to hold similar views, but he surprised me by declaring that it would be much better to use *romaji* entirely than a restricted list of *kanji* and *kana*, which he felt was a compromise without the advantages of either system. He deplored the loss of the beauty of *kanji* but said that *romaji* had practical advantages.

In the English lessons at school that term, I was teaching my class western etiquette: introductions, the attentions that women expected, letter-writing, and so forth. At one point I divided the class into groups of three and set them a problem which they were to work out in the form of a dialogue. Ichiro Saito, sixteen, and his sister Kazuko, fifteen, meet John Jones on the Mejiro Street. John is a friend of Ichiro's but has never met Kazuko. What happens?

The resulting brief dramas, acted out with zest in the front of the classroom, were most amusing. When the Crown Prince's turn came he took the part of Kazuko, and surely never was a Japanese younger sister treated with more courteous deference as Ichiro introduced John to her, they all three engaged in suitable light conversation and then decided to go to a concert together, both Ichiro and John assisting Kazuko into the streetcar and establishing her in the only available seat.

As part of the private lessons alone with me the Prince memorized the Gettysburg Address. He could recite it all, at one point, and I entertained hopes that some day at a diplomatic dinner he would be able to dazzle the American Ambassador by an apt quotation from Lincoln, but the rapidity with which he forgot it quashed that hope, though perhaps some tags will remain and something of its fundamental thought may become part of the climate of his mind.

Now that the Prince was not at Koganei these lessons were held for two or three weeks in a room on the third floor of the Imperial Household Building which had been Marquis Kido's study in the years when he was Lord Keeper of the Privy Seal. It was a corner room, handsomely furnished, with books lining the wall at one end, many of them books in English on history and government and scientific subjects. I never felt quite easy there. I felt that the owner, in Sugamo Prison under life sentence as a "war criminal," might well resent my presence.

After his house was burned the Prince spent four days a week in the dormitory and three in Prince Masahito's house. But this arrangement did not last long. I soon heard that a house was being sought for Prince Akihito in Tokyo outside the Moat, in which he would live with his chamberlains as he had lived at Koganei, dividing his week between that house and the dormitory.

The place decided on was the Tokiwamatsu villa, then being used as the Imperial Household Club. It was a large and attractive house with a garden on the edge of a bluff in the section of Tokyo called Shibuya, about a fifteen-minute drive from the Gakushuin campus and not more than ten minutes from the Palace. It had been built for a prince in 1925, but it was in no sense a palace, just a large city house with a wall around it.

Downstairs it was all western style; upstairs it was part western, with a Japanese wing, where the bedrooms had *tatami* on the floor, the sliding doors were beautifully decorated by Japanese artists, and the southern sunshine streamed in on a little gallery. Below was the garden with lawn, trees, rocks, and a pond, and a tennis court at one end behind shrubbery. The Crown Prince would sleep in one of the Japanese bedrooms, but his study, also on the second floor, was western and so was the room next to it, designated for his private lessons.

Furniture was brought from the imperial storehouses. There was no central heating. Small gas heaters were lit in the western rooms, usually just at the moment when they were to be used; *hibachi* served the Japanese rooms. It was cold in winter but not nearly so cold as the Koganei house.

I saw it first on the second of February; by the twentieth

the Prince had moved in, and we had our lesson in the room set aside for that purpose. There was a blackboard, a square table in the center with straight chairs, a piano, and a cabinet with ornaments. The windows looked out over the garden and the roofs of the city that stretched out below. It was the first time the Crown Prince had lived where he could see the dwellings of ordinary people, and I wondered if he took any interest in the life he saw there.

When I urged that Prince Masahito come to share this house with the Crown Prince I met with some encouragement. At some indefinite future time it might be possible!

The Crown Prince's affairs were managed by the board of his chamberlains, called Togushoku, the Board of the Eastern Prince, with guidance from the Advisory Council. Prince Masahito's, on the other hand, were handled by Jijushoku, the Board of Their Majesties' Chamberlains, who had many other concerns besides. There were now hopes that the two princes might at least be cared for together by Togushoku, with Dr. Koizumi taking responsibility for the younger prince's education as well. This was highly desirable on every count, and probably also a necessary preliminary to the moving of the two brothers into one house.

That the Crown Prince liked his new house was evident from the first. He told one of his classmates that he liked it best of all the houses he had lived in, including the Akasaka Palace. He liked it, he said, because it was an ordinary house, not a palace, and because it was "old."

Among his private lessons now he included French, which was taught him by Dr. Yoichi Maeda, who had grown up in Geneva when his father, Tamon Maeda, had been with the League of Nations. The French lessons during the winter were a compromise characteristic of the Crown Prince. When the new term began in the spring, his class would have three choices: to concentrate on English, to begin the study of German, or to take up French. It had been the tradition at the Gakushuin that the least capable students did not venture on a second foreign language, and the most capable took German. The Crown Prince naturally wanted to line up with his friends, most of whom were electing German. Those about him, including Mr. Nomura, formerly a professor of German, believed that French would be more useful to him, but they also felt that it would be good for him to make his own decision. The question was put up to him and he decided to try out French with a few private lessons during the winter: then if he liked it he would continue it in the new term; if not, he would switch to German.

That put a challenge to Dr. Maeda, which he met with ease. He was a charming and intelligent young man and a respected professor at Tokyo University. When the time came the Prince elected French in school and also continued the private lessons with Dr. Maeda.

Dr. Maeda and I had worked together on the committee which planned the International Student Seminars sponsored by the American Friends Service Committee in the summers of 1949 and 1950 at Tsuda College. From both of us, at one time and another, the Prince heard a good deal about the seminars.

In 1949 Mr. and Mrs. Thomas A. Foulke had been sent to Japan by the A.F.S.C. to open a neighborhood center in a housing project where the repatriates and bombed-out people living in tiny shacks might find a warm and friendly center, with sewing machines, a library, a kindergarten, classes and discussion groups of all kinds, and a welcome for people of every religion. While they were working on this they also served as host and hostess for the International Student Seminar. About seventy students gathered at Tsuda College for two weeks in August; half of them were Japanese; the other half was made up of Americans, English, Canadians, Chinese, Koreans, Indonesians, Formosans, Indians, Dutch, Turkish, and Siamese. With the aid of lecturers of various nationalities they studied the Foundations of Peace, and through work and play together acquired an understanding of one another's national viewpoints and problems and laid a few foundations themselves.

Since Thomas Foulke was a busy lawyer, who had put aside his work at the behest of the A.F.S.C. to serve without salary, as is the Quaker way, he could not stay more than a year, to the grief of their many Japanese friends, who had found in their devoted and warm-hearted service a source of strength and hope. The Foulkes went home early in 1950. The second summer their place at the seminar was taken by another attractive and vital Quaker pair, Mr. and Mrs. Henry Perry, who were making a visit of six months to Japanese Friends. The work at the neighborhood center was carried on by a lively young couple, Mr. and Mrs. Neil Hartman.

In the winter of 1950, while the Crown Prince was making his first acquaintance with French and hearing about the first of the international seminars, the two-year service of Edmund Blunden in Japan had run past its limit and he and his wife were preparing to return to England. Because Mr. Blunden had lectured on *Hamlet* to the Crown Prince and the other boys in the dormitory and because of his generous efforts for the Japanese people, it was decided that the Crown Prince should give a farewell dinner party to the Blundens in his new house.

The Crown Prince's first dinner party in his own house! The first time that he was host in the adult international world! It was a great occasion and called for much preparation and thought beforehand. Akiyama San, the Emperor's chef, was to be responsible for the dinner. The Department of Ceremonies gave advice about all the arrangements, and more skilful people socially can scarcely be found than the gentlemen in that department. I had been asked also to help, but my sole contribution was in talking the party over beforehand with the Crown Prince. I reminded him that royalty was expected to initiate the topics of conversation and that, furthermore, Mrs. Blunden, who would be sitting on his right at dinner, was shy and he must make her feel comfortable. I asked him what subjects he thought she might be interested in, and he suggested several.

The seventeenth of March was the day. The invitations had read:

Grand Master of the Crown Prince's Board
requests the honor of the company of

———————————————————

at His Imperial Highness's Dinner
at Tokiwamatsu Villa
on Friday, March 17, 1950, at 6:00 P.M.

At six, then, we were all gathered in the drawing-room at Tokiwamatsu: Mr. and Mrs. Blunden, Dr. and Mrs. Koizumi, Mrs. Matsudaira, Mr. and Mrs. Goto of the Department of Ceremonies, Mr. and Mrs. Blyth, Mr. Nomura, two chamberlains and I. The drawing-room had been brightened up with gold screens and flowers, and there was a great air of gaiety and expectancy about it.

[273]

Mr. Blunden was a slender man of fifty-odd, with a large and pointed nose, bright, darting, blue eyes, thick light hair rather long in the back. He had a quiet, unassuming, humorous way of speaking, questioning, understating, qualifying, yet revealing knowledge of his subject and confidence in his own opinions. The whole effect was very disarming and persuasive. On an earlier occasion, when Mr. and Mrs. Tajima had entertained for the Blundens, Mr. Blunden had said of the first World War, "The English people had a very simple idea about it all. Here were our old friends the Germans, whom we'd always liked. Now they'd shown their true colors and they were very wicked people. I can't say I could agree, but that was the way most people felt. And the Germans *were* a bit abrupt, weren't they? Going through Belgium that way. It was a bad mistake."

Mrs. Blunden, considerably younger than her husband, had fair hair, clear, serene blue eyes, a little straight nose, and the rose-petal skin that we think of as characteristic of English beauty. At mixed Japanese and English parties she was rather like a Japanese wife in her gentleness and stillness; though she was a graduate of St. Hilda's College, Oxford, and though she was the mother of three enchanting babies, she neither volunteered opinions on intellectual subjects nor talked about her children, but followed the general conversation with quiet interest.

The drawing-room at Tokiwamatsu is divided into two sections, the smaller of which, being part of a square tower, is set off a little with windows on three sides. Here the ladies of the party congregated with their cups of Japanese tea, while the gentlemen smoked in the larger part.

When everybody had assembled, the Crown Prince came in and greeted his guests with considerable aplomb.

The dining-room was a long room with French windows on the terrace, over which the curtains were now drawn. The long table was beautifully set, and each chair bore the imperial chrysanthemum in gold on its back. Fourteen sat down, the Crown Prince taking his place at the center of the table with Mrs. Blunden on his right and me on his left. Mrs. Matsudaira sat opposite him with Mr. Blunden on her right and Dr. Koizumi on her left. The Prince was well fortified if he needed help—but he did not.

[274]

He talked as much as anyone would wish a sixteen-year-old to talk. With shy poise and an open friendliness he drew Mrs. Blunden out and gave answers to her questions or responded to contributions from across the table with comments that went well beyond the "Yes" and "No" that he sometimes stuck at. The talk, which was general and all in English, was of poetry, travel, and the national cooking of different countries.

After dinner when we were back in the drawing-room, the groups divided again, this time with the Crown Prince beside Mr. Blunden on the sofa in the tower part and Mrs. Blunden among the ladies in the other half of the room. A *shikishi* was brought and Mr. Blunden was asked to write on it. A *shikishi* is a square of fine cardboard, usually tinted in some color and spattered with gold, on which the Japanese write poems in their best calligraphy with brush and India ink. Parties often end with the guest of honor being asked to write something on a *shikishi* as a memento of the occasion.

Mr. Blunden, after commenting on the way a *shikishi* facing one immediately drives all poems from one's mind, wrote in his distinguished hand—with a fountain pen—Robert Bridges' "I love all beauteous things," which had a private interest for me because that was one of the poems I had taught my English Club and the one which most frequently came to my own mind when a *shikishi* in all its pristine blankness appeared before me.

When the poem was written and passed around for everyone to see, the Crown Prince presented some flowers to Mrs. Blunden, said good-night to everyone, and withdrew. The rest of us stayed on a little longer to talk, and then departed, with the usual bustle of cars drawing up to the door under the porte-cochere, servants running, and chamberlains bowing on the doorstep.

The next evening a postal came to me by special delivery from Dr. Koizumi. It said: "Wasn't he splendid! How he spoke English well and charmingly! I concede that your impartiality is more than fully grounded. With congratulations and thanks."

My championship of the Prince had been a recurrent small joke. Now Dr. Koizumi was also an "impartial."

CHAPTER THIRTY-FOUR

PRINCESS KAZUKO WAS now twenty. During the previous summer, she had flowered suddenly into beauty, as girls will. With her wide, softly shining eyes, her fair skin, and the smile which reflected her loving, inarticulate heart and her deep longing for goodness and simplicity, she had the innocent mystery of a tightly furled rosebud. The women's magazines had been busy all autumn with rumors of her engagement to a cousin, but she had caused them to be denied. Her marriage, like the great majority of Japanese marriages, would be arranged, but she would have the right of veto.

One cold January evening about six, Mr. Tajima arrived at my house and told Tané that he would like to speak to me alone. After she had left the room he drew his chair up close and said, "I have come by the express will of the Emperor to tell you about the marriage of Princess Kazuko. His Majesty ordered me *himself* to tell you.

"She is engaged," went on Mr. Tajima, "to the son of ex-Prince Takatsukasa."

I had not met Toshimichi Takatsukasa, but I knew his parents and two of his five sisters. His mother was a direct descendant of the last of the Shoguns, and his father, a gentle, thoughtful man with white hair and a shining look, was chief priest of the Meiji Shrine and one of Japan's foremost ornithologists. My copy of his *Birds of Japan*, in English, was worn from constant use. Their only son, Toshimichi, had had all of his life a passion for railways. He was still a small boy when the subway in Tokyo was opened, and he got up long before dawn, crossed the city by himself, and waited in line to get the first ticket issued and have the first ride. His knowledge of railways and his interest in model trains had led to his present work in the Railway Museum, where he displayed and explained the models, which he himself had helped to collect, to the thousands of schoolchildren who visited the museum. He was interested in music, too, and had done some composing. Altogether he was a very out-going, happy-hearted person with a host of friends.

Two days later the public announcement was made and the newspapers had a field day. American headlines screamed, "Emperor's Daughter to Wed $20-a-month Clerk," and featured a photograph of the princess wielding a broom. It was true that Mr. Takatsukasa's salary at the Railway Museum was the basic salary for government workers, at that time about seven thousand yen, but the young couple would not live on twenty dollars a month, nor would the princess confine her activities to sweeping.

When I went to call on Princess Kazuko and take her some flowers, I found her very smiling and happy. Princess Shigeko, her elder sister, now Mrs. Higashikuni, was there that day, and little Princess Takako, enchanting in a red and white kimono, was flying about very much thrilled over this romantic development.

The wedding day was set for May, and in the intervening four months there was much to be done. A house must be found, a trousseau provided, and wholly new arrangements made for the ceremonies themselves, since for the first time in history, an imperial princess was marrying a "commoner." Most important of all, the engaged couple must become acquainted with each other.

They had barely met when the engagement was announced. The Emperor and Empress had never met their future son-in-law, though his father was a cousin of the Empress Dowager. The arrangements had been made by Mr. Tajima and Mr. Mitani.

Now began a series of formal and informal meetings. Toshi-michi Takatsukasa and his parents went to Hayama and were presented to Their Majesties, and Princess Kazuko of course was there. On the third of March, the day of the Doll Festival, formal betrothal gifts were exchanged. At ten in the morning Princess Kazuko was with her parents. Mr. Takatsukasa's brother-in-law, acting as his representative, came to the Palace and delivered to Mr. Tajima a fish made of red silk, a *tai,* which is the emblem of congratulation, and a bottle of fine *saké*. Mr. Tajima took these gifts on a tray and presented them to Their Majesties and Princess Kazuko. Some messages were exchanged, and Mr. Tajima returned immediately to the representative and reported. At eleven Mr. Tajima, as the Emperor's representative, went to the Takatsukasas' house and presented gifts from the Emperor and Empress. In the afternoon Mr. Takatsukasa and his parents went to the Palace to pay their respects to Their Majesties and Princess Kazuko. That evening both families celebrated the engagement with a party—separately, the Imperial Family at Obunko, the Takatsukasas in the caretaker's small house on the grounds of the Meiji Shrine which has been their home since their own beautiful house was burned during the air raids.

The formal meetings were more easily arranged than the informal ones. Whenever Princess Kazuko stirred outside of the protecting Moat the news photographers were lying in wait and the glare of publicity attended her wherever she went. One evening in March, though, she slipped out in the car with Miss Natori and went to the Takatsukasas' house. All of the sisters were there, and she spent an hour in that lively and affectionate household before she and Toshimichi San and Miss Natori came on to our house for dinner.

She was aglow with happiness when she arrived, and it was evident as the evening went on that even though the engagement had been arranged in what was to western minds a dry and formal manner, youth will have its romance and the two had fallen promptly in love. They were a charming couple, the pretty girl in her bright coral kimono decorated with flowers and birds and the gentle and smiling young man, not handsome, with his rather long jaw and round spectacles, but pleasant-looking, with an air of good sense and kindness.

Princess Kazuko heard every word he said with wonder and respect and radiated joy when he spoke directly to her. When they left, Mr. Takatsukasa stood back to let Princess Kazuko precede him into the car, but she, already showing a good Japanese wifely spirit, waved him on, and he got in first.

After that evening they met several times at our house. The newspaper people knew that Princess Kazuko came regularly on alternate Tuesdays for an English lesson and they paid no attention to that. When the lesson was over, a little after five, Mr. Takatsukasa would come walking up the driveway to join us at tea.

On the afternoons that her elder sisters had their lesson, Princess Takako was now having an extra lesson with Tané, and long before five she would begin to watch for Toshimichi San. The new big brother was already adored by the younger sisters and the tea hour took on a new gaiety.

When Princess Shigeko had been married, even though it was wartime she had had a full imperial trousseau. At the Okura porcelain works one day I was shown samples of the china that had been made for her, decorated in a rich blue and gold, four dozen of everything. Princess Kazuko declared that she wished to keep her trousseau simple, that she would not need many things in the kind of life that she was entering and would rather have the money spent for records and radio and other things which she and her husband could enjoy together. The Emperor, hearing of her decision, was pleased, saying, "That is the right spirit."

Simple though her trousseau was, she was generous with it. When a fire in the Palace grounds destroyed the house in which some of the ladies-in-waiting lived and with it all their clothes, she gave to each one some articles out of her own supply.

The wedding dress itself would be borrowed from her elder sister. It would be the costume made in the thousand-year-old style of the Heian period which the Empress Dowager had given to Princess Shigeko for her wedding six years earlier.

It was decided that the young couple were to start their married life in one of the houses in the compound where several court officials lived. It was a modest house in the western style, with one Japanese room and a rather overgrown garden, but it was well situated, not far from the Palace.

Early in May the pre-wedding formalities began. Although the date had been set for some time and talked about by everyone, on May third a messenger from Mr. Takatsukasa went to the Palace and informed Mr. Tajima that Mr. Takatsukasa would like to marry Princess Kazuko on May twentieth. Mr. Tajima then went to Obunko, where Princess Kazuko was waiting with the Emperor and Empress and reported to them this desire of Mr. Takatsukasa. After the formal setting of the date there followed a series of parties not given *for* the prospective bride, as they would be in this country, but given *by* her, her farewell as an imperial princess.

She gave a party in the Imperial Household Building for all her former teachers and classmates of the Joshi Gakushuin. Almost all of the girls came in their prettiest kimonos, and as two o'clock approached, the scene outside the Palace looked like an old print, with the bevies of bright butterflies against the great gray walls of the Palace reflected in the blue waters of the Moat.

She gave parties for all the ex-princesses and princes, for her own family, the Dowager Empress and the imperial uncles and aunts, for the chamberlains and doctors, for the teachers who came to give her lessons at Kuretakeryo.

Because she had come to my house for lessons, there was a special party for my sister, Tané, and me, even though I had been included in the Joshi Gakushuin party. This was held at Kaintei, and to it came the Empress, the Crown Prince, and Prince Masahito, as well as the two younger sisters. The Crown Prince was in very good form that day and took most of the burden of the conversation, both in Japanese and English. I noticed that when we all sat down, he waved Princess Kazuko into the place of honor on his mother's left, which was rightfully his, saying with a smile, in English, "Today is your day." It was the gesture of a young man, not a boy, I thought; how he was growing up! His mother's eyes followed him, as if she too were seeing him in a new light; her love and pride shone out.

After tea Princess Kazuko was persuaded to play on the piano a composition by Mr. Takatsukasa called "Spring," while her two sisters sang the words. Princess Atsuko was almost inaudible, but Princess Takako, after smothering some giggles, produced a sweet, clear little pipe. Mr. Takatsukasa, it seemed, had composed some sixty pieces. One composition, when he was still in school, had won a contest and was taught to children all over Japan. Princess Kazuko, then in sixth grade, learned it dutifully, with no idea that she would some day meet and marry the composer.

The only party that was given for her, so far as I know, was the farewell concert in which the Imperial Household musicians

[280]

chose the numbers especially for her, Overture to the *Marriage of Figaro*, Mendelssohn's "Wedding March," and Strauss's "Southern Roses."

Besides the parties, she had duties to her ancestors. One rainy day she went to the Emperor Taisho's tomb at Tama, about fifty miles from Tokyo, and paid her last respects as an imperial princess to her grandfather. One day, in the week before the wedding, she dressed in the court costume of the eleventh century, with the long trousers that trail behind like trains, and went to the Kashikodokoro, the shrine in the Imperial Palace grounds, to do honor to more remote ancestors. Only a handful of court officials were present. It was a very solemn ceremony, Mrs. Takaki told me afterwards, and very quiet; there was just the sound of approaching feet on the pebbles of the path, and the wind in the trees.

In former days the wedding ceremony itself would have been held in the Kashikodokoro, but that was not possible now because Princess Kazuko was marrying a "commoner." That Toshimichi Takatsukasa was a former prince and that, with the erasure of the peerage, the only people in Japan who were not commoners were the Emperor and his immediate family, made no difference. The wedding ceremony was to be held at the mansion which formerly belonged to Prince Takamatsu and was now available for various kinds of functions. On the other hand, under the new order of things, the Emperor and Empress and Empress Dowager were now free to attend the ceremony outside of the Palace, as they could not have done before. They could not, however, go to the reception which was to be given the following day by the groom's family.

Only twenty-five people were to be present at the actual ceremony, nine for the bride and sixteen for the groom, but hosts of others assembled at the Palace to see Princess Kazuko start off to her wedding. As we drew near the great gate we saw the lines of people approaching, a group of Joshi Gakushuin girls in their school uniforms, gentlemen in morning clothes, ladies in kimonos, a troop of marching policemen. Around the door of the Imperial Household Building people gathered to sign in the book. In our waiting-room we could hear the constant sound of scurrying feet in the corridor. Everyone was given a place to

[281]

stand, in the driveway along the path of the imperial cars or inside the Imperial Household Building.

Soon Mrs. Takaki came for us and led us at a run upstairs and along the long corridor to the door which Their Majesties used and from which Princess Kazuko was to leave. At the end of the hall, against a screen directly to the left of the door, we took our stand. At the door the dark red Packard with the gold chrysanthemum was waiting. Part way down the hall, in a sort of niche, the Crown Prince's chamberlains stood. While we waited, three ladies-in-waiting in long, 1890 dresses of blue, green, and wine, came around the screen behind us, walked the length of the hall, carefully hugging the wall like little creatures shy of the light, and disappeared behind the screen at the other end.

Next, from the other end of the corridor a whole troop of court officials in striped trousers came walking toward us, led by the Vice-Grand Steward and lined up on the steps beside the car. The Grand Steward and the Grand Chamberlain came around the screen at the far end and took their positions directly in front of it. Now everything was ready. There was a breathless silence, broken only by the sound of the rain dripping on the stones of the little courtyard outside the door.

At the far end of the corridor, the Honorable Leader of the Way, the *Go-Sendo* appeared, Mr. Takatsukasa's emissary, and walked slowly and with immense dignity down the corridor toward the door. After him came Princess Kazuko, beautiful in her ancient costume of claret-colored *hakama* and many-layered robe of rose and green, her hair arranged in two wide wings framing her face. She looked serenely happy and she moved with a lovely girlish dignity, as formal as a picture on a scroll and yet herself. She bowed very slightly to the people; she passed and gave me a little smile. Miss Natori, in lavender-gray court kimono, walked behind and after a little space came the Crown Prince and Prince Masahito, in school uniform, and the two younger sisters in scarlet kimonos with brown *hakamas*.

The bride got into the car, her robes were carefully tucked in, Miss Natori took the jump seat facing her, everybody bowed, and the car moved off. The younger brothers and sisters turned away; they had had all of their sister's wedding that they were going to get.

[282]

We were invited with some others to drink the bride's health in *saké* and eat the congratulatory rice with red beans and dried squids prepared in some special way, and then we saw the Emperor and Empress leave in their car for the wedding.

After the ceremony, which lasted half an hour, Mr. Tajima removed Princess Kazuko's name from the Imperial Family register. Later Mr. Takatsukasa would go to the Shinjuku Ward Office to add his wife's name to the register of his family.

The reception was held next day at the Meiji Memorial Hall, the favorite place for fashionable weddings. The day was fresh and sparkling after the rain. I went alone and was glad to join Miss Natori and Mrs. Hoshina at the door and go in with them. In a big room with paintings on the walls, the Takatsukasas were receiving some three hundred guests, including about fifteen westerners. The bride's aunts and uncles were there, and her elder sister and brother-in-law, but not her parents or her younger brothers and sisters. She wore a light green kimono decorated with peonies and pheasants, every blossom and bird with its own especial symbolism, and sometime during the crowded hours since the ceremony of the day before she had found time to have the camellia oil washed out of her hair and have it curled and arranged in western style.

Tea was served at tables in the adjoining room, where the guests sat down in relays, since to the Japanese mind our western way of walking about with food in our hands and gabbling furiously is both uncomfortable and absurd. After tea people drifted out onto the lawn in the sunshine.

Most well-placed Japanese couples have a honeymoon, but in this case it was decided to postpone the wedding trip until the fever of publicity had somewhat died down. They had, moreover, many duties to crowd into their first few days of married life: formal calls on all the many relatives on both sides, as well as a trip to the Tama Mausoleum to pay their respects as a new family to the tomb of the Emperor Taisho.

At every point their footsteps were dogged by the zealous representatives of newspapers, magazines, and radio, who followed them everywhere with their cameras and microphones and their questions. What were Mr. Takatsukasa's "impressions" of the wedding? What were Mrs. Takatsukasa's hopes for the future? The latter question was put with no warning, no chance

[283]

for preparation, but the answer, when it came, could not have been bettered. Princess Kazuko thought for several moments before she replied in a low voice into the waiting microphone, "I hope to build a simple yet solid family."

CHAPTER THIRTY-FIVE

WE FIRST READ about the Korean War in the morning paper on Monday, June 26, 1950.

The headlines, when I saw them, gave me the same sick feeling of disaster as those other headlines down the ominous years: Japan's attack on Manchuria, Hitler's march into the Rhineland, Mussolini's war on Ethiopia, the terms of the Munich settlement. I wondered at once if this was the spark that would set off a third world war.

My schedule went on as usual, and between lessons I watched anxiously for news. There were no special broadcasts, no commentators, just the regular brief Army news reports. We heard that the U.N. Security Council met and ordered North Korea to cease fire and roll back the invasion army, which had crossed all along the thirty-eighth parallel and taken several towns. The 1,700 Americans in Korea were to be evacuated. Supplies and munitions were to be sent to the South Koreans, with planes to guard them.

I saw Dr. Koizumi for a few minutes after the Crown Prince's lesson. He gave it as his opinion that Russia did not want war then; we talked about the possibility of localizing the struggle. On the way home I went into the center of Tokyo to do some errands and passed the Dai-Ichi Building at the time when General MacArthur was expected to come out. After nearly five years a crowd still gathered to see this daily spectacle; today the crowd was much larger than usual. As this was one of Tokyo's sights that I had never seen, I stopped to watch.

The big Cadillac with the circle of five stars on the license plate was waiting at the curb with the door open. Japanese policemen stood on the steps of the building and eyed the crowd. There were perhaps a hundred or so on each side of the path the General would take, two thirds Japanese and one third American, including two colonels and several other officers.

A two-star general of the Air Force came out first, very lean and rather fine-drawn. The American guards flanking the door gave him brisk salutes and he vanished quickly. Now two guards marched down the steps and stood beside the Cadillac. General MacArthur and Colonel Bunker, talking together, came slowly down the steps, crossed the sidewalk, and got into the car. The General looked quite fatherly and smiling, Colonel Bunker was pale, as if he had missed a night's sleep. The guards stood at attention and the car moved off. The crowd melted away.

It was very quickly over and all quite matter-of-fact and ordinary: two rather tired and preoccupied men going home late to their lunch, while a lot of people looked at them, yet I thought that the unusually large number that had gathered that day when there was so much tension and anxiety showed a need of some kind of reassurance and that they had got it from the air of confidence which the General exuded even in that brief moment.

The next day Seoul was reported as "entered" before I went to the Palace for the Empress's lesson, "holding" when Prince Mikasa came to my house for his lesson, and after the party which I gave for Princess Takako, "fallen."

The Emperor's youngest brother, Prince Mikasa, had been coming to my house for a weekly English lesson during this spring. He was a student of history at the University of Tokyo, and he came very informally, driving himself in his tiny Japanese car or sometimes walking from the railway station. He had the Empress Dowager's bird-like profile and something of her personality. His mind was very open and keen and I was always much interested in his frank and uninhibited comments on affairs. He did not, however, commit himself on the subject of Korea.

This afternoon I had invited three eleven-year-olds to come and play with Princess Takako. They were Jill O'Brien, her running mate Sarah Edna Dees, and Sharon Vaughan, who lived next door to me. For nearly a year I had had really friendly neighbors in the family of Air Force Colonel Lloyd S. Vaughan, his warm-hearted, motherly wife, and their two daughters, of whom Sharon was the younger.

[286]

On Wednesday we heard that President Truman had ordered air and sea forces sent to the assistance of South Korea but that no ground forces were to go. American evacuees from Korea were reaching Japan with only those possessions which they could snatch up in an hour before leaving. They were crowded into American billets and clothes were collected for them.

General MacArthur flew to Korea and back. He ordered the bombing of North Korean airfields. President Truman announced that the United States was not at war; it was carrying out police action for the United Nations. Now ground troops were to go in.

The Japanese whom I knew were very calm about the situation, even to the point of seeming indifferent. The boys at school talked very little about it; the Crown Prince and two other boys when they came to my house would make no comment at all. Mr. Shimizu told me that few adult Japanese were saying much. Disarmed and occupied, they were helpless; they waited impassively to see what was going to happen. The old nightmare terror of Russian domination of the Korean peninsula was awakened by the new fear that the United States might walk off and leave Japan at Russia's mercy. When the United States began to send troops into Korea, the relief among the Japanese was evident.

Events moved swiftly those first days. The American enlisted men whom we had seen drifting about the Ginza disappeared overnight. The PX one day was full of naval fliers, most of them incredibly young-looking and very sober, who disappeared in their turn. Planes were overhead constantly and Army people began to say that this was the strangest war they had ever known, fought by commuters who left in the morning, fought all day, and came home for dinner at night. Well-known correspondents began to pour into Tokyo. One was captured in Korea. "Fluid" was the current euphemism for describing the military situation. It was reported in the *Nippon Times* that two hundred thousand Chinese Communists were massing on the North Korean border, that eighty Russian submarines had gathered in eastern ports. A transport full of "dependents" who had started before the war began arrived in Yokohama; the young wives were met by members of the Special Services Division bearing neat little boxes of flowers and the news that their husbands were in Korea. All ship sailings were held up for the next few weeks, but some people were beginning to pack up. Promises of help from other U.N. countries were reported every day, but a "long and bloody struggle in Korea" was prophesied.

Occupationaires were determinedly calm; they repeated one another's opinions and watched to see the effect. An economic expert was certain that the war could be localized. A distinguished German refugee in the Legal Section was quietly pessimistic, seeing a general conflagration in a matter of months and the end of civilization soon thereafter. Though the occupying troops had all been sent to Korea and the civilians were left in an occupied country without protection, no one entertained any fears that the conquered Japanese might rise up and take revenge. There was complete confidence in the friendliness of the Japanese people.

On the fourteenth of July we went downtown to get our mail, and when we passed the Dai-Ichi Building we saw on its roof, flying in the sunshine beside the Stars and Stripes, the clear blue and white flag of the United Nations, which had been put there in a brief ceremony only a few minutes before. I shall never forget the lift that that sight gave to my heavy heart. For a time at any rate I envisioned a United Nations, effective and determined to keep peace, and in it I saw the only hope that there is for the world.

The next day we left for Karuizawa.

The narcissus flycatchers were like jewels in the fir trees. The cuckoos called in the early mornings when long fingers of light came through the balsams; the bush-warblers sang their "crossing-the-valley-song" at noon. The trees about the house had been thinned out so that now on very clear days we could see snowtipped mountains in a serried line on the blue horizon. Looking down we could see the road below, where a woman in a kimono led a white goat by a string, a jeep roared by in a cloud of dust, or an old man passed with a load of brushwood on his back.

The Crown Prince had liked Karuizawa so much the summer before that this year they took a house for him on a hill about four miles away for the whole month of August. The villa, which had formerly belonged to a prince, had been made into a rest hotel under Japanese management for the Occupationaires. It was small for a hotel, and all of its eight rooms were taken for the Crown Prince and his entourage. It was beautifully situated at the end of a curving driveway, which was easy to guard, with glorious views of Asama towering eight thousand feet in the air and the lower and nearer Hanareyama, which, according to the legend, was the bowl out of which the devil who lived in Asama used to eat his fermented bean soup.

Now began for the Prince the kind of summer experience which I had wished for him ever since I had been there and which I had feared was impossible. Two chamberlains and a doctor were with him, but there was none of the formality and rigidity that seemed to cling inevitably about the imperial villas. Part of the time he had two of his friends visiting him, Akira Hashimoto and Tadahiko Senge, both of whom were keen on riding. Horses were hired for all three boys—the Crown Prince's was a white one belonging to a farmer who had bought him from the Army at the end of the war—and they rode every day. Instead of the beautiful but formal exercises of the *haute école* riding in the riding hall, the Prince had good gallops along the back roads. Other classmates were staying at their families' summer cottages round about, and the Prince dropped in to see them casually whenever he felt like it, sitting on the *tatami* with them, reading or talking or playing cards. He played tennis on the public court in Kutsukake and for a time his tennis coach, Mr. Imai, a boyish and attractive man with whom he was on very friendly terms, came and stayed in the house with him. When his classmates left, Prince Masahito came to be with him.

Because the entrance examinations for the universities were beginning to loom up like a menace, though they were still a year and a half away, all of the good students were spending at least part of their vacation time in studying. Prince Akihito too went on with his work. I went three mornings a week to work with him in English, and Madame des Roziers, the delightful young wife of the naval attaché at the French Mission, who was spending the summer in Karuizawa, read French with him for his pronunciation. In the English hours we studied *Julius Caesar*. The Prince read the standard Japanese translation and then we discussed the play in English and read some of the famous passages in the original.

The Prince went to tea at Madame des Roziers', he had Madame des Roziers for dinner at his house; I was there twice for dinner. He came to my house one evening with five or six of his classmates. Mr. Toda and Dr. Saburi came with him but left him there while they went off to see some friends in the village. The boys played Contract Rummy, and after refreshments they discussed what to do in the time that was left. The Crown Prince wanted another game of Rummy, the others a Japanese game. One boy suggested settling it by vote, and they proceeded to vote the Crown Prince down. He accepted the majority decision as a matter of course and joined cheerfully in the game.

Another evening the two princes, with Mr. Nagamasa Murai, Prince Masahito's chamberlain, a very serious, good, young Christian of one of the fundamentalist sects, came to dinner at our house. With them I invited Mr. and Mrs. Merrill Vories Hitotsuyanagi.

More than forty years ago Merrill Vories, a young architect with a vision, had come to Japan as an independent missionary, had been led to establish himself in a little town on Lake Biwa, where with the help of a handful of ardent young converts he developed the Omi Brotherhood, a Christian group who lived like the early followers of Christ with all things in common. His skill as an architect was soon in demand all over Japan, he trained young men to work under him, and the proceeds of architecture financed the other projects of the Brotherhood, the church, Sunday School, evangelical missions, the kindergarten and training school. In the course of time Merrill Vories married Maki Hitotsuyanagi, the daughter of a feudal lord who had been a childhood playmate of the Emperor Taisho. Maki Hitotsuyanagi was a lovely and independent spirit; educated in the United States, for a time at Bryn Mawr, she had thrown over the cramping formalities of her upbringing while cherishing the high standards of behavior of the old Japanese aristocracy. Some time during the 1930's Merrill Vories had taken Japanese citizenship and his wife's name. The story of the Omi Brotherhood and of the devoted partnership of the Hitotsuyanagis would fill a book—and indeed has already done so—but more impressive than any written words are the singularly winning personalities of this amazing pair themselves: radiant, gentle, full of humor and wisdom. The previous autumn I had spent a week-end with them at Omi Hachiman and had come away thrilled by the sight of a religion not preached about but alive in every phase of daily life.

That evening at our house, the talk at dinner was in English, but after dinner in the living-room as we sat around the big, low coffee table made of a single piece of polished horse-chestnut wood, it drifted into Japanese, as Mr. Hitotsuyanagi reminisced about his early days in Japan. The two princes listened enthralled, for he was an excellent teller of tales, and he could paint a picture of their own country that was entirely new to them, of the trains of those days with *tatami* on the floors, the adventures of a foreigner who knew nothing of the language or customs, his early struggles and successes. If it is true, as I believe it is, that religion is caught, not taught, they were exposed to it that night in its most contagious form.

Several weeks later I was told about a composition which Prince Masahito wrote as part of his summer homework. The subject assigned was "A Dream," and the fourteen-year-old boy wrote roughly as follows: "There are two kinds of dreams. One kind you have at night while you are asleep. The other is a dream for your life. I know a man who had a dream for his life." (Then he retold in considerable detail Merrill Vories's story.) "I think it is important for everyone to have a dream for his life. To make a good dream you must know God."

On the twenty-ninth of August I went to give the Crown Prince his last English lesson of the summer. It was a rainy morning and the mountains were veiled. We sat facing each other across a table near an open window, through which we could see near-by trees and bushes, glistening with moisture and as depthless as stage scenery against the mists beyond. When we had finished talking about *Julius Caesar* I told him that in the autumn I was going home to the United States, not for a visit, but to stay. I had been in Japan for four years, I said; in that time he had grown from a little boy to a young man. I felt that I had taught him all I had to teach him, and that it was time for me to be in my own country again.

His is a reserved nature; he does not speak his thoughts easily in Japanese, still less in English. I wondered what he would say.

He looked sober. For a moment he made no comment, and then he asked: "Will you come back to Japan some day?"

I said that I hoped to, for I would always be a little bit home-sick for Japan. I told him that I hoped also to see him in America, and his face lighted up. I said I hoped that he would study there, if only for a little while, because he could understand the people and the life so much better than just by traveling about and looking at it from the outside. Again the look of pleasure spread over his face, as he said that he would like that.

The next day an excursion to Sunset Point was planned, partly for the princes' own pleasure, partly for me, and partly for the people of Karuizawa, who so far had had only the most fleeting and casual glimpses of their Crown Prince.

From the car in which I rode with Prince Masahito I watched the cavalcade pass along the village street between the rows of shops and the hastily assembling people; first came a local police-man on a bay horse, then the Crown Prince on the farmer's Shironishiki (White Brocade) a white horse faintly dappled with gray, then Mr. Kuroki, Sakai San, the intellectual-looking body-guard, and a groom. We stopped briefly at the tennis tourna-ment, which was in full swing, in order to give the horses a head-start, and then we began the climb up the steep hill.

At the top, where there was a very old hamlet around a famous shrine, the houses were all hung with new Japanese flags and the priests of the shrine were lined up, bowing. Sunset Point itself is an open ledge with views of fantastically jagged moun-tain ranges on three sides. The Japanese manager of the Mampei Hotel had sent up tea for the party, and tables were set out just where the view was finest. Alone at one table with the two princes, I had one of the most satisfactory times with them that I remember. Prince Akihito chatted freely about his summer and about things and people that we both knew, unhampered by difficulties of language, friendly and unself-conscious, while his brother followed his every word, intent and happy.

After tea the Crown Prince mounted Shironishiki and on the wide level space he put his horse through his paces for me, showing me the steps that he had been learning in the riding hall. Against the background of distant mountain peaks, framed in leaning pine trees, the handsome boy on the prancing white horse made a picture to remember.

On the return the car was to go first. I said good-by to the Crown Prince before I got in, for I was not to see him again until we were both back in Tokyo. As we shook hands he surprised me by saying with sudden emphasis, "Thank you for the summer."

In the car we rolled and jolted slowly down the winding rutted road, and when we reached the bridge over the little river at the top of the village of Karuizawa, got out to wait for the cavalcade to catch up and pass us. The word had got about that the Crown Prince was returning, and all the people who missed him the first time were out to see him. Among the children there were two small, red-headed, freckle-faced American boys in blue jeans. One of them went up to Dr. Sato and asked him what was going on.

"The Crown Prince is coming," replied Dr. Sato.

"The Crown Prince?" said the boy. "What's that?"

CHAPTER THIRTY-SIX

THOUGH I WAS to stay until the end of November, and though the public announcement was not to be made for two or three weeks, now that I had told the Crown Prince about my plans I felt already half gone. I had been pressed to stay another year and I had persisted in my decision, feeling that it was the right one both for the Prince and for me, yet the breaking of ties of affection and the pulling up of new roots were painful. I longed to return to my own country, which four years away had taught me to love more deeply and consciously than ever, and yet I was grieved to leave this beautiful and fascinating land where I had met so much kindness and made so many friends. The three months that remained were a bitter-sweet time, poignant as Indian summer is poignant, with a sunny warmth made more precious by the knowledge that it must soon end.

We went back to Tokyo on the most beautiful day of the whole summer. A typhoon had washed the atmosphere clean, the sky was a deep blue with enormous puffy clouds, and the mountains so clear that each tree stood out separately.

Tokyo itself was still wrapped in the heat of summer. Sponge gourd vines with big yellow blossoms grew on trellises over the doors of the little wooden shacks, making pools of shade in the midst of the ruins of walls and gates and foundations. The sun poured down on the crowds of men on bicycles carrying everything from live goats to parlor organs, patient housewives standing in line for the ration, swarms of small children playing in the dust of the streets. Our house was serene and orderly and welcoming. Persimmons in the garden were beginning to turn red, a few yellow leaves drifted on the surface of the pool. At dusk people passed on their way from the public bath with towels and basins in their hands, the bean-curd man's melancholy whistle sounded along the lane between the hedges, and the insects sang of autumn in the cool dark.

Lessons began again as usual. The Crown Prince and I read together *Pilgrim's Progress* in the abridged edition with Robert Lawson's beautiful illustrations. At school I dictated to the boys each week a quotation which they were to memorize for the next week, and after dictation and recitation they took turns reporting in English on books they had read. I was interested to see what sort of things they were reading: translations of French, Russian, and Scandinavian novels, books on science and philosophy, no travel and very little biography, but on the whole a more mature selection than their contemporaries in the United States would be undertaking. The quotations I gave them were Shakespeare's "To thine own self be true," Penn's statement on government, Washington's words during the troubled sessions of the Continental Convention in 1789: "If to please the people we offer what we ourselves disapprove, how can we afterwards defend our work? Let us raise a standard to which the wise and honest can repair. The event is in the hands of God," and Robert Bridges's "I love all beauteous things."

Princess Kazuko came to my house with her sisters as she had done before she was married; Mr. Takatsukasa joined us at tea. Twice a week I went to the Empress. Two or three times the lessons were held in the Kaintei, where I talked into a wire recorder, so that the lessons might continue after I had gone.

One day Mr. Tajima came to my house with a message from Their Majesties. During my remaining time in Japan, he told me, they wanted me to put the lessons second and my own interests first; and they wanted me to see something more of the country before I left. I was to have a trip, wherever I wished to go.

After Mr. Tajima had delivered the imperial message, which he always did directly without anybody else in the room, Tané was called in to interpret and we talked about my successor. The position as I had held it would come to an end, but they had asked me to recommend someone to give the Crown Prince two hours of English conversation a week. Esther Rhoads was my immediate choice. Her character and personality, her long and successful experience of teaching English in Japan, her work for LARA, which had taken her all over Japan and had given her a knowledge of present-day conditions that would bring something new and valuable to the Prince, all these made her, I felt, the ideal person. She was already doing the work of two or three people, as a part-time member of the LARA staff, and principal of the Friends Girls School, and she was not at first sure that she should take on this added work, but in the end she consented. It was arranged also that once a month she should have a lesson-tea with the princesses and that Tané should carry on their weekly lessons. Now the public announcement of my departure could be made, and this was done on September twenty-fifth. The Emperor's very kind and more than once expressed concern that my last days there should be happy resulted in a succession of imaginative and generous acts to give me pleasure that fairly overwhelmed me.

One evening Mrs. Hoshina, the chief lady-in-waiting, telephoned that some singing insects had just been received from Nara and that the Empress was sending some over to us. A little later they arrived: two enchanting little wooden cages, one shaped like a boat and the other like a miniature birdcage. Inside were cricket-like insects, *matsumushi*, pine insect, and *suzumushi*, bell insect, which are very much cherished by the Japanese for their songs. These had been captured on a certain hill in the ancient capital of Nara and sent to the Imperial Palace, a custom centuries old. When they arrived in our living-room they promptly went into a sulk—"Evidently they feel they have come down in the world," commented my sister—that lasted for the rest of the evening, but after we had gone to bed they tuned up and their trills rippled out on the night air. Whenever any of my students wrote me letters at this time of the year they always commented on the cool sound of the singing insects after dark. I often thought how characteristically Japanese it was to take a sensitive joy in something which in other lands might go unnoticed, and also to build up a charming paraphernalia and tradition for the enjoying of it.

One afternoon there was a riding exhibition at the Palace riding hall. This was the Crown Prince's own idea and was the first thing of its kind.

The whole affair was very gay and lively, and somehow much more European than Japanese. The big cavern of the riding hall with shafts and spots of sunlight on the tanbark, the royal box where the Empress sat with her children and her ladies-in-waiting, the court officials, and a very few favored guests, the nineteenth century waltzes and marches that jingled out of the amplifier from time to time, the two young princes, looking very smart in their riding habits, who watched from the royal box when they themselves were not riding and who had many important errands back and forth between the box and the door to the stables, where there was always a great bustle going on: it was all reminiscent of a continental novel of the 80's when each country had its court and cavalry officers were figures of romance.

The program was full and varied, and though Prince Masahito and seven of his classmates, the members of the Gakushuin Riding Club, and a number of court officials all took part, the Crown Prince was the dominant figure. No doubt partly because of the ability he showed that afternoon he was soon after elected president of the Gakushuin Riding Club, and led it to victories in athletic meets with other schools.

After the demonstration of *haute école* riding by Prince Akihito on Shirafuji (White Wisteria), a handsome and spirited Arab, accompanied by Mr. Higashizono, and several jumping events, there was a rather sedate relay race in which Prince Masahito took part, and then two games of musical stalls. This is like our Going to Jerusalem, with stalls instead of chairs. There were ten contestants in each game, and I noticed that, except at the very last, two stalls were taken away each time instead of one, and I thought that must be due to the Japanese regard for the individual's pride, so that the first defeated ones need not go off the field singly, but in pairs. In this the Crown Prince was riding Sakurakage (Cherry Shade), his first horse, a bay, and he was playing to win, going slowly when he was alongside of the stalls, racing around the ends, scrambling for a place when the music stopped. It must have been a temptation to whoever was managing the music to favor the Prince's position a little, but I could not see that he yielded to it. The Prince won, but he worked hard for the victory. His prize was a basket; numbers two and three got a paper umbrella and a box of cakes respectively.

One afternoon my sister and I went to a concert with the Empress. One evening we dined with Prince and Princess Takamatsu. One day Dr. and Mrs. Koizumi took us to lunch at a little *tempura* restaurant, where shrimps and lobster and white-bait and other delectable things such as fresh ginger stalks were dipped in batter before our eyes, delicately browned in a deep kettle of hot fat, and popped onto our plates in a state of un-imaginable crispness and tenderness. Afterwards we went to visit a doll factory, where the tenth generation of dollmakers continued the family business. We watched the whole process, paying especial attention to the cutting of the eyes, for that, we were told, was the most delicate and critical operation of all. A dollmaker, it seems, cannot help reproducing the eyes of the woman he loves, and his fellow workers, by looking carefully at his dolls, can tell whether his wife or someone else holds his heart.

As we talked with the proprietor and his wife and son over the coffee and apple pie which they provided for us, they told me that when the Crown Prince was born they had made the gift which the Joshi Gakushuin gave him but they had heard that it was burned during the war. It was, they said, a small Noh theatre made entirely to scale.

"Oh, no!" I cried, "that wasn't burned! I see it twice every week!"

It was of course the one in the Empress's lesson-room. The school's gift had been the theatre. The arrays of dolls in the cabinet representing characters in all the famous Noh plays had been ordered separately by the Emperor and had also been made by this workshop. They had still three duplicates, and they brought out one, a doll four inches high, with a scarlet and gold robe of a minutely patterned brocade, the simpering mask of the female Noh character, and a gilt headdress with tiny tinkling ornaments, and they gave it to me. For my birthday the Empress had given me an ivory carving of rabbits on a lily leaf boat, to remind me of the lesson-room, and now I had this second treasure to bring back vividly those hours which I loved.

On my last day at the school Prince Akihito was in bed with a cold. As I had asked to continue with his private lessons up to the time of my departure, this was not the final lesson for him, but nevertheless he sent Mr. Shimizu to the school especially to see me and tell me that he was sorry to miss my last class.

I was to see the other boys again too, singly and collectively, before I left, but this was the final time in the classroom and I felt sad as I faced them. They recited the quotations that they had memorized and then I said to them:

"I have asked you to learn these great words by great men, because I hope you will remember them all your lives. When I was in school I had to memorize many poems and most of them I still remember. I have forgotten much that I have learned since then, but what I memorized when I was your age has stayed with me. The parts of two poems that I learned in German are almost all the German I know now, but I often think of them. So I want these great thoughts to be part of the permanent furniture of your minds.

"These are great thoughts of great men, but I want also to give you something from myself." (They sat very still and attentive and there was an electric quality in the silence. They were very different from American students, who begin to squirm and think of something else whenever there is any threat of preaching. The Japanese, on the other hand, like homilies from their teachers; they even ask for them.) "I want you to try always to think for yourselves. Don't believe everything you hear, no matter who says it. Don't believe all you read in the newspapers. Don't take other people's opinions without examining them. Try to find out the truth for yourselves. If you hear a very strong opinion on one side of a question, try to hear also an opinion on the other side, and then decide what you think yourself. In these days there is a great deal of propaganda of all kinds. Some of it is true and some is not. It is very important that young people all over the world should learn to find out the truth for themselves."

Then I wrote "Think for yourselves!" on the blackboard and we spent the last few minutes playing a word game.

During these weeks before the farewells began I had a number of conferences with Mr. Nomura, Dr. Koizumi, and Mr. Tajima about the Crown Prince's future, his education after he should graduate from the Gakushuin, and even his marriage. Five or six years before the actual marriage was none too early, they thought, to begin to consider the matter, to lay down the broad principles upon the basis of which the choice would finally be made. In former days the Crown Prince's bride must be chosen from among five families: now the field could be widened. The principle was established that character, rather than pedigree, was the primary essential.

I love to remember one conversation that I had along these lines with Dr. Koizumi. He sat in an easy chair in my living-room, beside the table where there was always a flower arrangement, the Crown Prince's photograph in a silver frame, and some books. The sun came in through the long window open on the garden.

"What kind of character," he asked me, "do you think the Crown Prince's bride should have?"

I launched into a description of the paragon: she must be good-looking, because the Prince had an eye for beauty; she must be intelligent but not opinionated; she must have wide interests and be able to talk well about them, because the Prince liked to be entertained and amused; she must have real depths of sweetness, because her position would demand endless sacrifices of her own desires and inclinations, and at the same time she must be a girl of spirit, for it would be a great mistake if she were to make a doormat of herself; she must have a sense of humor, or she would be overwhelmed by it all, and she must have charm, or none of her other good qualities would be of much use to her.

"I agree with you perfectly in theory," he replied when I finished this impressive portrait, "but *name one!*"

"*Makemashita!*" I said, which is the Japanese for "You have me there!" and we both shouted with laughter.

In the realm of more immediate possibilities we talked—once more—about the Crown Prince and Prince Masahito living together. Since spring they had tried as an experiment having Prince Masahito spend two nights a week at Tokiwamatsu and it had been obviously and admittedly a success. Now I pressed for more. The Crown Prince spent three nights a week at the dormitory, but that still left four in which the brothers might be together. If Prince Masahito's things were all moved to Tokiwamatsu and if he were there all week he would feel more settled, would really be living there instead of visiting. Nothing immediate came of this, but a month later, in November, when I heard that Dr. Koizumi had been put in charge of Prince Masahito as well as the Crown Prince I began to have hopes that before too long it would come about.

These hopes were fulfilled in the spring of 1951, after I had been several months at home. Prince Masahito finally moved into the Tokiwamatsu villa, and both princes spent four days there and three days in the dormitory. Even before I left Japan the building of a new dormitory had begun, and this was completed when the new school year opened in April. It is a comfortable, modern building on the Mejiro campus, with central heating.

On the eighteenth of October Tané and I departed on the trip which Their Majesties had urged me to take and in which they had taken a personal interest that, Mr. Tajima emphasized to me, was quite unprecedented.

We went by day train to Kyoto, because I wanted once more to see that wonderful stretch of sea and mountains and farming country, spent the night at our favorite inn, the Tawaraya, had a day in Nara, and went on by night express to Yonago, where the round-faced, jolly, kimono-clad mayor met us and took us up the mountain of Hoki Daisen, to have lunch in a Buddhist temple with the most extraordinary views of mountain ranges and the coast of the Japan Sea. From there we went to Matsue, the little town which was Lafcadio Hearn's first love and about which he wrote with poetic exuberance. The inn where we stayed, the Minamikan, overlooked the Shinji Lagoon, and after a bath we ate dinner in our bathrobes looking out over the water where a fisherman in white trousers and blue *happi* coat was poling a boat, against a background of island and mountains.

All the next day we rode in the train along the top of pine-clad cliffs looking down on the Japan Sea, which has not been written about so much as the Inland Sea but is, I think, even more beautiful. It is wilder, less visited by tourists, less self-conscious. Almost every time we stopped at a station, someone, the mayor or the chief of the city council or the station master, appeared to bow and wish me well or to thank me, as so many others had done in the four years, for coming to teach the Crown Prince. When dusk fell, after a day in which I was almost surfeited with beauty, the sea was silver between dark clouds and black cliffs, and among the islands moved the golden lights of small boats coming home.

We spent the night in Fukuoka and went on next day to Hitoyoshi, accompanied by a prefectural official and a plain-clothes policeman whom the Governor of Kumamoto Ken had detailed to take care of us. Hitoyoshi is a very old city on the Kuma River high in the mountains of central Kyushu. There we were met by Mr. Hideyoshi Mikami and his daughter Keiko, friends of Tané's, who had a most interesting and original little school for the children of charcoal-burners and wood-cutters still farther away in the mountains.

The inn where we all stayed was the Nabeya, which ranks with the Tawaraya among the most delightful inns I have known anywhere. Tané and I had the room called Kirinoma (the Misty Room), overlooking the river, the rapids, the bridge, and the hill formation called the Sleeping Buddha, site of the ruined castle of Saga, the old feudal lord of the district. The Mikamis had planned our entertainment, and filled the hours with vivid interest. They were a delightful pair themselves, the father a writer, a man of vision, humor, and determination, the daughter a beautiful girl, ardent and happy and gentle, talented herself both with her pen and brush.

That evening we saw the shrine, of which the present building was erected in 1601 but whose foundation went back to the dawn of history. We were purified by a priest who chanted before an altar some prayers for our safe journey and shook over us a wand tipped with cut paper streamers. When we came out into the dark garden after this ceremony, the stone lanterns were lighted, a mist had risen from the river, and in the sky we saw a moonbow, very faint but clearly arched.

The next day began with breakfast at quarter past six, included a three-hour ride over the mountains in a car, an hour ride in a tiny aluminum gasoline car belonging to the Forestry Division up a logging railroad to Hachigamine and the Mikamis' school, where we had two wonderful hours with the children and some of their parents, fine stalwart, weatherbeaten people with the pride and independence of mountain folk everywhere, and after the return to Hitoyoshi a ride to the village of Suyemura, in which John Embree lived for a year and of which he wrote. After stopping briefly at the high school of the district, we abandoned the car and got into a long narrow wooden boat manned by three boatmen, in which we shot the rapids in the gathering dusk. The moon came up as we sailed swiftly along, and when we passed the bluff where the *daimyo's* castle stood a plover sang his liquid trilling notes, plaintive and a little lonely. The boat brought us, a little later than we were expected, right to the river entrance of the inn, where we found our good innkeeper out pacing up and down and praying to the Sleeping Buddha for our safety. It might have been a little dangerous, they said, because the boatmen did not like to shoot the rapids after dark. But, as Mr. Mikami later wrote me, "If there are no thrill, one cannot immerse in the bosom of nature," and certainly I would not have had one moment of that glorious day changed. The mayor entertained us at dinner that night, with a speech of welcome by himself, and folk dances and singing by two maids from a neighboring inn.

From Hitoyoshi we returned to Kumamoto, where we took the train across the island to Beppu, climbing the foothills of Mount Aso, the southern volcano, which towered above us most of the way. Here the scenery was on a larger scale than any I had seen in Japan before, wide valleys, big fields, and great mountains with rounded tops.

In Beppu we stayed at the same inn where the Emperor had stayed the previous year, indeed in his very suite, were visited by an emissary from a goddess who claimed to be the reincarnation of the Sun Goddess, toured the "hells" (hot springs, red, green, and mud) in the company of the mayor, and left on the little steamer next afternoon to sail up the Inland Sea. We watched the sea and the sunset from the deck of our little cabin until sleep overtook us, and the next morning before dawn I saw the island-dotted water bathed in moonlight.

At Takamatsu on the island of Shikoku, we stayed with my friends Rebecca and Walter Pedersen for two or three days, saw the famous sights in that vicinity, and talked long about America and Japan and the books and poetry that we all loved. We talked too about the Korean situation and the future.

After the desperate struggle of the summer, when the U.N. troops could do no more than cling to their toehold in Pusan in the southwestern corner of the peninsula, the tide had turned at last, the Inchon landing had been made, and Seoul had been given back to the government of South Korea in a simple but impressive ceremony that came over the radio punctuated by the sound of shattering glass in the damaged hall in which it was held. When we talked in Takamatsu at the end of October, the

U.N. armies were sweeping triumphantly northward, but military victory, I thought, could not settle all the problems that loomed so sombrely over these eastern countries.

"What about the national police reserve?" I asked.

Under the Occupation, Japan's police force had been decentralized and stripped of power. Most of Tokyo's policemen were fresh-faced boys, excellent directors of traffic but not very effectual against organized crime. Now the activities of the Communists and the threat of violence made necessary a central police force strong enough to put down riots if they should occur. A national police reserve of 75,000 men was created with the encouragement of the Occupation.

They went into training at once in various places, and since we had come down from Karuizawa I had seen them about, at Kamakura, at Nara, at Fukuoka, at Takamatsu. They did not look as I had imagined they would look, like the Canadian Mounted Police or like our state troopers, formidable men but a civil force devoted to the guarding of the law. They lived in camps like soldiers, they were trained like soldiers, in their free hours they drifted about in uniform seeking amusement like soldiers, and they looked like soldiers, in American Army surplus khaki and marine boots.

That was why I asked, "What about the national police reserves? Are they policemen or are they an army?"

There was a moment's silence in the room, then someone answered, "Nobody has called them an army—yet."

It was profoundly distressing to me. Japan had renounced war in her new Constitution. We had preached to her in a thousand ways, had sent experts of all kinds to impress upon her, our belief in a sacred Constitution assented to by the people, amended by their elected representatives if necessary, but never circumvented or overruled by a military group as Japan's militarists had done to her destruction in the years that led to the war. Were we now helping her to set up an army, in flagrant disregard of her Constitution, and pretending that it was not an army?

CHAPTER THIRTY-SEVEN

WHILE I WAS in Takamatsu the news came out over the radio and in the newspapers that the Japanese government would bestow on me a "decoration," the Third Order of the Sacred Crown. This was, I learned, a rather rare order, given only to women; there were eight degrees and only imperial princesses received the first and second.

Three or four days after I returned to Tokyo the order was presented, on a day so full of extraordinary honors and privileges that I moved through it in a daze, not at all sure that I was actually I and that it was all happening to me and not to someone else.

At ten-thirty in the morning, with Tané in attendance, I presented myself at the Prime Minister's official residence, a many-tiered building of mustard-colored brick rather reminiscent of the Imperial Hotel. Through various stages I came to Mr. Yoshida's office, where he greeted me smilingly, congratulated me, wafted me onto the sofa and himself sat down in an easy chair with a round table between us. He showed me the decoration in its lacquer case and presented it "in the name of the Japanese people," adding with a twinkle in his eye, "This is a decoration given only to ladies. It is not a military order."

As a child I used to pore over the colored plates in the ninth edition *Encyclopaedia Britannica* in my father's library; the pages devoted to foreign orders seemed to me especially brilliant and splendid. Little did I imagine that I should ever hold one of these in my own hands. It was a beautiful piece of enamel-work, the crown with a phoenix in gold in the center, on a background of brilliant blue, surrounded by two rows of tiny seed pearls and a border of enameled cherry blossoms. The ribbon on which it was hung was striped yellow and red, and there was a

tiny ribbon rosette to wear on ordinary occasions. That day, however, I was told to wear the order itself, and Tané pinned it
on me.

After a few minutes' chat, in which I tried to express my
thanks, Mr. Yoshida said that he had to go to the Palace to
report to the Emperor that he had given me the order, and I was
taken into another room and turned over to the photographers.
Then I went home, changed into my best black dress, and sallied
forth to luncheon at the Palace, arriving exactly at twelve-twenty
as I had been told to do.

A distinguished company was already assembled in the big
drawing-room in the Imperial Household Building; Mr. Yoshida,
whom I had seen a little earlier as Prime Minister, was now present as Foreign Minister, and all the members of the Crown
Prince's Advisory Council were there, as well as Mr. Tajima and
the top officials of the Department of Ceremonies. Soon the
Emperor and Empress arrived and we went in to lunch, I with
the Emperor, Mr. Yoshida with the Empress.

The table was beautiful, with great silver vases filled with orchids, white chrysanthemums and maidenhair ferns, and in the
next room the orchestra played softly. The program was on the
table in front of me, with the menu, and the last number, I was
sure, had been chosen for me: "Waltz: Over the Waves." I sat
on the Emperor's right, with Mr. Matsui, his interpreter, beside
me, and Mrs. Matsudaira beyond, on His Majesty's left. Though
the occasion was very formal and everything was done with the
utmost ceremony, the conversation was easy and happy, and I
enjoyed myself thoroughly, somewhat to my surprise.

As we went back to the drawing-room after lunch Mrs. Matsudaira whispered to me that this was the first time since the
war that the orchestra had played at a luncheon. "It's all come
back!" she said softly.

Speaking through interpreters the Emperor and Empress both
thanked me for my work with the Crown Prince, and the Empress spoke especially of the atmosphere of happiness which she
said I had created for him. I replied that it had been my prayer
that he have a free and happy growth to his fullest capacities
and that I felt he had very fine potentialities of mind and spirit.
The Emperor said that he felt happy but *hazukashii* (shy) to
hear his son so praised. I remarked that it had troubled me some-

times when I praised the Crown Prince in interviews and magazine articles because I knew that he would see some of them and
I thought it wasn't good for young people to read compliments
about themselves, and so I usually tried to phrase it in such a
way that he would feel that he had something to live up to. On
the whole, however, I thought he was essentially level-headed
and modest and I did not think praise harmed him.

As we came out of the dining-room we had passed a table
with two tall vases on it, but I had been looking at Their
Majesties and had not noticed the vases. Now the Emperor said
that he wanted to give me a memento, and we all turned to look
at them. They were beautiful pieces of cloisonné so exquisite
that it is difficult to see how they could be made by human
hands. Both had backgrounds of clear, soft blue; both had fishing scenes, with nets drying on a shore under pine trees. On one
a red *tai* (congratulatory) showed through the meshes of the
net; on the other a silver moon shone down on the beach. The
box in which they were to be put away was beautiful in itself,
padded inside with white damask, and to cover them there were
two royal purple *furoshikis* with the imperial chrysanthemum in
white. I thought of the craftsmen who had worked patiently on
these beautiful vases and the years of their lives that had gone
into the work and I felt truly as the Japanese so often say: *"Mot-
tai nai!* It's too good! It's too much!"*

When the Emperor and Empress had withdrawn, I talked
with the rest of the group for a little while, before I went to my
regular waiting-room where Violet and Tané had come to join
me. Together we went on to the Music Hall, where there was to
be a command performance by M. Lazare-Levy, the French pianist, then visiting Japan.

A number of people were already in the room when we were
led in; others followed, from the French Mission, then M.
Lazare-Levy with his two pretty Japanese pupils who were also
to take part. The imperial party came in last; the Empress Dowager all in black with a little black toque, the Empress in gray-
green, having changed from the lavender and gold of the
luncheon, the Crown Prince in school uniform, the four princesses, and Princess Shigeko's two older children, a five-year-old
boy in dark blue shorts and sweater, and a three-year-old girl in
a white knitted dress and pink sweater, her enormous eyes very

roguish. They behaved beautifully throughout the hour; Fumiko San sat for part of the time on her mother's lap playing with her pocketbook and had to be gently restrained from premature clapping.

The amazing day ended with dinner at Mr. Tajima's. Princess Chichibu was there, and Mrs. Matsudaira, Mrs. Tsuji, a fragile and lovely person of great distinction, Miss Jodai, of the Japan Women's University, Dr. Koizumi, Mr. Maeda, and Mr. Yamanashi. The talk swung round to the land reform, which was perhaps the most radical and the most successful reform of the Occupation.

Before the war the majority of Japan's farmers were tenant farmers, and the fruit of their labor was swallowed up by rent and taxes. From the agricultural population had come many of the ultra-nationalistic young officers who had sought to change by military dictatorship and overseas expansion the impossible conditions under which their people struggled. After the war this class offered a hotbed for communism, which to economic discontent added the appeal of pent-up nationalism. By the land reform laws, which got rather slowly under way but were fully implemented by 1948, the landlords had to yield all of the land which they, with their families, could not work themselves. The land thus freed was sold to the former tenants at pre-war valuations. Though the landlords were paid for their land, inflation had so reduced the value of the returns that it was practically confiscation and worked hardship upon many. It was natural that they should be bitter. What was surprising was the spirit in which many of them accepted it.

That evening at Mr. Tajima's I told of my visit to Mochizuki the previous summer to speak to a thousand farm women and of the tea and discussion afterwards with some of the leaders among them. One of them was the wife of a man who formerly had been a big landholder with a number of tenants and whose land was now reduced to three or four acres. He had taken a job in the city and his wife, an attractive graceful woman, well-dressed, worked on the farm, deep in the mud of the rice paddies. She had to work very hard, she said, but she was glad that it was this way; she felt self-respecting and productive; her neighbors did not look down upon her as an idler, and the new system was best for Japan.

Miss Jodai nodded and said that the same thing had happened in her family. Her brother had got caught in the land reform and had been very bitter at first but was now convinced that it was the best thing both for the farmers and for the country at large. She thought that attitude was rather widespread.

I asked if the Occupation had worn out its welcome yet, and one among the company replied: "No, we have got used to it now. We do not want it to go away now. We feel safer when it is here. And now people really understand the purposes of America and its unselfishness to fight for Korea and Japan."

"I should like to keep the clause renouncing war in the Constitution," said another. "I should be sorry to see Japan have an army again. But I cannot think it is right to ask others to die in defense of us."

These ideas I heard reflected in many other conversations also. They no doubt inspired the many Japanese who contributed to the blood bank, among whom was Prince Takamatsu, and who made presents for the wounded United Nations soldiers who were filling the hospitals in heart-rending numbers.

As November raced past, the days were crowded with farewells of all kinds, letters, calls, gifts, parties, and innumerable thoughtful acts of kindness.

One day Violet and I were invited to the Empress Dowager's for tea. One evening the Crown Prince and Prince Masahito gave a dinner party, to which Violet and Tané, Mrs. Matsudaira, and all the chamberlains and doctors came. After dinner Mr. Motofumi Higashizono showed moving pictures that he had taken. He had been the Crown Prince's chamberlain before he was Prince Masahito's, and his pictures went back to the days when the Crown Prince was an adorable three-year-old, running about the lawn at Nasu, peering at the carp in the pool, trailed by two ladies-in-waiting in long dresses, a doctor and a chamberlain. I asked him if he could remember that day and he said, "Only the fish swimming around." His very first memory, he said when I asked him, was of the Imperial Palace and of his father "standing—but it is too difficult to explain in English."

Other reels showed him in Hayama, a sturdy four-year-old with a look of mind and ability, going out with a net to get specimens from the pools among the rocks. We saw him come out of the house, wearing short dark blue trousers and a dark felt hat with streamers down the back, and get into the waiting car while two ladies and two gentlemen bowed very low. When they reached the beach they let him scramble over the rocks quite freely and he was happily absorbed and unself-conscious. The Governor of Kanagawa sent him two large live lobsters and he picked them up by the feelers without hesitation and examined them thoroughly before he dropped them into a tub of water. We saw him eating his lunch at a little table and then getting into his rubber boots at the step, unaided, before he went out again.

The next series had to do with his riding and covered several years. First he rode an Okinawan pony, then a small Arab, then the full-sized Sakurakage. He was nine years old in the last pictures, and the war was on. "It all looks very peaceful, doesn't it," commented Dr. Koizumi, as the little boy rode along the paths of the Akasaka Palace grounds, a groom in front, a groom walking beside him with a lead-rein, and his instructor, a colonel in the cavalry, riding behind. But I thought I saw a difference, a tenseness in the child's correct military salutes, a general air of repression and rigid discipline.

In all of the pictures he was with chamberlains and ladies-in-waiting. How much his parents were missing, I thought, all those years!

One afternoon our flower-arrangement teacher, Miss Taira, and a great company of her pupils gave us a wonderful party at the Meiji Memorial Hall. It was the one day of the month when the gods do not like people to get married and so, as there were no weddings there that day, the hall and its lovely garden were available.

The Prime Minister—or perhaps he was Foreign Minister that night—gave a dinner party for me. The order of the Sacred Crown was spoken of and there was much laughter and joking about whether he should have kissed me on the cheeks in the French manner when he presented it.

During dinner he said to me: "When Mr. Grew was in Japan he and I became friends. I said to him, 'You have known only the upper class in Japan. You say very kind things about the Japanese people because of those you have known. You should know also some laborers.' That is true of you also," he pointed out. "You have known only the people around the court."

I agreed, but spoke of the farm women that I had met and the many teachers.

"The Japanese women are wonderful," he agreed. "I have great respect for them because of my mother, my wife, and my daughter. But the Japanese men, including myself, are not so good."

Someone brought up the remark he had made recently to a reporter, which had brought him much indignant publicity: "Baseball is a coolies' game."

"Daddy likes to say things to shock people," commented his daughter, Mrs. Aso, from the end of the table.

"I had been beginning to suspect that," I said.

Mr. Yoshida chuckled. "It's a coolies' taste," he said calmly.

"I quite agree," said Mrs. Aso severely.

One day I was lent the Imperial Household bus in which the ladies-in-waiting were transported when they all had to go some-where in a group, and I took my English Club girls to Aisenryo, the little orphanage in Saitama Prefecture which they had adopted. Miss Kücklich, who was its "Mama San," showed us with joy the new church, a beautiful little building in which every detail spoke of love and thought. On the day of its dedica-tion, eighteen people had been baptized, including the architect who had worked so closely with Miss Kücklich through the de-signing and building of it.

A farmer in Saitama, who wrote poetry and at whose house I had watched the preparations for the New Year, came to say good-by and to bring me a gift of sesame seed. The wife and children and mother-in-law of my former chauffeur, who was now the prosperous owner of two public baths, arrived in a taxi with gifts of flowers and fruit and a carved wooden bear.

On Thanksgiving Day my boys at Gakushuin, who had al-ready sent me a gift of a silver bowl with a very nice inscription, gave me a farewell party in the school's newly built auditorium. Several rows of seats in front near the stage had been taken out and tables set up for tea. Here we sat in groups of eight, drink-ing tea and eating oranges, *o sushi*, sweet cakes and crisp rice wafers, while the program rolled along smoothly on the stage.

They had planned and executed the whole thing themselves and it was a remarkable achievement. It was all in English, and everybody took part. There were three hours of songs, readings, plays and speeches. The Crown Prince read the part of Antonio in a scene from *The Merchant of Venice,* there was a drama of Noguchi's life, and Dunsany's *The Lost Hat.* Speeches were made not from the platform but from different tables, as one boy after another rose, as if spontaneously, and talked about some phase of the work that we had done together during the four years. One boy said, "You have not only taught us English, you have taught us thoughts."

My heart was full as I sat there in the midst of my boys, every one of whom was dear to me. They had been a joy to teach, and throughout the four years I had never come away from their classes without a lift of the heart. Could I at their age, I often wondered, have received a foreign teacher from an enemy country with one half the coöperation and the sweetness of spirit with which they had received me? I doubted it. In these boys, and in the young people all over Japan whom they represented, I saw hope for the future, which often looked so dark. The thanks which they were so generously pouring out to me should have gone the other way, and I tried to tell them so.

After a period of "free conversation," in which I signed a great many autograph books, we closed the day by standing and singing "Auld Lang Syne." I crossed my arms in the Scottish way and took the hand of the Crown Prince on one side of me and of the boy who had been master of ceremonies on the other, and soon the chain of linked hands went almost all the way around the big room.

The next evening I dined alone with the Crown Prince. We talked together in his study before and after dinner, and we dined just the two of us in the small dining-room, a more comfortable and informal room than the large one. Mr. Shimizu stuck his head in once to say that the cakes had been especially sent by the Empress, and I noticed that the fruit knives and forks we were using were the gold ones that I had seen more than once at Kaintei.

On the night of the big party at Tokiwamatsu the Prince had given me a silver and lacquer ornament of a cock on a drum, symbol of longevity and also a reminder of the Crown Prince himself, who was born in the year of the Cock, but this night he gave me something that he had made himself, one of his poems which he had written out in his best calligraphy on a gold and white *shikishi.* It was a poem about the birds returning to the Akasaka Palace gardens after the war, and it was especially appropriate because his grandmother had given me a picture scroll with a painting by Kawai Gyokudo, one of Japan's foremost contemporary artists, of the pond in the Akasaka Palace grounds. The chamberlains also gave me that evening a wonderful album which they had filled for me with photographs of the Prince, poems, and sketches, and the Prince autographed in Japanese the first portrait in the book.

Dr. Koizumi had come in after dinner, and we went downstairs and chatted with him and Mr. Nomura for a little while before I said my thanks and left, very sad to think that this was the last time I would walk down this wide hall to the door, the footmen running ahead to open the door of the waiting car, the chamberlains coming to bow in farewell. Tonight all were there on the wide doorstep, the Crown Prince himself, Dr. Koizumi, Mr. Shimizu, Mr. Toda, Dr. Sato. Mr. Nomura, who lived near my house, got into the car with me, the tires grated on the pebbly drive, the policeman at the gate saluted for the last time.

The next afternoon the Empress went to Kuretakeryo to stay with Princess Takako, so that Miss Natori could go to the party which Esther Rhoads gave for me. In the evening the Tajimas and Koizumis came to my house for dinner for the last time. On Sunday afternoon my sister and I went to tea at Kaintei with the entire Imperial Family.

We went in through Inoui Mon, and the long driveway which in spring was bordered by foaming cherry blossoms was now softly brilliant with the red of maple and the gold of ginkgo leaves. The sun shone on the gray-purple stones of the great walls, glinted off the inner moats, warmed the green of pine needles to brightness. It came in shafts through the leaded glass windows at Kaintei.

Mrs. Matsudaira and Mr. Mitani were there ahead of us. Soon the Imperial Family arrived, all the family, the Empress Dowager, the Emperor and Empress, their six children and two sons-in-law. It was the only time I had ever seen them all together.

At tea we sat at two tables, the three Majesties, the Crown

Prince, Mrs. Matsudaira and Mr. Mitani, who were both interpreting, Violet and I at one, and the young people at the other. I felt sorry for Prince Akihito, stuck at the table with the grown-ups when his brothers and sisters were having a hilariously good time at the other. Their gay laughter punctuated our more sober conversation, though we laughed too from time to time. The Empress Dowager was the focus at our table; her personality was vibrant, her mind keen, her humor quick. The Empress was always gently deferential with her mother-in-law, and the Emperor was happiest watching his family and saying little himself. The Crown Prince talked well to my sister about her interests in Japanese matters and once called across the table to me that a lady whom we both knew had taken a spill in the horse show that morning.

The final farewells were something of an ordeal. All who had been my pupils had made something for me, even the Empress, who had made an exquisite picture, in silk, of peach blossoms (for herself) and bamboo (for the Emperor). The elder princesses had written poems, the Crown Prince gave me the English translation of his poem, which he had made himself and written on a *shikishi;* Prince Masahito made the wooden frame, shaped like an American eagle, in which was a signed photograph of himself on horseback; Princess Takako had designed and made, every bit of it herself, an album with photographs of herself in kimono and *hakama* and of her brothers and sisters. Each one made a separate little speech of farewell in turn, the elder people in Japanese, the younger ones in English, as we went around the circle saying good-by, and the interpreters, one behind my sister and one behind me, translated in reverent whispers that intensified the solemnity of the occasion.

The next morning I sent my small farewell offerings, with notes of thanks and good-by, around by messenger.

On Tuesday the twenty-eighth I had an appointment to see General MacArthur to say good-by. On Monday, however, Colonel Bunker telephoned to say that something had come up which would make it "inconvenient" for the General to see me on Tuesday and could I come on Wednesday instead.

Tuesday afternoon at ten minutes to three we stopped in at the Dai-Ichi Building to get our shot clearances from the dispensary there and learned that the General had still not gone home to lunch. From that circumstance and from the air of tension about the building, we knew that something critical was in the air, and that afternoon the *Stars and Stripes* came out with ominous headlines. Great numbers of Chinese soldiers had broken through in Korea, and the U.N. troops were retreating all along the line.

The next evening at six-thirty, the General received me and talked with me for over an hour. He looked tired and rather drawn, his fine, clean-cut features were more chiseled than ever, but his color was good and I thought it amazing that a man of seventy could have the resilience and power that he had.

The conversation, which was entirely under his leading, ranged wide over the world and back over the years. After a while he spoke of Korea. There were 200,000 Chinese in Korea then, with 300,000 more ready to pour down. He had 125,000 men and had been told he would get no more. "I can't throw these educated, carefully nurtured boys against hordes of coolies," he said. The suffering and death weighed heavily on him. He spoke of one group of fine youngsters who had gone into battle and only ten per cent of whom had come out again.

The Chinese, he thought, wanted not so much recognition and membership in the U.N. as Korea itself.

He spoke with compassion of the plight of Korea. "It is pitiful. Pitiful. Fierce fighting men pour down from the North and then up from the South, and now down from the North again. Each house has a North Korean flag and a South Korean flag, and most of the time they don't know which to wave. Both sides line them up and shoot them down. The country was poor to begin with. They will be destroyed, utterly destroyed."

He spoke warmly of his faith in the Japanese people and the way in which it had proved to be justified. With all the occupying troops removed to Korea, there had been no riots or disturbances in Japan whatsoever. Labor had coöperated by cutting out strikes. "This," he said, "is the proof of the pudding."

Other farewells crowded the last days. "Farewell is a monster among words," wrote Lady Murasaki in *The Tale of Genji*, "and never yet sounded kindly on any ear." The Neighborhood Center and the Tokyo Friends Meeting, the Meditation Group, the dear friends at Tsuda, the Friends Girls School, the neighbors whom we had come to know, and a host of others loaded us with kindness.

I was anxious about the Inoues, the fragile little family who had served us in the house so faithfully these years and who had been plagued by serious illness of one kind and another, but they were to stay on in the house as caretakers until they could make other arrangements. Michiko San, who had suppressed literary aspirations, now got a job with the *Bungei Shunju,* one of Japan's most popular magazines, which had published some of my articles. Masako San later found work with the Botts.

Takenaka San would go back to driving for the Imperial Household.

Tané was to be Peace Secretary for the American Friends Service Committee in Tokyo, working under Esther Rhoads, and would go to Kuretakeryo once a week to teach the princesses English. We were making plans for her coming to the United States later.

We embarked at length upon the *Peter Maersk,* a Danish freighter which carried twelve passengers and made them very comfortable. Sailing was delayed because the Army needed all the available stevedores, and the ship could not be loaded on schedule. While we lay in the harbor at Yokohama, the Crown Prince and Prince Masahito came down to say a final farewell on the ship.

About forty photographers gathered to record the occasion. We shook hands in one part of the lounge, we shook hands in another part. I thought it was finished, but there was a chorus of Japanese protests that I did not understand. "They want us to shake hands again," said the Prince to me in English. Laughing, we went through the pantomime once more, and this turned out to be the picture that friends everywhere clipped and sent to me.

"Did you realize," said Tané to me in an awed voice afterwards, "that the Crown Prince was *interpreting* for *you?*"

Our friends were very kind to us during the day or two that we were held there waiting for the loading to be finished. Many people visited us, the Koizumis, members of the Friends Meeting, girls from the Joshi Gakushuin, schoolboys, others. At the actual moment of sailing, Tané and Takenaka San, who had brought her down in Esther Rhoads's jeep, were there alone.

Mount Fuji had withdrawn behind a cloud the day I left Japan as she had done the day I came. Tané and I clung to each other for a moment before she went down the swaying steps onto the dock. As the stretch of gray water widened between the ship and the little figure tirelessly waving a white handkerchief, my mind went back over the past four years.

I had seen extraordinary things. I had seen a broken and bewildered nation pick itself up from its ashes, make an about-face seldom if ever equaled in history, and start a new life in a new direction with determination and vigor. I had seen, in the unlikely soil of war's aftermath and military occupation, the growth of friendship between former bitter enemies. I had seen the great, nail-studded gates of the world's most secret court swing open to admit a foreigner to a position of trust. I had seen a chubby small boy develop into a poised young man.

What of that boy, who will some day be the Emperor of Japan? What promise does he offer for the future? He will not have political power, but in a free Japan he will have great moral influence. What kind of man will he be?

What he is not may in some ways be as important as what he is. The lack of initiative that troubled me when I first knew him, he has to a considerable degree overcome. With his great natural dignity is combined a shyness which sometimes seems like hauteur; and the ability to suffer fools gladly, which is so great an asset to any public figure, is apparently missing. The charm which is his when he makes an effort to please will bring him friends and also expose him to the resentment of those for whom it is not manifested. On the other hand, he is not facile, and he is not fanatic, not a person of easy agreements for social purposes or of sudden enthusiasms and coolings.

 He gives his faith slowly, but once he has given it he is steadfast. He is honest, with himself and with others. He is modest. He has a better than average mind, clear, analytical, independent, with a turn for original thought. He has a strong sense of responsibility and a deep love for Japan and her people. He is aware of his destiny; he accepts it soberly. Cautious and deliberate, he has the true conservative's ability upon occasion to break radically with tradition. He has a sense of humor, that invaluable balance wheel and safety valve, and he has that quality without which there can be no true greatness: compassion. One of his friends wrote to me—and it is unusual for one sixteen-year-old to see it in another sixteen-year-old—"He knows pity."

I had come to Japan hoping to make some contribution, however small, to the cause of peace. Now Korea was aflame and no one knew where the fire might spread next. The United States and Russia were on the verge of a war that would be the final disaster for both, and I saw Japan's new democracy in danger of being crushed in the struggle between the giants. The very spirit of reconciliation which seemed so good and so desirable might draw her into war as America's military ally.

I had been asked to open windows on to a wider world for the Crown Prince. I had tried, but who can say to what extent I had succeeded? But certainly many windows had been opened for me—and perhaps through me for others—both on Japan itself and on that ancient, ceremonious, hidden world within the Moat. Through windows, whichever way they face, comes light, and light, I thought, is good.

POSTSCRIPT

When we had been back in our own country about six weeks and my sister and I had unpacked our things and were getting settled in the little old house which we had rented from a friend, we had a visit from an imperial emissary.

Mr. Shiro Sumikura, who had been the Crown Prince's chamberlain when I first went to Japan and one of my earliest friends there, and who was now head of the legislative reference division in the Diet Library, had come to the United States on a government mission. He had also another charge. He had been asked by the Empress to see me and bring me messages from her and letters from the imperial children. He wrote to me that Tané had suggested that I might be visiting friends in Washington and perhaps he could see me there, but that, he said, would not do at all. He must come to our house, in order to deliver the messages and letters properly and also because Her Majesty wished him to see us in our environment and report back if I was comfortable and happy. So to our great pleasure Mr. Sumikura came and spent a week-end with us.

I drove to a railway station about ten miles away, for we were now living in the country, and brought him to our house. After we had exchanged greetings and news and had tea in front of the fire, he brought out the precious letters, each in an envelope and wrapped for further protection in fine white handmade paper.

Each of the imperial children had written me a note, so carefully, so well. They were New Year's greetings, a little out of date now, for they had been a long time on the way. I had heard in the intervening time from the Crown Prince directly, and as time went on I was often to have letters from him and from Prince Masahito and the princesses. They belong to the new world and they may write letters to be dispatched through ordinary mails.

The Empress's messages must be delivered with due formality, through intermediaries. She gave them to a chamberlain at Obunko, the chamberlain sent for Mr. Sumikura to come to the Imperial Household Building, and repeated them to him. Mr. Sumikura wrote them down in Japanese and translated them into English, and finally, many thousands of miles away and several weeks later, he delivered them. They were numbered one to six. Four of them were, in Mr. Sumikura's careful translation:

1. Her Majesty feels lonesome that she has no longer your lesson of English which she has been very much enjoying.
2. She gets your picture on her desk and thinks as if she were seeing you every day.
3. She is now reading your book *William Penn* with much interest.
4. Last year she recollected that you taught a Christmas carol to her and her daughters and they sang it after the dinner at the Kaintei on December twentieth. At that time you said that you would teach it again the next year but, to her sorry, you have gone "the next year."

A silence fell in the room.

In spite of all the formalities and the distance, the Empress's personality came through to me, and for a moment I was back in Japan once again within the Moat, in that sunny room with the carved rabbits and the Noh dolls.

The next day Mr. Sumikura took many photographs, in order to make an album for Her Majesty. I answered the Crown Prince's letter by air mail.

FINIS

32526

DS
889
V5

VINING, ELIZABETH
    WINDOWS FOR THE
CROWN PRINCE.

DATE DUE	
8/19/21	
9/14/21	